MW00617200

My Rock From Stoneman

A 20TH CENTURY LOVE STORY IN THE NUCLEAR AGE

Dolores Tate

Upswing Publishing

SAN DIEGO, CALIFORNIA

Copyright © 2016 by Dolores Tate.

All rights reserved. No part of this publication may be reproduced, distributed or transmitted in any form or by any means, including photocopying, recording, or other electronic or mechanical methods, without the prior written permission of the publisher, except in the case of brief quotations embodied in critical reviews and certain other noncommercial uses permitted by copyright law.

For permission requests, email the publisher
with the subject "Attention: Permissions Coordinator"
at orders@upswingpublishing.com

Upswing Publishing
San Diego, CA
www.upswingpublishing.com

Ordering Information:
Quantity sales. Special discounts are available on quantity purchases by corpora- tions, associations, and others. For details, send an email with the subject "Special Sales Department" to the address above.

Publisher's Cataloging-in-Publication data

Names: Tate, Dolores, author.

Title: My Rock from Stoneman : a 20th Century love story in the nuclear age / Dolores Tate.

Description: San Diego, CA: Upswing Publishing, 2016.

Identifiers: ISBN 978-1-942628-04-0 | LCCN 2016946379

Subjects: LCSH Tate, Dolores. | Married people--Biography. | Teachers--Biography. | Man-woman relationships--Biography. | Marriage. | Parenthood--Biography. | BISAC BIOGRAPHY & AUTOBIOGRAPHY / Personal Memoirs.

Classification: LCC HQ734 .T256 2016| DCC 306.81--dc23

Dedication

To our children—-

Christina, Barbara , Patricia and Carolyn.

And to our grandchildren—-

Cameron, Cortland and Christopher.

Acknowledgements

The idea for this book came from Mary Kay Lane of Pittsburg and Antioch, California, a friend of mine since high school days. She had also known John and was familar with our courtship and marriage. Since she was seeking a love story that originated from a serviceman stationed at Camp Stoneman, she asked if I would write ours. I was intrigued by the idea and consented.

My present husband Simon Mayeski said, "You need to write the full story of you and John." I was encouraged by my daughters also.

I will always appreciate my deceased mother for many reasons, but also for having saved what seemed to be every letter I and my children ever wrote to my parents. It was this huge supply of correspondence that helped provide some of the details of our family's lives that I couldn't recall well enough for this book. Reading her usually optimistic letters with her beautiful handwriting and skillful language was a joy.

My good friend Viv Phillips was the only person I had to help me confront, sort and organize my mountain of paper materials necessary for my research. That included not only boxes containing family education and employment histories, but also our medical and government records. There were seemingly endless amounts of greeting cards, letters and photographs. She was a very diligent and pleasant companion who helped keep me from being overwhelmed.

Once I was actively engaged in writing my story, Simon displayed endless patience and kindness in reading the many details of the Tate family as well as solving problems with my computer. After consulting with designers Patricia Hall and my daughter Patricia, he and I worked together on finalizing the cover. Bill Stephenson provided valuable insights for the story.

Marie Anne Mayeski, Professor Emeritus at Loyola Marymount University in Los Angeles, provided excellent editing assistance. Any remaining failure in story, structure or spelling is the result of my work, not Marie Anne's.

Simon's superior technical, editing and publishing skills completed the tasks required to put everything together.

I thank all from the bottom of my heart for helping to make *My Rock from Stoneman* a reality.

Introduction

THERE IS A JEWISH tradition of using stones and rocks as symbols of important memories. With a sense of gratitude, I have borrowed that idea for John's and my love story that spanned 47 years—44 of them in marriage to a magnificent man.

Obviously, John — often "Johnny" when we were younger —was my Rock. I admired his physical and mental strength greatly. What kept me most grounded was his spiritual commitment to what was important to both of us— lives of service to family, God and society.

Recalling some of the memories was, at times, emotionally painful and delayed the writing process.

I didn't expect to take six years to write the full story.

I didn't cling to my Rock. We strode freely side by side, supporting each other during the challenges and joys of our lives together.

This book is my last gift of love to him.

Contents

1. LADDER

IT STARTED WITH A phone call for me on July 30, 1982:

"Dolores, this is Eric, the teacher working with John. Maybe you should sit down while I talk to you."

"Why—is something wrong?"

"Yes, John has had an accident. He's alive, but injured." That sinking, sense of dread like I had upon learning of Carolyn's accident, started. I braced myself. "He just fell 20 feet off a ladder in the Taft annex gym!"

"Oh my God! Help!" I was too nervous at that point and started to cry.

"He landed head first, so his head is bleeding some above his right eye. We just put some ice on it to keep swelling down. He's lying down until the medics arrive, and he's disoriented. We don't know where else he might have other injuries. As well as John, I and two college students were painting for the school system for summertime pay. He was putting masking tape around a light when the ladder fell out from under him! Oh, the paramedics just arrived! They said they'll be taking him to Timken Mercy Medical Center."

"I'll meet them there. Thank you so much, Eric."

Before the medics left the hospital, I thanked them and the one named Fred, said, "He was in a stupor and disoriented when we got there—he didn't quite know what had happened. He's lucky! If I fell 20 feet and landed on my head I wouldn't expect to be here to talk about it!"

By the next day the diagnoses were: mild brain concussion, fractured hip and elbow. He had stitches on his forehead, a cast on his arm and would be using crutches for weeks. All his injuries were on his right side. His memory had come back and the neurosurgeon declared that part of him "fine". One of his doctors said John was very, very lucky, also saying he was a strong man to have taken the fall as well as he did. I attributed it not simply to luck, but to his strong will, healthy diet and nutritional supplements, and probably, how and where he fell. I was so full of joy and thankful that I still had my husband and our girls still had a father.

And his students still had their teacher. By the end of the year, that same Eric wrote him a note at school, with a strong acknowledgment of John's work: "John, This is one of the best planning books I have ever seen. You are such a true professional! You do such a super job here at school! Eric."

2. A STRANGER AMONG US

Sweet Summer Day
That we should meet—
A slim chance among so many;
He a guest—
Myself a part of the group;
He an Ohioan—
Myself a Minnesotan;
But happen it did—
On that sunny day in California

I DON'T KNOW WHICH were louder—my shrieks, or the surf! The Santa Cruz shoreline was great for viewing, but the lapping Pacific waves were gruesomely frigid for swimming—a challenge to enjoyment in swimsuits until numbness set in. It was an overcast but warm-enough June Day in 1951 so we high school girls were still determined to frolic in the ocean between screaming on roller coaster plunges and feasting at the beach picnic.

We were down for the day from the luxuriantly forested Santa Cruz Mountains, on break from a retreat at the Mount Herman Christian Conference Center. It was an idyllic place for contemplation and commitment where a little creek rambled and groves of coastal redwoods stood as quiet sentinels, adding peacefulness to our questing spirits.

Don Allen, our non-denominational church's minister, and his wife Lucille had made the arrangements for our young people's group of high school and college-aged members to attend. Among us were three college-aged servicemen from Camp Stoneman, who were attendees at our church in Pittsburg, California. (This river town is located just beyond the convergence of the San Joaquin and Sacramento Rivers to the east, and Stoneman was at the opposite end of town from the river, near the hills.) Bud, a tall, good-looking Air Force Protestant chaplain's assistant from Chapel Number One on base was one of the three with us. All of us there were just casual friends and acquaintances at that time. However, back home in Pittsburg we girls found it more interesting and fun to be with the servicemen at church than with our male classmates at school. Eventually, some of us did pair up for church activities, which included Bud with me.

3

By the latter part of August, I had turned sixteen and was looking forward to another group outing and seeing Bud. Everything was looking good that sunny day for our planned swim event at Mitchell Canyon. It was a recreational area near Pittsburg with a large pool nestled near the oak studded, beige rolling foothills of Mount Diablo, east of San Francisco.

The gathering place from which we would all leave was the residence of the hospitable Vriend family. I only remember what happened when the front door opened and I entered the living room. Immediately my gaze fell upon a handsome young stranger, sitting at the end of the crowded couch. His gorgeous, soulful eyes,—darker than my aqua ones—attracted me as well as his black hair—wavier than my naturally straight blond.

Other events I remember that special day included being in the pool and watching the quiet stranger's graceful laps across the pool. Slender, tall and broad shouldered, he was lithe as an athlete when he walked, which created another attractive scene! We all occupied ourselves with small talk and snacks while sunning ourselves on the grassy knoll.

By the time everyone said good-by that evening I wanted to know this unassuming, somewhat quiet Johnny Tate with the pleasant low voice better. We learned that he was also a chaplain's assistant, and that Bud had brought him. Within weeks Bud became less important to me, and I thanked him for having brought his "fly-boy" buddy because Johnny and I were clearly gravitating to each other.

Getting better acquainted was easy and enjoyable with this new person in our group.

"I'm nineteen and a 1949 high school graduate from Canton, Ohio. I thought at that time I might want to become a Catholic priest, but my parents were adamantly opposed to it. Not happy at home, I rebelled and joined the Army. But after my written tests, I was switched to the Air Force and sent to Lackland Air Force Base in Texas for my basic training and clerical school in Wyoming. I was willing to go to Korea, so was stunned when I was told I was more valuable in Pittsburg for processing those who *were* leaving and coming back.

"Nearly all U.S. units and replacements for Korea are being processed and staged at Camp Stoneman for both the Army and Air Force. The river here is an important conduit for getting the men to and from San Francisco."

He continued, "I have a sister who is almost sixteen. My mom, a daughter of Romanian immigrants, stays home and my dad works at the Ford Motor Company in Canton. He's a member of the Autoworkers' Union and was born in Romania."

"Romania? I'm sorry — I don't even know where it is and don't recall having met anyone from there before. You are my first Romanian friend!"

He scratched his head. "Some people wonder what I am, and ask me if I might be Greek, Spanish or Italian, but I seem to be taller than a lot of those I've met. My mom is 5'4". Even my dad is only 5'9", and I'm 6'1". Most people I've met aren't familiar with Romanians."

"Your background is fascinating to me. My paternal grandmother's parents came to the United States from a community near the Arctic Circle in Finland in the 1800's. My paternal grandfather arrived here in the late 1880's from a community near the middle of that country. My mother's parents were immigrants from Sweden in 1910. All of my grandparents ended up in Minnesota, so that's where my mom, dad, brother and I were born. I was seven when we moved to California. I'm also the oldest child in my family. My brother is three years younger than I. My mom is a nursery school teacher and my dad is a painter-decorator and belongs to the painters' union."

By Thanksgiving, Johnny spent time not only with me, but with my family. After dinner, Dad gave him the keys to our car for a ride, so he and I went over the nearby hills to Concord. We both enjoyed it until we had a flat tire and he had to change the tire in his blue dress uniform. It was time for him to buy his own car!

By the end of the year, he had it—an older coupe with room for two inside, and two outside in the rumble seat. In the interim, he had been walking several miles from camp to my house.

While I was having fun and getting more attached to this intelligent, reliable, honest and good-looking guy, I felt I could trust what he said and how he behaved. I found myself singing along with the pop tune recordings of "Johnny is the Boy for Me" while also worrying that I didn't want to "go steady" with anyone because I was planning to go to college. Going steady in those days meant that you dated only the same person, and I believed I was too young to limit myself in that way. Yet the romantic pull was there. I enjoyed his company and kisses!

By Christmas, his mother included this lovely heartfelt note in her card:

Dear Dolores:

—Just a few short lines to say hello and to thank you for keeping my son from being homesick. He tells me of the good times you both have, and how nice your parents treat him. That makes me feel so good, because I worry so over him. I hope you and your parents have a Merry Christmas. This is the third year without him. I miss him so, but with you, he won't miss us so much.

Love, Mrs. J Tate

3. EXPLOSIONS AND EXPRESSIONS OF LOVE

BY SPRING OF '52, Johnny had been assigned as a guide to top military and political personnel viewing atomic bomb explosions from a dignitary observation post in Mercury, Nevada. If there was much danger associated with that viewing neither the government, he nor other members of the public admitted or knew it. Las Vegas casinos were even advertising views of the nuclear blasts as entertainment for their customers! Johnny too, was caught up in the wonderment of the spectacles.

In his April 17 letter to me, this is how he described his situation:

"They are trying to give us a complete course in nuclear physics in a few hours. It was very interesting. We studied about radiation. What it was—what caused it— how to work with it. It is extremely dangerous. It can cause severe burns and even death, if the source is strong enough. Our work will be such that we will be safe. We are allowed to be exposed to radiation only for so long, then, we are taken off the job..."

He thought his experiences there were awe inspiring: *"You know, studying about atomic energy is like studying about God. It is so amazing and mysterious all these things that go on before us and we can't see them that one could not help but believe in God."*

Sunday, April 20: *"Today the press and radio are getting prepared for Tuesday's A-Bomb. This will really be some spectacle. The previous bombs have been very small—only 1.25 KT. This one will be about 33 KT. That is equivalent to about 33,000 tons of TNT—lots of noise from that! Maybe you'll hear it on radio and TV. Troops will participate in it. I should be there too. In fact, I know I will."*

From Mercury, Nevada 1952

6

We were at the point of signing our letters, not only with our names, but also with love. In his April 20 letter he also wrote about the weather:

Today is another beautiful day. The sun is out and it's nice and warm—was like this yesterday. I'm trying to get a tan before I leave here.

And tan he was when he surprised me with his June arrival back in Pittsburg! I was at my summer job as a clerk at the National Dollar clothing store, when he "popped" in! As I accidentally saw him enter the front doorway, I gasped! I was so ecstatic, and happy to see him! It was so easy to be thrilled as he was *gorgeous* with his jubilant smile, reddish-bronzed tan and dressed in his summer khaki uniform! Our embrace came in an instant! Later, since we were together in Pittsburg again, we made sure we had more photos of us taken.

Pittsburg, CA 1952. I'm wearing my first gift from John:

Pittsburg, CA 1952. In front of my house.

After receiving my '52 yearbook and having had student friends autograph it, Johnny decided he wanted to add his:

Dearest Dolores, You're the sweetest and most wonderful girl in the whole world. You have really been a blessing and a joy to my life. I thank God for you. It's been less than a year since I've known you but what a wonderful year. It is my hope that the rest of our lives may be spent together.

All my love to you always, Johnny

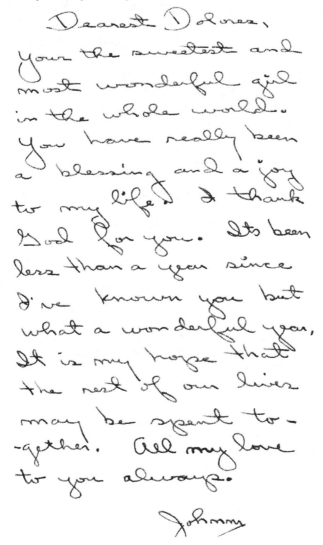

Pittsburg, CA 1952. Johnny's surprising autograph in my yearbook for my junior year.

His heartfelt words were so surprising and touching to me. I didn't expect such sentiments so soon. It was also an indication that he seemed ready for a strong commitment to a long future together. This was already more involvement than I expected. (But, he was twenty, and both my parents and his dad had married at that age. His mother was 19.) I was so emotionally involved with him, I didn't want to push him away, but because of my age and college plans, I couldn't express the same kind of commitment at that time.

We both wanted more time together, though. Usually it was with friends and relatives and sometimes just the two of us, as on Fourth of July. It was such a great day in San Francisco! The weather was gloomy and chilly, as a San Francisco summer day often is. Like the words from a song, though "... we had our love to keep us warm" while walking on the beach near the Seal Rocks, laughing our heads off at the amusement park, and exploring the streets of Chinatown.

In August I spent my seventeenth birthday with a surprise party at Eleanor Collett's. It was also the month for another significant event in my life—the arrival of my maternal grandmother, Ida Christopherson. She and my mother Peggy arrived via the San Francisco airport from Minnesota where my mother's brothers had been caring for her. At seventy-nine years old, it was Ida's first plane ride, and she enjoyed it to the fullest! I grew to appreciate my Grandma even better as I learned more about her. I had to share my bedroom with her, but it worked, partly because I was so busy, I didn't spend a lot of time there. In terms of temperament, I couldn't have asked for a more pleasant personality within that personal special space. And who could have guessed that she, a Baptist, also meditated? I started taking her to church with me on Sundays, which she liked a lot. She was thrilled when my family and Johnny took her to experience the awesome redwoods in Muir Woods.

It was my senior year and Johnny took a furlough in September to visit his family. While he was gone, I went to the California State Fair with our church "gang", and also spent some time thinking of my romantic situation. I felt that I loved him, but what did I know about deep, abiding love that is important for the long haul? Was I too young to have experienced it? What was it that I called love and signed my letters to him with it? I was somewhat worried at how fast he and I were connecting our lives, so would it help to date some people while he was gone? To find out, I dated a couple of people. I gained a gift of a personally autographed baseball from the one who was a baseball player for a professional farm team. Aside from that, neither experience was really very interesting or enjoyable, compared to what I had experienced with Johnny. They just didn't compare to him, and I missed him. Before he came back, I wrote to him about the other dates and how I reacted to them, so he could start to deal with his feelings about it then. I don't remember how my parents felt about this, but I had greatly irritated my usually quiet and mellow Grandma. In her wisdom, she had sensed that he was very special in many ways, and that I had no business "cheating" on him. It had been a good learning experience for me, and I was ready to go steady with him when he came back. Just picking him up at the train station had been a great event!

A marriage talk in one of my Problems of Democracy classes by Episcopalian priest Reverend Sandercock helped me better understand what love encompassed. Our English language has only one word to indicate it, which can be confusing when speaking of lovers or thoughtful attachment to country, siblings, and parents. He pointed out that the ancient Greeks, in their wisdom, divided the concept into three words: Eros for physical, emotional, sexual love; Philia for friendship, sibling and parent-child love relationships. Agape was for Divine, unselfish concern for people, God and causes. In Johnny's and my future years together, we were touched by all three.

4. RACE AND WRITING

I DISCOVERED I ENJOYED writing in English class of my junior year. Miss Lurana Lord, my teacher, encouraged me to enter a Jaycees' essay contest on "Americanism—the Key to World Democracy." Besides mentioning the positive aspects of living in a democracy with responsibilities here and to the world, I pointed out that there was a race problem involving Negros and whites in America and that it needed to be addressed.

It bothered me once I learned of it in junior high school. Racism—junior high? Yes! Strange as it may seem, I wasn't aware of it until then because thankfully it didn't exist in my home. When my dad Arnie started employment with the Contra Costa Housing Authority as a painter in 1946 our family moved over the hill from all-white Concord, California to integrated Pittsburg. Through summer 1949 we lived in the Columbia Park housing project, my mother Peggy taught nursery school there and Warren and I attended public school. All three were integrated and I was unaware that there were any conflicts.

After I did become aware in ninth grade, I searched the downtown library for information on racism but found none. By the eleventh grade, I had learned enough to submit my paper. I was stunned when I won first prize and was awarded an engraved trophy. It was presented to me at a banquet in June with Miss Lord at my side.

Earlier that year, Sam, a senior letterman and Galleon newspaper staff writer was elected student body president for the spring semester. It was the first time a Negro had been so honored at Pittsburg High.

In the fall, I told my Problems of Democracy class teacher, Miss Virginia Mabey, of a book I had just finished reading, recommended to me by Rev. Doran, my parents' Methodist minister in Pittsburg. It was Alan Paton's beautifully written novel "Cry, the Beloved Country" about the racial injustices and tragedies of apartheid in South Africa. It moved me deeply, so Miss Mabey had me write a term paper on it. I did it passionately and well.

Rev. Doran, originally from England, was the first person who introduced me to the Christian concept of social justice. Unfortunately, he was eventually relieved of his ministerial position because he was called "pink", associating him with Communists instead of Christianity. It was the dismal time of Senator Joe McCarthy's extremist hunts for "Communists" behind every figurative telephone pole! Doran had Negro servicemen from Stoneman at his worship services along with the white people and that wasn't acceptable to some. My parents were so upset with his forced departure that they left that church (where Dad was on the board but outnumbered), and didn't attend *any* church for years.

At *my* church I became upset one day when my Sunday school teacher replied to my concern about the lack of Negroes there. He justified it by saying they were of the tribe of Israel that was cursed by God.

Kay, Paula, John B., Eleanor T. and I were school newspaper editors who published a special 1952 presidential election issue about candidates Dwight Eisenhower and Adlai Stevenson. Our *Galleon* won the National Scholastic Press Association "All American Journalism Award." We were one of the five best high school newspapers in the country out of 5,000 evaluated! The criteria were not only mechanical excellence, but also vitality, creativity, and imagination. In addition, we were recognized in the national magazine "Student and Publisher" with an article and photo. Credit also goes to the rest of the students in our class, and our advisor, Mr. Eugene Phillips, who said the most important part of journalism was that we learned how to think for ourselves, which certainly helped in this endeavor.

5. GOOD-BY STONEMAN, HELLO SANTA BARBARA

ON NOVEMBER 21, 1952, Johnny was honorably discharged from the U.S. Air Force and Camp Stoneman. Then he had to leave Pittsburg all of a sudden for Ohio to mediate a crisis within his family. His sister Mary Jean, who was a few months younger than I, had eloped across the border into Indiana with her boyfriend Johnny, who was a year older than she. They were married on November 10. I never found out how her father reacted, but her mother Mary exploded, not only for running off and marrying a boy she didn't like at that time, but also because she was recuperating at home after major surgery. She felt that her daughter should have stayed home to continue helping her. It wasn't long before *my* Johnny had them sort of reconciled to one another, and the daughter was helping her Mom a lot. As far as the marriage was concerned, they have continued with it, have raised three sons, are grandparents, and are still married as of this writing.

While Veteran Johnny was in Canton, he was able to get a job the first week of December, and except for family duties was not interested in doing much else. His letters also indicated that he missed me a lot. I was feeling the loss big time too, was addressing him "Dearest Johnny" at the beginning of my letters and signing them with "Love and Kisses". I didn't feel like going out much either, so became a homebody except for church and special events, like the talk on peace that I attended with my parents in a Berkeley Methodist Church. I wished Johnny could have gone and wrote that I thought he would have liked it.

* * * *

It was raining a lot, with some flooding, but Mt. Diablo looked beautiful with snow! Christmas Day was uneventful for me; I just stayed home. I wrote to Johnny that I was thinking of him morning, noon, and night every day! But prior to that there were some pleasant outings. Mom took Grandma shopping to buy her grandchildren presents, while Dad headed for the Pittsburg hills with Warren to collect mistletoe.

I caroled with the church choir, sang with the "Harmonettes" quartet for chapel and the Serviceman's Club at Camp Stoneman, plus Pittsburg High's Christmas program. Greta joined us on college break to sing as an alumnus. We continued with the quartet singing Christmas carols for our local radio station. Guiding us on the radio was our former junior high choral director, Mr. Phillip Jones. Because he was from Wales, he took us to his church in Berkeley to experience beautiful music in the Welsh language, and where the whole congregation sat divided in the pews according to their choral

14

musical parts! I was blown away! I thought it was the *coolest* thing, and still do.

* * * *

When I picked up Johnny at the train station in February, we flew to each other to smother each other with hugs and kisses! I took him to kind Mrs. Nellis's where he rented a room. That year he worked at a couple of jobs to support himself until he could go to college on the G.I. Bill. He worked at Continental Can on the assembly line, and then at what he enjoyed most of all: assisting a surveyor along the river area, boating and surveying the lands on and out of the water.

June 12 was a big day for our family. Warren graduated in the morning from Pittsburg Junior High and I graduated from Pittsburg Senior High, along with 158 others at seven o'clock in the evening. Our high school football field was used for both ceremonies and Johnny was there for mine with my family. I was awarded a small scholarship for the teaching profession from the Pittsburg Civic Club. It was a complete surprise to me and the other graduates as Mr. Billeci announced it. In happy shock, it took me a moment to compose myself before I could walk down the bleacher rows in high heels to receive it! I had wanted to be a teacher since my junior high school days, so I was very grateful then and always have been for that assistance.

To earn more funds for college, I worked all summer in the office of the Bechtel Corporation, as a clerk-typist. Thank goodness I didn't have to do it very long. I found it so boring I was fighting sleep every afternoon. But because I appreciated having a job, I stayed with it.

Nancy and I had completed our plans to enter Westmont, a Christian College, but Johnny had a problem with his quest. He wanted to go to Cal Poly in San Luis Obispo to study engineering or architecture, but when interviewed there was told he had not met enough science and math requirements to enter at that time. While in high school he had excelled in some of those (which he loved), had been teaching college level drafting classes to classmates, was mechanically inclined and had the necessary drawing skills. However, he hadn't had the right guidance at school; his parents hadn't known how to guide him; and his clerical work in the military was unrelated.

So, what to do? If he had gone there, we probably would have seen each other on college breaks. If he went to Westmont, we'd probably see each other a lot more. We really didn't like the idea of being separated for very long, anyway. He visited Westmont, was favorably impressed, applied, and was eventually accepted. By September, Nancy, Johnny and I moved there to begin dorm life and studies.

Pittsburg, 1953. My Pittsburg High School graduation day photo.

Dorms weren't co-ed. Nancy and I shared a large room with a fireplace on the first floor at Emerson Hall with four other girls: Jan, Betty, Joy, and Lucy. What a dorm! Emerson was a large, beautiful gray stone, former mansion with a small reflective pool on the patio, palm trees, and terraced foliage. It also had a large flat balcony porch on the second floor where we girls used to sun ourselves and "fry" our skins with baby oil to get tanned. Our room, with tall doors full of curtained square windows off the patio, soon became the quiet gateway through which late students would sneak in after the ten o'clock curfew to avoid disciplinary measures by Mrs. Leonard, our "Dorm Mom".

My dresser had three framed studio photos on it, and they were all of Johnny! And where was he staying? Because he enrolled late, there wasn't room in the regular men's dorms, so he was put into a cottage with eleven other students, including Hal, another vet. Fortunately for studying, they all had individual rooms. (We girls used our dorm library.) It was within walking distance of Emerson. We both found part-time jobs—he with campus landscaping and I with window cleaning chores at Emerson.

There was so much beauty to behold in Santa Barbara. Off campus, and because Johnny had a car, we explored Montecito, the mountain foothills, and the ocean beach areas soon after we arrived in the fall. We swam in the ocean and visited the Santa Barbara County Courthouse, which, with its Moorish-Spanish architecture and murals was the most exquisitely beautiful building we had ever seen. We loved it!

On campus, situated off of Sycamore Canyon Road in affluent Montecito, we were surrounded by lush landscaping. Walks with special people could be very romantic, as it was for us. There was a semi-tropical "greener than green" little spot which we called "the jungle". It was surprisingly quiet at times considering it was just moments away from Kerrwood Hall, where there were classrooms as well as administration offices. With early evening sunlight peeping through the leaves, there was a little gray stone bridge where he asked me, and we pledged our love for marriage, for I was ready by then! He was a gem, and a living treasure I didn't want to lose. The sealing kiss was such bliss.

While still there we also discussed practical conditions. After obtaining his college degree, I was to return and get mine. I would be willing to work while he studied. Since some of our family backgrounds were similar, they helped us in relating to each other, and we had common interests in education, the arts, and spirituality. We loved children and wanted a family sometime in the future. We had almost no money, and I don't recall how we justified getting married at that time, but jobs were easily available then.

I didn't get a ring that twilight evening. He had decided prior to that time that he wanted me to help choose it. Soon we both went to a jewelry store on State Street and chose an inexpensive but beautifully crafted filigreed white gold set with a modest diamond and diamond chips on each side of the engagement ring and three little sparkly diamond chips in the wedding band. We were so happy and looking forward to revealing all to our families on Thanksgiving break.

My major in the fall was elementary education but Johnny didn't have one yet. I don't remember which classes were his favorites, but mine were the sessions with education professor Miss Campbell, speech and English with Mr. Cleath; Dr. Monroe's biblical history; psychology with Mr. Harley and of course, choir with Mr. Beasley. I was elated when I passed the audition to sing alto in the choir!

President of the college was Dr. Roger Voskuyl, a dignified yet pleasant man whom we didn't know, but with whom we would exchange friendly greetings in passing. He was highly respected on campus, known for his personal integrity, interesting conversations, and his own accomplishments in science studies, particularly chemistry. At graduation from Hope College he received high honors, which propelled him to Harvard, where he received his Master's and Doctoral Degrees. Since he was interested in Christian higher education, he accepted a teaching position at Wheaton College in Illinois after he finished at Harvard. He interrupted that at the request of the federal government to work at Columbia on the Manhattan Project, which developed the atomic bomb for World War II. He left after two years because his work was more valuable for scientific research methods than for atomic reactors. (We did not know of his involvement with the Project while we were at Westmont.) After serving as dean and interim president at Wheaton, he came to Westmont's campus as president in 1950. He was president until 1968.

I was pleased with my life on campus except for one unsettling question. Where were our Negro students? When I queried the registrar about it, he said, "There are people who wouldn't send their children here if we accepted them. There are even some who won't send them here because we teach psychology!" (It was okay to sing their Gospel songs and spirituals, but not have them living among us and studying as our equals. It was a culture of America, and shouldn't be of Christianity.)

* * * *

There was no opposition to our happy marriage news to our families and friends. My mother simply said, "You're grown up now." I was a bit puzzled over the fact that there wasn't more of a discussion of it. After she had passed away in 2007 I learned that she *had* wondered about it when I found some of her writings from January 1953, soon after her return to college. She wrote a paper for her psychology class entitled "Marriage or an Education?" Her paper began:

My problem primarily belongs to my daughter, her boyfriend, and the many young people that find themselves in similar circumstances...What started as a casual friendship has blossomed to something much deeper and he writes that he would like to marry next summer...Sometimes it seems as that would be the easiest solution but there are many conflicting emotions, especially on her part. She is graduating from high school in June and will be 18 in August. She has been taking a college preparatory course and is looking forward to going to college in the fall. Johnny, who is 21 years old, plans on studying under the G. I. Bill. He wants marriage and his education.

She continued to ask relevant questions, and then continued:

It has been widely discussed as to whether the necessity for an education has a detrimental effect on the emotions of young people when it requires them to wait so long for marriage. I frankly do not know the answer as it is difficult to be matter of fact when the problem is so close to one's personal interests.

She analyzed financial considerations, then asked,

What would be your advice?...I am no closer to a solution, but I do wish we could give her some concrete advice as to whether they should get married or wait until later...if they wait for even one year it may help them to see things from a better perspective.

The written advice from the professor was to

...never give advice. Your function as a parent is to supply information so they may think the problem thru, based on all available data...to see the problem from all sides. It must be their decision.

He advised counseling, which Johnny and I didn't do, but we read about marriage and discussed it with friends.

Jan, one of my dorm roommates, and I started planning our weddings during the 1954 winter break. She was a sophomore. Nancy, whom I had known since sixth grade would be my maid of honor; Eleanor my bridesmaid; Bob Ramsey, Johnny's best man; and my fifteen year old brother Warren, usher.

Johnny and I both felt spiritual needs to grow in our faith. So, when we were back in Santa Barbara, we continued to attend Westmont's chapel services and visited various churches off campus. First Presbyterian held our attention for a while; then we discovered more affinity at Trinity Episcopal for Sunday morning worship and early evening vesper services. We attended Mass once at the Santa Barbara Mission, but I didn't appreciate it like he did, because I didn't understand the Latin liturgy. I bought the little book "Your God Is Too Small" by Anglican J. B. Phillips at the Westmont student book store, and it still sustains me today.

In April, our choir went on tour. We had a special bus with a beautiful hand painted sign in Old English on the outside. It said, "Westmont College Choir" and had been created by one of our singing buddies, Sophomore Joe. On the road, there was always someone goofing off, and we traveled 1500 miles in 12 days.

We gave mostly *a cappella* concerts of sacred classical music in churches up and down the state of California as far north as San Francisco. When we needed instrumental accompaniment, Mrs. Beasley, wife of our choir director played organ. I was pleased that Mom and Dad drove to Walnut Creek for that performance. My only lament was that Johnny wasn't there also.

The tour was both musically and spiritually enriching. While on a visit to College of the Pacific in Stockton we visited the Methodist chapel. While there, I had a moving, meditative experience when I looked up at the beautiful rose stained glass window. I don't know if anyone saw me, but I spontaneously fell on my knees, deeply touched by the splendor of its multi-hued, intricate patterns. An overwhelming realization came to me: I craved visual artistry, as well as the drama of beautiful music with processions and symbolic ceremonies. All of these things taken together impart a sense that something important is happening.

The conclusion of our tour was singing on the national radio broadcast for Easter Sunrise Service at the Rose Bowl in Pasadena (another rose connection for me).

With the abundance of Westmont's music that year not only did my voice sing, but also my heart! Greta, Nancy's sister and editor of the 1954 Citadel yearbook, dedicated it to a music theme and Fine Arts Chairman John Hubbard. Because of Greta's singing background it wasn't surprising to me, then, that she presented Westmont as "Our Singing Campus". Besides the choir's Christmas concert at First Methodist Church and participation in the city wide Conductors' Choral Festival there were scenes and words depicting hymns in chapel, "singspirations" in the lounge, songs at the basketball games and off campus at the beaches. There were the male vocal quartet and pianist, who were considered "travelin' good will ambassadors" for the college. Even when there wasn't singing, there were classical music concerts with small group instrumental ensembles, and also a rally band.

We choir members sang at the Friday Baccalaureate service and the outdoor graduation ceremony at Emerson on Saturday, the fifth of June. Not only did Greta and the other graduates get their degrees, but so did some of the wives of graduates, as Dr. Voskuyl conferred "P.H.T. Degrees" (Putting Hubby Through)."*How cool,*" I thought, since I would be doing that soon as well.

Nancy, Johnny and I returned to Pittsburg where I had a bridal shower with close female friends and family. The wedding plans continued as Eleanor's mother Marian, a professional seamstress, made my white bridal gown. The wedding was to be Saturday, June 19 at 5:00 PM, but no one from my beloved's family would be there since we would be moving to Canton soon after the wedding where they were planning a reception for us. We had decided to move there temporarily, because Mary, my future mother-in-law, was not in good health.

6. MARRIAGE

THE LITTLE WHITE WOODEN Methodist church with a pictur-esque porch and simply furnished sanctuary would serve us well for the early evening ceremony and reception. It was also the church my parents had attended; I had gone with them occasionally. Since most of my and Johnny's attendance had been at the church where formerly non-denominational Don Allen was now a Baptist minister, he would marry us. (He had also arranged for my baptism when I was fourteen years old). Don would provide the instrumental music, for he was an outstanding concert pianist, and his wife Lucille, who had a beautiful soprano voice, would sing.

As I arrived at the aisle and set my pace to the pulse of Mendelssohn's music, I placed my arm on my dear dad's arm. Through my white cloud of veiled vision the glow of the candles lit up John's smiling face, making my joy as sweet as the scent of the beautiful blossoms. As our eyes met, I knew I was making the right decision. Our brief, traditional ceremony with commitments to love each other with implied faithfulness, plus the unifying Our Father prayer of all Christians, made our transformational relationship feel so real and sacred.

The only food was cake, coffee and punch. But there were 71 special people to share it and our happiness! Grandma Ida was especially pleased to be there. With evening slipping away, we departed soon for beautiful Marin County and the beginning of our married life, happy to be that night in a San Rafael motel on the "Redwood Highway" section of U.S. 101.

I was a bit subdued the next day in San Francisco. My hair even went limp from the damp air, but my honeymoon husband graciously didn't care. Exploring the sights was interesting, but the highlight of the day for me was an exquisite dinner, which completed our wonderful weekend celebration!

Returning home to say good-by to my family was the only difficult part of my new life. I hoped it wouldn't be very long before I'd be seeing them again. I wasn't fearful of our future though because I felt secure with my man, my *Rock*—whom I trusted fully to take care of me. I also felt, in a sense, like I was going back to my original home which was in the Middle West, because Ohio was there too. My relatives in Minnesota were a must-see part of the trip plans.

Our first honeymoon day on the road ended with a perfect night of love in a perfect place—a small cabin in a forested area near Lake Tahoe. It seemed like paradise to us! By morning we were refreshed, and looking forward to the next adventures northward.

Pittsburg, 1954

John loved driving across the country. Of all the states involved in the trip, I was most fascinated with Wyoming and South Dakota. The Grand Teton Mountains were awe inspiring with their craggy majestic beauty. In another area, Johnny stubbornly continued to drive through a raging Wyoming thunderstorm, even though we could hardly see. He ignored his wife's objections while more sensible drivers were parked by the sides of the roads!

South Dakota was full of many splendored scenes. The contrast of the iron rich red soils with the summer green plants and grasses were so vivid it seemed almost unreal—as though an artist had chosen colors that were exaggerated in intensity. Added to that were the placid chestnut colored ponies and large chocolate hued grazing bison. When we reached Mt. Rushmore in the forested Black Hills, we couldn't help but feel respectful of the sculptured scene. The enormous carved presidents' heads were awesome. We felt it was a fitting shrine for America.

7. CANTON AND ANAHEIM

WE WERE GREETED WITH warm hospitality in Canton also. Johnny's parents, John and Mary, held an informal wedding party for us in their back yard for friends and relatives. Their older neighborhood friends were such a delightful mix of Americans from Spain, Croatia, Romania, Italy, and Germany. Socializing, food, and gifts were the main ingredients for the happy affair. Mom and Dad gave us a large GE refrigerator-freezer and I felt rich!

The yard was modest of size but with two lots. One had the house, a Buckeye tree in the front, and in the back, another large tree with our toddler nephew's swing and the nice, separate one car garage built by my father-in-law. The sidewalk bordered that corner lot with one of two streets surrounding it. The adjacent lot facing the other street was lovely, with lush grass sporting a bird bath, a metal framed hammock, a redwood colored wooden picnic table with attached benches and two Adirondack lawn chairs in the back. In front was a colorful vegetable garden bordered by flowers, mainly planted and fertilized with lime by my father-in-law and visually similar to those created by other Canton Romanian immigrants who thought gardens were important. It was an inspiration for my subsequent organic gardens, which started in 1956.

Ohio experiences were pleasant, but not the humidity! There were no air conditioners, so I felt hot and sticky most of the time—even at night, so I lost my usual energy for our first two weeks there. The promised summer job for Johnny at a machine shop wasn't there when we arrived, so we stayed a little longer with Mom and Dad Tate than we had planned.

Soon after the wedding party, we were immersed in "Life in the Tate House." The chores were shared, so we were "enlisted" too until our jobs and school took over our lives. It didn't matter if one was female or male. Johnny helped, as he did as a kid, and since his dad worked the swing shift at the factory, he too was considered available. Not much rest for him!

Mom and Dad had bought their modest but pleasant three bedroom house after previously buying and selling a smaller one in another part of town. They had the downstairs area remodeled to enlarge the narrow rectangular doorway between the living and dining areas. The replacement—a great improvement—was a broad, arched entrance. Cleaning their place was done daily, especially the staircase leading to the upstairs, since it was not carpeted. The house was always spotless, well organized and tastefully furnished. It was a pleasant environment, planned mostly by Mary, who was particular about it and had some talent for accomplishing it. No wonder Johnny was so neat! Home and military life both insured it.

Mondays were dedicated to laundry, and considering the circumstances, it was understandable how it took up the full day, year round. It began in the morning in the basement, where there was a ringer-washing machine, a large laundry tub and full sized kitchen range, which was used not only for occasional cooking, but for laundry — some clothes had to be boiled! Colored clothes could fade, so they definitely had to be washed separately from the whites. After squeezing the water out in the wringer, the heavy wet clothes were carted upstairs, and then outside to be hung on the lines with clothes pins. There was nothing else comparable for giving the clothes that fresh, clean fragrance. If the temperature was cold enough to freeze, the clothes froze too, stiff as boards. In extremely cold weather or rain, clothes were hung in the basement, making them less fragrant, but making the chore much easier. The ironing board was up and ready to press the clothes as they came off the line. I was amazed that my mother-in-law even ironed sheets and my father-in-law's boxer shorts, convincing me even further of another good reason for Johnny not to wear boxers! I was thankful that he didn't, but I wasn't going to iron them anyway.

My mother-in-law Mary became her most vivacious when she was in the kitchen pleasing her son with the foods he loved so much! His favorites were the Romanian specialties she made so well. Topping his list was stuffed cabbage rolls (sarmale)—cabbage leaves filled with ground meat and rice, then covered with sauerkraut. Then there were stuffed green peppers (also with ground meat and rice) with tomato gravy, cornmeal mush, sour bean soup with tarragon, chicken noodle soup with vegetables and farina dumplings. Best loved pastries were rolled yeast nut roll, dessert crepes, and placinta: sour cream yeast dough filled with a pineapple, cottage cheese and egg mixture. We were both enjoying ourselves to the fullest with the delicious food fare, especially since my sparse cooking specialties were toll house cookies and banana bread. The one custom that surprised me when we first came was Dad's way of eating bread—that good unsliced Italian bread delivered to their door by the bakery truck. Where was the butter, I asked? Instead, it was "bare" bread, cut or pulled into chunks, and when eaten was often a "pusher" accompaniment for the food on the plate, or a "soaker" for dipping into gravies, soup or stew broths.

I hardly knew what TV was like. I hardly took the time to find out. But after we moved in with my parents-in-law, I discovered two programs my mother-in-law watched regularly that I learned to enjoy. One was Dick Clark's "American Bandstand" (my mother-in-law's favorite), and the other was the popular Catholic Bishop Fulton Sheen's "Life Is Worth Living", sponsored by a women's bank in Cleveland. He seemed very intelligent, knowledgeable, and articulate- a gifted orator, as well as sincere, dedicated to Christianity, people, and his church. His bishop's brightly colored garb seemed a bit melodramatic, especially the cape, but he was a dramatic man with piercing eyes. He seemed to inspire people toward developing their better selves. He spoke of inner peace and happiness, serving God and others out of love, relevant subjects for all people. I gained an additional appreciation of community when I heard him speak of Jesus as Our Lord, when in my past experiences I had heard only My Lord and, he ended each program with "God Love You". He left me with an indelible example of compassion when he said that at one point while traveling he had struggled with himself greatly, refusing for a while to touch a leper. He acknowledged he didn't have enough love until he was able to overcome that fear and embrace the man, which he finally did.

Staying that summer with Mom and Dad helped us a lot toward independent living. I was hired as a shoe salesperson at Stark Department Store where we x-rayed everyone's feet to get the proper fit! Johnny started receiving his G.I. Bill money for Kent State University (KSU), which was some thirty odd miles from Canton, so he became a commuter. He liked Kent State and appreciated a family connection in that his father's first cousin, Professor John Popa, was head of the Eastern European Studies Department.

Even though neither of us could ballroom dance very well, we had a delightful evening dancing under the stars at Moonlight Ballroom at Meyers Lake Amusement Park in Canton. A Big Band performed, one of many broadcast nationally on the radio at that time.

By fall we found an apartment. Early morning people we were, so we could eat the large breakfasts Johnny craved, and the new bride was happy to create, to please her husband. It wasn't long before Johnny found part-time work with the security company, ADT. In this job he was required to carry a gun when out on alarm calls. Soon he told me of a job opening at Western Union, in the same building and huge room where he worked. I was quickly hired, probably because I had typing skills. Large breakfasts went by the wayside since then I had to catch a bus to work across from where we lived at 7 A.M.

That job, though, was what I needed at that time in my life. It was more interesting than the prior one. I was still working with the public, but this time it was taking messages and money at the counter and typing or singing phone messages. Another task was sending teletype business messages directly to machines at manufacturing firms in the area, such as the Bliss Company, Diebold and the Timken Roller Bearing Company.

The most interesting of all the machines I used was the reperforator. This was used for all outgoing telegrams. I and the other women sat while typing on keys which punched holes on a wider tape. We had been trained to read those holes that meant letters for words. These tapes fed directly into a machine at our hub, Cincinnati. Receiving the incoming messages from Cincinnati meant sitting and sliding the wet, narrow, gluey tapes with printed words from a hand held round tool with water onto the papers with Western Union's letterhead at the top. Then, they were ready for delivery to the public. I also trained an operator for working a reperforator at Sears.

The only unpleasant task I had in our office was selling "Santagrams" in the fall, over the phone. I thought it was hard on poor people, especially children. To synonymize goodness with gifts and bad behavior with none or a lump of coal could make poor children look worse than the more affluent ones. Besides, it was teaching a poor motivation to be good. I explained my view to my manager, and he graciously allowed me to quit the task. I decided then and there that if I ever had children, they would be told the truth, in that their gifts, including the filled stockings, were from family members and whoever else gave to them at the time. Eventually, maybe our daughters had felt deprived of the Santa Story, because of the three who have had children, they chose to teach their children about Santa. Even so, I still believe the same about the Santa Story and prefer the beautiful birth story of the infant Jesus, to whom many children can relate, regardless of their economic status.

On the days that Johnny worked at the ADT office we flirted across the large room during spare moments between my various jobs!

Besides necessary furniture (which meant a console radio-phonograph, too), another important purchase was *Laudate Dominum*, Gregorian Chant by the Trappist Monks of The Abbey of Gethsemani in Kentucky. It's a four record set of 78 RPM records produced by Columbia Masterworks, which I still have today. The program notes were written by Thomas Merton (Father Louis). This was my introduction to Merton, the monastery, and monastic music. Johnny had read Merton's autobiography, *Seven Storey Mountain*, but I had not yet, so my main interests at that time were Father Louis's commentaries and the music. I was enthralled with the beauty, flow, and skill in the singing of plainsong.

Thanksgiving and Christmas, 1954 began many holiday seasons of celebrating food and family with Johnny's relatives. I loved his family!

I missed my own family, so we communicated with letters. I was puzzled when mother wrote that she, Dad and Warren had moved rather quickly to Long Beach, California soon after Johnny and I left Pittsburg that summer. My dad's two youngest brothers and their families relocated to Long Beach from Minneapolis a few years before, so he thought it might be worthwhile to live near them as well as explore job possibilities in the greater Southern California area.

Mom and Dad rented a pleasant Spanish styled two bedroom house with a nice large back yard. Both Dad and Warren obtained jobs constructing Disneyland before Warren had to attend Long Beach High in the fall. Warren met Walt Disney when he was painting Walt's apartment above the fire station at Disneyland. Walt was friendly and nice to Warren, complementing him that day after checking out both the paint job and the young and only painter. Warren's other decorating job was wallpapering the Main Street music store with individual sheets of real sheet music literature on the walls and ceiling. Dad found working on the Fantasyland Sleeping Beauty Castle with artists especially gratifying. Every time I see that castle and walk on Main Street I think of Arnie and Warren with pride!

Walt Disney gave a grand opening celebration to all the workers who built Disneyland and their spouses. He then opened it soon afterward to the public on July 17, 1955. It wasn't long before Dad was made a top foreman.

8. THE LOSS OF IDA

GRANDMA IDA DIDN'T MOVE to Long Beach with them. She refused at first, and then said she wanted to go back to Minneapolis to be with her boys. Mom and Dad paid for her flight back to live with her second oldest son "Gunny" (Gunnar) and his family. On June 2, 1955, we lost my beloved grandmother at age 82 of cardiovascular problems, and mother was so traumatized, she couldn't go to the funeral. Dismayed over that, I took a bus the next evening to Minneapolis to represent my family.

The funeral was on June 5 at Mother's birthplace, Cokato, and was a beautiful one. The chapel was packed with people and an explosion of flowers, with all arrangements lovingly planned by my extended Swedish American family. The service was led by a young Baptist minister who had a Swedish name: Rev. Howard T. Olson, and included a piano-accompanied song sung in trio form by three of my sister cousins, Barbara, Bonnie, and Gayle.

In writing to my family in California I said, "One of the things the minister said was that he did not have the privilege of knowing her, but he had been told that even during her times of financial troubles and other trying times, she didn't complain, but remained faithful to God and was cheerful. In describing Grandma, people used such adjectives as sweet, easy-to-get-along-with, kind. There were others too but it's hard to remember them all." People commented afterwards about what a good person Grandma had been, and while conscious, how cheerful she was in the hospital, even though being fed intravenously while also on pills and shots for pain. She never complained. I wrote, "If I ever have any sickness or suffering I hope I can take it the way Grandma did. She has been a wonderful example to me."

Everyone at the funeral seemed to respect and/or love her. Even the hospital medical personnel sent a letter of sympathy which surprised the family, because no one had previously experienced that.

Her Christian faith, prayer and Bible, which she read daily, had meant a lot to her and sustained her through the various stressful traumas in her life, such as her serious case of the 1918 influenza, death of two sons and permanent separation from her husband in the 1920's because of his drinking.

Ida was buried in the Cokato Baptist Cemetery with her husband Andrew (Anders) who preceded her in death by five years, by their newborn son at birth and by son Herman, who died at 19 in an alcohol-related car accident.

That last incident had been devastating to Grandma. Herman was the elementary school aged son with whom she had stayed up all night by his bed to pray for his life and care for his wound when he was shot accidently. It had happened while out shooting small game with his young brothers. She had rejoiced after he had recovered. The second time, however, had been impossible to save him. He was killed instantly as a passenger in his older brother's car driven by his drunken cousin who crashed into a tree. It was like having her heart ripped out of her chest and yet she forgave her nephew who survived, and begged him to change his lifestyle. What another good example for me.

Her third oldest surviving son, Hilding and his wife Sadie were also there, as well as sisters-in-laws. It had been Hilding's car that Herman was in when he died. It was so devastating to Hilding that he never drove a car again.

It had been better for Ida to have died back in Minnesota rather than California after all, with more of her descendant family around her. Her surviving children, minus one, plus all the grandchildren except two and her great-grandchild, helped make up for the large family of parents and siblings she had left in Sweden, never to have seen them again. As indicated by the few letters we have to her from Sweden, they were close, full of affection, and missed one another— great losses, then, on both sides of the ocean.

We were both pleased I had gone, but Johnny and I were so disappointed we had just missed seeing her before she passed away. We had planned to see her and I had already been given three days off from work to go there, but she died the week before our trip. He couldn't attend the funeral that week either because of college finals.

9. FINDING OUR WAYS

BEFORE MUCH LONGER, JOHNNY needed to declare his major at Kent. Around that time, he discovered the Christopher Approach, established by James Keller, M. M. in his book "You Can Change the World". It was published in the late forties, after the carnage of the two world wars and the Holocaust. There was such a great need to make the world a better place.

Believing that it was better to light one candle than to curse the darkness, to overcome evil with good, and through love carry light into darkness, the Christophers adopted these aims from the Chinese, St. Paul and St. Francis. The name Christopher was taken from the Greek word Christophoros, meaning Christ-bearer, believing that the good life of the Prince of Peace harmonized with the previously mentioned sources.

Keller was looking for ways in which average people, individually and responsibly without fanfare, could achieve practical accomplishments in the influential fields of education, government, labor-management and writing. There were no memberships or dues, just admonitions to love all people, pray and do well in the field of one's choice, working for the common good of all through beneficial ideas. He quoted Cicero: "What nobler employment or more valuable to the state, than that of the man who instructs the rising generation?"

Johnny was hooked—he declared his major as education, on the secondary level, in the area of social sciences. He loved history and geography and hoped he could help kids understand themselves and their places in the world better because of these and other social science classes. He eventually made a career of teaching in the public schools, with a keen recognition of the separation of church and state, while at the same time imparting responsible rights, duties and positive ideals for citizenship and away from tyranny. He respected all of his students because he believed every human being to be a child of God. In teaching American History and Government, he could connect to Keller's quote of a letter written by George Washington to a Hebrew congregation in Rhode Island: "For happily, the Government of the United States, which gives to bigotry no sanction, to persecution no assistance, requires only that they live under its protection, should demean themselves as good citizens."

He appreciated deeply what had been given to him as a citizen, just by having been born here. His grandfathers and their families had enough of the problems in Romania, so they came to America. Also, just before World War I, in 1913, his grandfather George and his two brothers fled to avoid conscription in the Hungarian military in Transylvania, that part of Romania where both sides of his family originated. His father's young brother George died in the 1918 influenza epidemic there.

His father, at the age of thirteen, with two sisters and his mother, arrived here in the early 1920's after his grandfather finally had the money for it. One other sister, age 18 at the time, was detained by a government official and never made it to the United States. Instead, she married and bore ten children.

After praying and studying the various Christian persuasions, Johnny and I became Roman Catholics in spring of 1956. We still retained a respect for some of the insights and beliefs of the various churches in our familial backgrounds. On Johnny's side, there was Romanian Orthodox and Romanian Byzantine (Greek) Catholic. On mine, there was Lutheran, Baptist, and Methodist. Both of us were dissatisfied with the little church we had been attending in Pittsburg. Catholicism was a unifying element for us in our struggle for spiritual wholeness. It was also a deepening and maturing of my faith.

I enjoyed learning about the liturgical seasons and attending Mass Celebrations of Lent, Holy Week, Easter, Pentecost, All Saints, Advent and Christmas. I was delighted to attend the Christmas liturgy. I had been used to going to church on Thanksgiving Day (which I still do) but not Christmas. I had joyful peace at high masses with "the smells and the bells", processions, and artistry which sometimes included classical music. It helped satisfy the sensorial worshipful needs for me that I had discovered on college choir tour.

A major concern among some of my Protestant friends was if Catholicism was really Christ-centered. With the Stations of the Cross, the aforementioned liturgical seasons and of course the daily liturgy as the Mass is celebrated, the life, death and resurrection of Jesus are central to all. Communion, established by Jesus at the Last Supper, became even more important to us as we were not to have serious sin in our hearts to partake of it. We were to have a sense of oneness with God and people, and if we had grievances with others, we were to reconcile first before coming to the altar, as the Bible taught us. If people think they can hate others and then go to Communion, this separateness becomes an illusion as to what the sacrament is about. This central and most important part of the Mass with Communion became my main focus in Mass as well. As with other Catholics, I also came to appreciate this as primary for worship, and preaching was secondary. The meditations in the Rosary were on the Life of Christ. And Via Dolorosa, the path Jesus took as He carried the cross to Calvary explained the source of my first name. I didn't like learning that my name meant sorrowful, or sorrows, but once I associated it with the sufferings of Jesus and also His Mother (as in Michelangelo's *Pieta*), it was transformed for me as compassion to be shared.

I thought confession was spiritually good for all souls, as well as for psychological and emotional healing when there was a valid reason for it. Forgiveness, whether inside or outside a confessional place, is foundational for the Christian faith, and it helps not only the person receiving it, but also the person bestowing it. People who don't have a habit of an examination of conscience sometimes bury their guilt in their subconscious and can have unfortunate consequential, conscious behavior resulting from the lack thereof. There can be a joyful sense of freedom from forgiveness. I know. I've experienced it.

Catholics are big on buildings and blessings! I enjoyed gaining quiet, sacred spaces where I could walk in at any time of the day to pray and be at peace. The names of many churches had beautiful names of good, real people—those we call saints. (This is true in some Christian churches other than Catholic as well.) The benevolence that is imparted in blessings is wonderful, whether the recipients are people, other living creatures, places, or food!

Social justice, helping suffering people in unjust circumstances, was described in the Bible and is also found in later practices of the church. Some of the popes had written about it in their encyclicals.

I never heard the words "social justice" in our little Pittsburg church, but instead we were taught beliefs that prohibited social activities such as secular movies, the drinking of alcohol and dancing. When I became a Catholic, like many of my Protestant friends, I too enjoyed a drink or two at celebrations, and thoroughly enjoyed dancing. Obviously, many movies, including those that are not religious, are excellent, and some are trash and a waste of time, especially if vices such as violence are glorified.

We were instructed by, and accepted into the Church by Father Regis McCoy, a Benedictine Priest at St. Benedict's, a small mission church established by monks in Pennsylvania. Aunt Vic and Uncle John were happy to be our sponsors. The church was only a block from them, and only a few blocks from our first purchased house, made possible by Mom and Dad Tate. They took out a second mortgage on their house to help us live next door to them, with those two lovely lots between, and room in the back yard for our own organic garden.

We had a few reactions by others than Johnny's family: We received some written comments: Eleanor, bless her, said, "Well, wherever the Holy Spirit leads you". Nancy was also benevolent. "Dear Dee, I admit I was very surprised to find out you had turned into a Catholic. Yet I know you haven't lost your salvation at all and are still saved. And, don't think for a minute that I would let our friendship end or become hurt because of it. We were too close for that and it will never change on my part." The last two were comforting to us. It was a huge disappointment, however, to my parents. Dad exploded into an emotional rage in his written response to my letter of my faith decision:

You write me a letter like that and expect me to take it lying down. You underestimate your parents' intelligence and patience!"

Not only was he adamant to me, but he also felt that he had failed as a parent.

I had always assumed that you would mature in the normal fashion, after Mom and Dad had planted a few seeds of reason. But apparently you are a dreamer and refuse to grow up. I thought I had raised a daughter to stand on her own two feet. I'm sorry to say I have failed miserably!"

He didn't think I had been thinking for myself.

You will never be a free person, either intellectually or any other way. You will always be a slave to one of the worst brain washings a human being can fall heir to.

I was, as a man, hoping you had married one. I'm sorry to relate the fact, that you are married to nothing but a mamma's boy and slave to a stupid religious doctrine. As a father I am not a bit proud of you or him.

Sadly I write this, Your Dad

He thought the Catholic Church hierarchy was corrupt and too authoritarian. But our focus at that time hadn't been on the hierarchy. Also, he blamed Johnny's mom, who attended church only occasionally and when she did, went to the Roman Catholic Church because she didn't care for the priest of her husband's church. What really did influence us, instead, were the positive, sweet spirits of Aunt Vickie and Uncle John, who helped a lot at St. Benedict's. Vickie, an immigrant child of eleven when she arrived in America, worshiped at St. George's Romanian Byzantine Catholic Church with her brother (Johnny's dad) and their parents until she married, and according to Romanian patriarchal custom, then had to go to her husband's church, which was Roman Catholic. Both the Orthodox and Byzantine Catholic Romanian churches practiced the Greek Liturgy; one recognized the pope as head of the church, the other didn't; both allowed married clergy. Johnny's maternal grandmother Mary was Byzantine Catholic when she married his grandfather Nick, and had to become Orthodox. This is why my mother-in-law Mary, child of those Romanian immigrants, was raised

Orthodox, but then when she married Johnny's dad, she also had to change to her husband's church. This, then, is how my husband had been raised in St. George's Byzantine Catholic, mostly attending with his dad, serving as an altar boy, and where his grandfather George was a cantor.

So, Roman or Romanian? We liked the international aspect of the Roman Catholic Church, where Latin was a common denominator for liturgical responses and not homilies, but was a hindrance for our own full participation. When English masses were established, we were big promoters of them. Since St. George's Catholic was still largely an immigrant church, much of the worship service was in the Romanian language, which was good for those people, because that was their first language. However, I didn't understand it, and Johnny understood it some, but could not speak it. As much as I grew to love some Romanian traditions, we both didn't want to spend as much time with them as we would have in the Byzantine Church. In the future, where and when we could make time for Romanian people and customs, we did, and enjoyed doing so tremendously! Eventually, after our decision, we made what we thought would be a friendly visit to Father Crihalmean, the Romanian born Byzantine Catholic priest, and a friend of John's, to tell him of our choice. Did I say friendly? It turned out to be anything but, as he threw a framed photo of Johnny at us, and shouted at us to leave! I was stunned. "What a way for a clergyman to act!" I said.

And getting back to my parents, what had my mother written?

Dear Dolores,

We want you to know that we do not approve of what you have done one iota.

She was extremely upset over the censorship:

They are afraid that it will open your eyes to the ignorance and stupidity whereof they preach in the name of The Creator. Since when are mere men supposed to tell you what and what not to read? I say read everything you can and then and then only make up your own mind.

Love, Mother

It was as though they had looked only at the beginning of my July first letter where I said, *"There are times in all of our lives when we must make important decisions. I have recently made one of the most important decisions of my life. I have become a Catholic."* For, they were so enraged nothing else I said seemed to register with them. Neither did they even consider any of my points of view. If they had read them, they couldn't be considered valid because of the "brain washing".

What else I had said was the following:

I know this statement might be a tremendous shock to you. It must also be hard for you to believe since you know I have always been so opposed to Catholicism.

For the last several years I have had questions about my Christian faith and have been searching for answers to them. I have sought solutions in five different denominations but have still been dissatisfied. I decided to investigate Catholicism, and much to my surprise, I discovered the answers to many of my questions. Now I can see that Catholicism is not what I thought it was. My views were colored by prejudice. Also, I found the expressions of many of the high ideals which you have taught me to be good and noble.

You have always taught me to be loving, kind, obedient, polite, and truthful. You have always taught me to regard the poor man and the poor man's job with as much respect as the wealthier position and job. All work is honorable, says the Church, and to love all men of all economic statuses and positions is our Christian duty.

Love of all races has been so clearly taught to me by both of you in word and deed. This too is explicitly taught by the Church. Love of our fellow men knows no color boundaries. Maybe you have read in the papers of the stand the Bishop of New Orleans has taken against segregation there.

I always have, and will continue to appreciate all you have done to teach me the right attitudes toward all these things. Thank you so much.

Please know that my love for you always continues to grow. If it seems that I have turned against you in this matter of conversion it is because this is so important a matter that it means life itself to me, and even the strong disapproval of my family will not deter me. Johnny didn't urge me to do this. I did it of my own free will after a lot of reading at home, and then after taking instructions at church.

There are many more things to be said, but more than I can include in a letter. However, I couldn't keep from telling you this much, regardless of the consequences. I want to share all my important experiences with you. I haven't told you sooner, because I wanted to make this decision myself without any outside influences from others.

Hoping you'll understand, I'll close by saying love to you and God bless you. Dolores

Out of all the letters Mom saved of our correspondences to her and Dad, the ones Johnny and I sent in answer to these blistering attacks are nowhere to be found. Maybe she found them too unpleasant. However, they both responded to our defensive replies.

July 23, 1956

(Dad) *"Dear Dolores and Johnny—*

First, let me say to you both—bravo! It was a complete thrill to find you both are thinking! I know now that so many of my assumptions were wrong. I humbly apologize for any aspersions I may have cast on Johnny or his parents' character.

However, I'm glad I wrote the letter the way I did. It brought out the best in you. Johnny, I wish you would concentrate on writing, for you do a beautiful job.

After being away from organized religion more or less for about ten years, Mother and I decided to give it another try when we joined the Methodist Church in Pittsburg. I was put on the Board of Trustees and served in that capacity for one year. There was so much hypocrisy and division in their thinking, it nauseated me. Rev. Doran was practically crucified when he "retired" because of his sociological thinking. And this by his congregation who professes to love God's ways.

Believe me, it has been hard for me to make my decisions. I like to believe Mother and I have had some ideals and principles. You have a right to believe that or not. I also like to believe that reason has had some part in my personality, instead of as you say, always emotionalism.

You both talk of me jumping to conclusions. Put yourself in my position for one moment and you will realize why I said what I did. Especially, if you will ever know that I love knowledge and respect the same more than any other thing in our universe.

Some of the books which created my opinions: Liebman's Peace of Mind; Overstreet's Mature Mind; Thoreau's Walden; Paine's Age of Reason; Marcus Aurelius' Meditations; Francis Bacon's Essays New Atlantis; Sinclair Lewis' Main Street; Henry George's Progress and Poverty and Social Problems; Bellamy's Looking Backward; Mark Twain's Huckleberry Finn." (Dad was amazing for all the intellectual reading he did through the years without the benefit of college.)

By the way, Dolores—how many women do you know in this society that has gone to college after raising two children, like your mother did? Why? She got all A's and B's, also. Your mother and I have also taken a partial course in Sociology and Economics in night school these past few months. Does that imply that we are not trying to learn or understand?

There is no point in any further discussion .You have a right to your opinions and we the same. Let me again ask your forgiveness for the personal insults. Believe me, my estimation of you both has increased considerably.

Much love and happiness to you all,

Your Father

P.S. Mother and I attended opening night at the Hollywood Bowl—all Tchaikovsky—It was an evening we will never forget.

(Mom) "Dear Dolores and Johnny,

We think Johnny wrote us a very informative and good letter which showed much maturity and we respect him as a man. Daddy was hurt of course, but admitted that many of your accusations are correct. He at least knows how you both feel about him. He should have made his letter more detailed to get his viewpoint across. The statement about Johnny's folks should have not been made, but was done in anger.

We know how M. (family friend) has been mixed up because of her religion. Catholicism encourages a woman to sexual relations with her husband, but M. said she could never enjoy their intimacies because if she practiced birth control she was doing wrong and when she didn't, she feared pregnancy because what intelligent working people want to have ten children to raise in poverty? Of course, the priest does not have to support them, but knows it will make the church more numerous. Their views on the subject make good Catholics either fools or hypocrites.

We know Daddy has been too emotional in discussions. He has tried to improve himself and I think he will overcome too much emotional arguing. Neither of you has had it too difficult, I believe, have not suffered the poverty he did as a child (one of seven children), a depression, and lack of opportunity for a good education.

Dolores, you have not lived too long, suffered too much, or read too much, so be careful before you say you are right. But, try to do what you think is right, which is all any of us can do. We are all products of our heredity, environment, and unique experiences and no two people have the same. It is small wonder that there is so much disagreement no matter how close your life is with another.

We feel we know so little yet and will not have the time to read one iota of what we desire but we want to learn little by little as we find the time. But when we were so certain that we knew all the answers, we argued about the pro and con merits of the Baptist and Lutheran faiths, having read nothing else.

When writers, artists, scientists, and educators cannot say the things that they must believe is truth and good for the majority it is time to investigate the Un-American Committee. Your educators in public schools should have freedom to tell what all isms represent without fear. If democracy or a religious belief is good we should have no fear of criticism or of having people learn different ideas for we should feel as former President Roosevelt, that 'we have nothing to fear but fear itself'.

We do not wish to continue a running argument on religion, so in our limited time have done the best we could to tell you how we feel so you can understand us better.

We love you both,

Mother.

10. A GOOD YEAR

Sunday, June 17, 1956

Dear Dolores and Johnny—

Thank you, thank you for remembering me on Father's Day. There is nothing in this world that could have thrilled me more than getting the book. I've read so many references lately about Dostoevsky's "The Brothers Karamazov". It has aroused my curiosity. It seems the older I get the more fascinating literature becomes to me. I am of the opinion now, that of all of life's thrills, there is very little that can take the place of good literature. Again, thank you both so much for your excellent choice of a gift for me.

Warren's graduation exercises were beautiful Thursday night. We truly missed you. You would have loved it.

Much love, Dad

WE WERE SORRY WE couldn't attend Warren's graduation from Long Beach High due to jobs, school and cost. Fortunately, we were able to plan a trip for me in the fall. Before I arrived, though, our family almost lost my seventeen year old beloved brother! He was riding with his friend Charles on a pleasant summer night in Long Beach with the windows down. The street went beneath an underpass, and just as they arrived at the top, a shopping cart was right in front of them! Charles suddenly swerved to avoid it, and as the hardtop convertible careened uncontrollably, Warren (no seat belts then) flew out the window and landed on a grassy divide as the vehicle rolled onto Warren's head. Just behind them was a police car from which the two policemen dashed out to help. Warren yelled, "Get this damned car off my head!" Well, they couldn't. Soon the ambulance arrived, and all the medical/police personnel were finally able to lift it off of him. Everybody was puzzled as to why he didn't have worse injuries. Warren later said it was because he landed on the grass, where there was enough flexibility and cushioning to save him. He stood up, but the authorities ordered him to "Sit down—you're too injured to stand!" So he did. Blood was oozing down his face, and Warren said, "My skull feels soft, like a balloon, and I can push my fingers into it!" At the hospital, it was discovered that he had a cracked collar bone, multiple bruises and cuts, but no serious injuries to his skull/brain area, so the doctors allowed him to go home. What a relief and thankfulness from our family! We used to joke about our family's stubbornness, but this was a new slant on it as his head refused to get too hurt. Maybe it was "Sisu", the word that Finns use to describe our mental attributes of stoic toughness, strength and will, that helped him get through it all.

On my first visit back with my family since my marriage, it was also my first plane trip that fall. I'll always remember that "red eye" flight. Climaxing it was the descent to the Los Angeles Airport. I had never been so high before, and the immensely beautiful, broad bird's eye view of L.A. with its tiny, flickering amber lights against the black pre-dawn sky was an awesome sight to me just as I woke up. Soon Mom and Dad greeted me, beginning my Visit of Multiple Joys.

There were no discussions about church issues. There had been reconciliation, so we just enjoyed being with one another, sharing our love. We started with a brief jaunt to Lake Arrowhead, and then Dad took a day off work from Disneyland to show us a great time there. A first for me was an all day trip to Catalina Island with Mom and Dad. Even the boat rides there and back were fun, for we Hills never get seasick! We drove up to Santa Barbara to see the now married Nancy and Paul. Nancy had left Westmont after her freshman year also to study nursing at Cottage Hospital in Santa Barbara. While she was in training Paul, a Westmont graduate, was teaching. In between, I was harmonizing old songs with my dad around the little fire pit bonfire in Mom and Dad's back yard, where there were more visits with our extended family.

Back in Canton, on November 2, Johnny wrote a letter to my Dad, Mom and Warren where he indicated some of my contribution to his education: *"I've just arrived home from school and have a few minutes before Dolores will be ready to come home from work. She sure has been a faithful worker in helping me finish school. I don't think a lot of people would have done it like she has. I really feel fortunate and am very appreciative of her."*

Also in November, at 21, I voted for the first time in the national election. In a letter to my high school Problems of Democracy teacher, I wrote:

"November 6, 1956: Dear Miss Mabey, Tomorrow is voting day. For the first time in my life, I am able to actually practice my right and privilege of voting."

I told her how as a senior in her 1952 class we students were energized by participating in a mock national election, complete with campaigns and issues for discussion. I confirmed that those activities helped create in me a vital interest in government and a feeling of responsibility for active government participation. *"I am writing this to thank you for taking such an interest in your students, teaching them about government in such a way that is both interesting and educational."*

On November 11 she replied:

Dear Dolores,

For a teacher, there are few thrills that can equal the one that comes from reading a letter like yours, and your timing was masterly!

Tuesday afternoon I was limp with exhaustion and wondering if a mock election is worth the expenditure of time and energy. Definitely yes—even if only one in a hundred or so students feel as you do. Yes, we held our usual election, preceded by discussion and bulletin board rivalry. I still find voting a wonderful experience and never take it casually.

Thank you so much for taking time from your home and job to write me such a morale-building letter.

Affectionately, Virginia Mabey

Another good happening in 1956: we became homeowners for the first time, having bought a pleasant place from the Pont family who had taken good care of it, so we didn't have to spend money improving it, and we loved it! The outside was an older style, but the inside was modern.

It had only two bedrooms, both with hardwood floors and located upstairs, but one was large, running across the full front of the house. The highlights for the living room were a fireplace with mantle and built-in bookcases on each side with glass doors. We had more than enough books for them, including a large, beautiful Catholic Bible with white leather covers and much colored art, which we had just purchased. The open living room, dining room area had beautiful sculpted, wall to wall carpeting, and the kitchen was up to date.

We had two lots, so had room for a garden beside the garage. Soon after we moved in we were rewarded with a visit from a young man on crutches, from whom we bought a subscription to *Organic Gardening Magazine*. I had remembered my mother had bought a subscription to it during WWII for her victory garden when I was in second grade.

11. THE ADVENT OF CHILDREN AND VISITS

IN SPRING OF 1957 I became pregnant, and we were elated over the prospect of parenthood! We pondered that this might be the first in our plan of raising four. We both had grown up with just one sibling, and thought it might have been even better to have had two or maybe more. After our parents and Warren, Aunt Vickie, Uncle John and Mike were next to be told.

Warren had joined the Air Force some months after high school graduation, and while attending school in Illinois, he visited us twice during the summer. That first weekend visit was such a great surprise! When I answered the knock on the door, he was standing there after having walked several miles from the bus station. He hadn't told us he was coming. He had managed to get a ride from one of the other fellows on base as far as Fort Wayne, Indiana, and from there took the bus to Canton. We enjoyed relaxing at home, amusement rides at Myers Lake, dinner at a restaurant and took him to the bus station early enough for him to get back to camp on time. Later that year he visited us again before being shipped overseas to a base near Tripoli, Libya.

I was feeling great, still working full-time and also doing all the regular chores of housekeeping and cooking. We accomplished the usual preparations at home for the baby, while family and my co-workers celebrated with us by giving me two showers.

What wasn't usual, however, was that I wanted to have our child delivered without anesthesia, so it was called natural childbirth. When I discussed it with Johnny, he said "I was born that way. I was delivered in my grandparents' home in Alliance, Ohio with only a doctor to attend."

No one that I was aware of was delivering that way in American urban hospitals at that time. I had bought "Childbirth without Fear", a contemporary book written by Grantly Dick Read, an English M.D. and obstetrician. He wrote that to arrive at the desired goal for delivery, this holistic prenatal process had proven better for the mother psychologically through less fear, emotionally as a fulfillment of love and nutritionally through improved diet and supplementation. Exercises were recommended, so I performed them by using the descriptions and photos of his patients in the book because they were the only sources I had. With this approach, his own patients had less maternal physical tension and pain. The alertness and stronger, earlier breathing without outside assistance was also a better start for the baby. So I had high hopes for a special kind of happiness, and good health for my baby. I was looking forward so much to being awake for the awesome event.

43

In 1935 when I was born in Minneapolis General Hospital, my mother had not been allowed this option, had been given ether, and was kept there for two weeks, as though she had been ill. My only inspiration was Dr. Read's book. I chose to deliver at Timken Mercy Hospital, to be ready for any emergency, if there would be one. I found a Doctor R. on their roster, a lady with only a few years' experience, who had no children herself but who was willing to accept me on the basis of having natural childbirth, even though I would be her first patient for it. I was elated, and very grateful for her.

In addition, I wanted to nurse my baby, which nobody I knew was doing either. Formula and bottles were deemed the modern way to feed babies. Dr. Read was an advocate of breast feeding, and my obstetrician would allow me to do so. I remembered that my mother said she had nursed both me and my brother in the 1930's. Mothers had been nursing their babies for millenniums, so I thought there was nothing odd about my doing it in the 1950's. It just made sense to me not to waste the milk that was the healthier choice for my baby.

I added to these plans a "Mother and Baby" course offered by the Red Cross. It wasn't about childbirth itself, but helpful for prenatal/postnatal care. I received the highest rating in the class for having the best and most varied diet. I cut down on salt intake, and took the physician recommended supplements of calcium and iron.

Through a friend of ours we met two Hindu Indian doctors. They were working at Aultman Hospital in Canton. Dr. P. in his early thirties at the time was married and a practicing physician in India, but was not allowed to practice the full scope of it because he had not been educated here. Dr. V. was twenty-five, single, and acquiring at least some of his medical education here, with a further goal of attending one of the major Ivy League medical universities to learn nuclear medicine. Both had been allowed only to deliver babies, which was not fulfilling enough for what they wanted to accomplish. Dr. V. was very surprised to learn that forceps deliveries were such a common practice with normal childbirths in the United States. He thought that method was not good; that they should be used only when necessary in some abnormal cases. He said that was the case in India, where forceps were rarely used. Dr. Read was of the same opinion.

V. also said he had seen poor people here refused medical help at the hospital because they didn't have money to pay. I was deeply moved when he said, "If people are sick and they can't pay, I'm not too happy about it, but as a doctor, I have the obligation to help them anyway, because my job is to help those humans who are suffering."

"You have your father's..." At the end of August I went to one of my routine maternity checkups and everything was fine except for one small exception. I asked Doctor R. to look at a small rupture of blood vessels in a small vein on my upper left leg. She said it was rather unusual to have the trouble that early with a first pregnancy. I told her that my dad had varicose veins, so she said I probably inherited the weakness for it. She told me to stay off my feet more and elevate them when I did. I decided to do that, because I didn't want the same problems he had experienced.

After thinking about that for a while, I recalled a statement made to me by my paternal grandmother when I was in junior high, living in Minneapolis, while visiting her and my step-grandfather, Alex. As I descended the stairs to the downstairs part of the house, she said, "You have your father's legs!" Unfortunately, I thought of this much later when I couldn't ask her these questions: "How in the world did she remember the shape of his legs when he was the fifth of her seven children? Did she remember the looks of all her kids' legs? Plus, she had been stepmother to her deceased sister's five children mostly before she had her own family. Did she remember how their legs looked also?" This was hilarious to me as I pondered her outstanding visual acuity. The unknown vein thing was not part of her observation, but it did continue to be part of my future in a negative way.

12. BARBARA

TO GAIN MORE INCOME for our expanding family because I was leaving my job at the end of November, Johnny acquired his first teaching position before he finished Kent State, also in November! There happened to be an opening for a sixth grade teacher at Genoa Elementary School in the Perry Township School System near Massillon, and he was accepted for it. How fortunate for us, but his remaining university studies would have to be part-time.

My due date had been estimated for New Year's Day 1958. Well, Baby didn't get photographed by the newspaper to welcome the New Year because it wasn't quite the right time for her to enter the world.

After my water broke the night of January 12 my doctor told me to go to the hospital, and we did. Johnny was with me for hours, but when it appeared I wouldn't be delivering for a while, he was told he could go home and then teach the next day, which he did. That first experience, with 18 hours of labor pains was intense and miserable. Our beautiful, normal daughter arrived at 4:07 PM, as though she had been waiting for his arrival, which was near the same time, but in the waiting room for fathers. She was 6 pounds, 13 ounces, with a lovely round head that had not had bruises or depressions because there had been no forceps used. I had worked so hard, my body responded immediately afterward with tremors, which lasted only minutes. The birth event itself exceeded my highest hopes! To see her as she left my body, and to hear her cries, brought me the greatest joy. This spilled into brief, tearful feelings of wellbeing and thankfulness to God for my part in the mystery of the co-creation of new life! After they cleaned her and wrapped her in a receiving blanket, she was given to me to hold. Once that happened, I had a surprisingly intense feeling of confidence. I was instantly transformed into my own "Mother of Confidence", feeling so capable of taking care of that baby. I wrote to my parents, "It's a glorious experience to be a mother!" I added, "Johnny is very thrilled and proud of her, too. I'm sure he's going to make a good dad."

That evening, her grandmother Mary came to see her first granddaughter through the glass at the neonatal nursery. Mom noticed that Barbara appeared somewhat pale, and a little blue. Because of Mom, Barbara was given oxygen that first night, and was fine the next morning. While I was taking a shower at that time, the pediatrician knocked, and since I was near the door, was able to stick my head out easily. What he told me was significant. "Good morning, Mrs. Tate. It's a good thing you didn't have any anesthetic yesterday, since your baby had the umbilical cord wrapped around her neck twice. She could have been severely damaged." Upon that revelation, I was determined to continue with natural childbirth if I had any more children.

We named her Barbara Marie; Barbara, because we loved the city of Santa Barbara so much for its beauty and the place of our engagement. We learned later that the channel and one of the islands there were also named the same, by navigator Juan Cabrillo who found the area lovely, too, on the feast day of Saint Barbara, December 4, 1542. Our baby's middle name is a form of Mary, the name of her paternal grandmother, and the mother of Jesus.

Fortunately, my mother Peggy was with us by the night of mother and baby's arrival home, six days after the birth of Barbara. She, however, didn't seem to appreciate the transition and cried all night, exhausting both Mom and me.

Mom with me for a week, and we "got going" with the nursing. One day soon after she left for California and Barbara was sleeping, I was standing in the kitchen, and suddenly, to my terror, something fell out of me and onto the floor! The only thing I thought it looked like was maybe a liver. I knew it couldn't be, but after the call to the doctor, I learned it was part of the afterbirth, which should have come out at delivery. I was shaken, but fine, then thought about my Indian doctor friends, Doctors P. and V.—maybe I should have had one of them for the birth.

13. BEGINNINGS

BARBARA AND I WERE getting along fine with her feeding until the third week, when I developed a cracked nipple on one of my breasts. I seemed to have enough milk, so I wanted to continue. I called the doctor, and she didn't know how to help me, so when I couldn't stand the pain anymore, she told me to quit the nursing. I was so emotionally devastated. It was possible to remedy the problem, but neither of us knew how. I nursed as long as I could on the one side while at the same time I was weaning her. It wasn't done well or slowly enough as my breasts became engorged with too much milk, hard as rocks, and excruciatingly painful. By the time I put her on formula and yogurt, I recalled that while I was in the hospital and the nurses brought my baby to start the flow of milk, they gave me alcohol to wipe my nipples so they would be sanitary enough! Neophyte that I was, I didn't realize soon enough how they were drying them out!

Barbara survived the change and did well.

Earlier she was baptized at St. Benedict's little church on one of the coldest days of the year and survived that well, too. With family and godparents at our home, we celebrated.

Beginning with this child as well as our succeeding ones, we incorporated them into our immediate families' tradition of being welcomed into God's family through water and blessing into the Christian culture of love and grace. Coming from my father-in-law's and his ancestors' baptisms in Byzantium and those of my ancestors in Northern Europe, northern United States and California were added as new baptism locales. In the various American baptisms were my mother-in-law Mary's Romanian Orthodox in 1911, my father's Lutheran in 1914 and Johnny's Romanian Catholic in 1931. Those were done in infancy. My mother, raised as a Baptist where infant baptism was not accepted, was baptized in 1942 as an adult by the Methodists, and as a teenager I chose to do so by immersion in the 1950's with the Baptists.

14. CANTON AND THE GREAT BEYOND

I RECEIVED THE CATHOLIC sacrament of Confirmation in April at St. Benedict's and Aunt Vickie was my sponsor. The diocesan bishop invited to do this spoke of our faith responsibilities and the diversity of gifts that are bestowed by that Good Spirit which we call Holy: love, peace, patience, kindness, faith, self-control and joy. By the time the bishop prayed to God to send down the Holy Spirit and give us strength to walk in love, I also prayed, not knowing what gifts would be mine, but I was thankful and full of peaceful joy. I took the name of Monica, also not knowing that I, like she, in praying long for the spiritual life of her son Augustine, would be doing the same for my children.

I went back to work for a few weeks in June while Johnny and his mom took care of Barbara on his break from teaching and university studies. He was only working his part-time job at ADT on Saturdays. By the middle of the month he started summer school at Kent. Barbara was happy with whoever was taking care of her!

By mid-July, Johnny was done with his summer studies, so we embarked on an almost unbelievable trip across the country, looking forward to seeing the ocean, mountains, and relatives again. By today's standards, it was more hazardous for our little six month old baby than we realized at the time, with "Mother of Confidence" me, and "Protector Father" he, naïve and unaware about the possible risks to her. In fact, worries about that were nonexistent in our minds. At that time, there were no seat belts for adults, and no reliable infant car seats like there are today. She sat between us in the front seat in a little, somewhat flimsy plastic car seat with a thin belt around her and a metal bar in front of her, with metal bars hooked over the back of the seat. Her bed was the top of her buggy on the back seat, with wheels in the trunk. Milk from the breast would have been more sanitary, but I only had bottles with formula. There were neither disposable diapers nor baby wipes so we would have to find laundromats along the way for our considerable laundry. Public restrooms didn't have changing tables for her, but the buggy was fine for that. What about car trouble? Sometimes we were the only ones on country roads, far from repair shops. Fortunately, we had no problems from our reliable sedan.

The vast Interstate Highway System implemented in 1956 by President Eisenhower was just in its earliest stages, so we took whatever roads available. I don't remember which roads we took from Canton to Chicago, which we traveled in a day, but from there on it was the two lane historic Route 66 Highway to L.A., with side trips to the Painted Desert and the Grandest of all — our national Canyon in Arizona. We arrived in the morning at one of the rims, only to be disappointed because we couldn't see it. In less than an hour, our patience paid off! While we were standing there, Mother Nature started blowing the cloud away and parted it in two as though she was pulling chords for theater curtains. As the scene appeared, we had our own breath phenomena—Johnny and I were breathless! The multi-hued terraces, rocks, trees and meandering Colorado River created the greatest panoramic "3-D theater stage scene" ever! If only Barbara would have been able to remember this "one of the greatest shows on Earth", too! Johnny was happy as a lark, as he always was, driving across the country and sharing special places along the way with me and now Barbara!

By the time we arrived in Los Angeles, it was just a quick trip to Long Beach and seeing Mom and Dad. Soon we happy five were off to the sequoias, King's Canyon, and Yosemite. It was Johnny's and my first visits to all three. Mom and Dad had driven to Yosemite once before from Long Beach. Even though our family was less than a day's car journey from Pittsburg to Yosemite, there never seemed to be an opportunity for us to travel to these treasures in the middle part of California.

We had always loved trees, and being in the quiet presence of those giant millennial redwoods in that trio of places gave us a respectful sense of strength and time, in a living, outdoor sacred space not experienced before. In Yosemite Valley, where Mom and Dad took care of Barbara while Johnny and I swam in the pine and oak bordered Merced River, the water was so frigid, we told our parents when we came out that we felt "ten pounds lighter and ten years younger!"

Everywhere we looked, there was awesome beauty, and we had only one day to experience it. We saw Yosemite and Bridalveil Falls from the valley, and Yosemite Falls was actually a three-in-one visual treat. The top part was the longest, the middle next in length, and the bottom the shortest, making it one of the largest falls in the world. We drove up to Glacier Point and saw more of the water wonderland—Nevada and Vernal Falls. They were at a distance, because of our high elevation, which also revealed Half Dome and more of the Sierra mountain range. Because of the vast scope of the majestic scene, the trees that were so large to us when we were down in the valley now appeared to be miniature toys. We spoke little, felt humble, small, thankful and pleased to have seen it. In seeing such vistas with John Muir, it's no wonder Theodore Roosevelt was inspired to protect Yosemite as a park!

After returning south to Long Beach, we visited briefly with relatives before leaving again. We three said good-by to all and then stopped next at Disneyland—John's first visit there. As we drove up the coast, we stopped in Santa Barbara to see Nancy and Paul, who were expecting their first child.

Eleanor was working another summer again at Mount Herman in the beautiful Santa Cruz Mountains, so we stopped to see her on our way to seeing friends in Pittsburg. Anna Marie was there too, working on her Master's Degree at UC Berkeley. Next we drove to the Bay Area, crossed the amazing Golden Gate Bridge and continued through northern California. There were more impressively beautiful ocean and redwood forest scenes, but also disappointing shabby mill towns and heavy blankets of smoke from lumber mills.

The southwestern part of Oregon was very pretty—greenery everywhere with rolling rivers and bubbling streams. So far on the trip we had slept in motels at night, but we arrived late at Crater Lake, so we slept in the car. We woke up at 6:30 in the morning to quite a sunny sight! It was a gorgeous aquamarine, smooth-as-a-mirror lake, reflecting its small Wizard Island within. Its 2,000 foot depth enhanced the color, and it was sunken enough below the crater rims to be somewhat protected from the winds. There were no boats on it. Next we crossed the mountains into eastern Oregon and spent that night in Idaho, another scenic state.

What's not to like about Grand Teton National Park, Jackson Hole National Monument, and Yellowstone National Park? Where Disneyland was the Land of Enchantment, these outdoor titans were Lands of Wonder for us as we discovered the wild beauty that was yet preserved in the mountains, canyons, rivers, glacial lakes, gushing geysers, forests and animals. Even though we visited areas where there were other tourists, we sometimes felt, as our photos show, that we were the only people in the area "privileged enough" to take in some of those awesome attractions without distractions. We had quite a thrill looking at a vast panorama from an 11,000 mile peak, as we continued into Montana. We arrived in Billings that night. Gene Hedrick, Johnny's cousin, and his artist bride Sybil welcomed us warmly. We spent a good part of the next day swimming in the local pool with Sybil, who was also a national swimming champion, while Gene was at school, coaching the football team.

After some time with both of them, we left the next day for Canton, driving night and day through the rest of the states. By the time we arrived home two days later, Johnny and I were hot, dirty and exhausted! Barbara was clean, happy and seemed okay, but two days later we noticed she was not so happy and had a fever. The doctor even came to the house! The diagnosis was a severe case of tonsillitis. He gave her a shot of penicillin, and I had to give her more medicine. Then we had to rethink about how we did the too long a trip (nearly 9,000 miles and seven national parks) with too young a child! The trips with one or more children wouldn't be that long again. Fortunately, her health returned to normal quickly; her parents were thankful and yet still pondering the risks we had put her through with some degree of guilt. This was only after we returned home, though, for while we three were traveling, we were experiencing bliss most of the time, with renewed appreciation by her parents of the natural splendor of our American West.

15. GRADUATION: 1959

BEFORE JOHNNY COULD GRADUATE, he had to do his student teaching at Kent. When that time came, he was looking forward to it, and was paired with a middle-aged lady to be his student teacher supervisor. It wasn't long, however that he discovered it wasn't a good match. Her goals, teaching content, and how to arrive at them were so vastly different from what he thought should be done, created an impossible situation, so he dropped out. He enrolled again the next time he could, and experienced a vastly different situation. He thrived beautifully with a male teacher with whom he related well supervising his teaching 10th Grade Social Sciences.

Finally—graduation! We were both ready for it. We were looking forward to that Big June Day when the plans were interrupted. Ross, a friend of John's family for many years, died suddenly from cancer. He had been like another grandfather to Johnny, had at one time rented a room from Mom and Dad Tate, and had been renting our other bedroom for a couple of years. He died in the hospital, and then we met with his family members who came from out of town to take care of his final affairs. The funeral was in little Tiltonsville, Ohio, hours away from where we lived. This was more important than the graduation ceremony, so the three of us went with Mom, Dad and Mary Jean. Kent State mailed him his diploma: Bachelor of Science in Education, History/Comprehensive Social Studies major with Secondary Certification for grades 7-12.

In July we were happy to see Warren again as he stopped at our place for a few days on his way back from Libya and on to his new and last assignment before getting out of the service, Norton Air Force Base in San Bernardino. One of the highlights at our place for him was trying out his new camera, one of several that would give him many future joys.

By November we had a reality check on what could happen with public school systems and teachers. In a November 6, 1959 letter to my parents, I wrote:

Things are getting better here. Fortunately at the polls Tuesday, the people in Canton and Perry Township voted for the levies enough to pass them. Last year, Perry voted no. Consequently this year, some of their classes were on half day sessions and the teachers received no annual increase in their salaries. In fact, Johnny has been working without his just salary for having graduated last June. Perry Township actually had to threaten the people in their area with school closures next year if the levy didn't pass; they wouldn't have had the money to operate.

16. PATRICIA

SINCE JOHNNY HAD HIS bachelor's degree, we decided we wanted to move back to California after he finished teaching at Genoa in June of 1960. We sold our house and repaid Mom and Dad. We also gave them the vacant lot between our houses, which was an extra bonus for them. We realized Mom was never going to be fully back to good health, but because she had Dad to continue to take care of her, we were told we should follow our dream. We would miss them, though.

I hadn't wanted less than two years between babies, so I could fully recuperate from childbirth, so we were pleased when we learned I was pregnant again at the onset of the sixties, which was when we wanted another.

The three of us plus "Little 6/9" drove in our station wagon the quickest route back to California, similar to the southwestern route in 1958. The immediate destination was Long Beach again, because I wanted to be near my parents for the childbirth. Barbara was so active outside the car, we sometimes had to chase and grab her (with my big belly slowing me down) to prevent her from falling down canyon walls!

Johnny had a sixth grade teaching job waiting for him at a nice school in the Long Beach Public School System: Starr King Elementary. He also acquired a part-time job with ADT in Huntington Beach.

By the time September arrived, I was more than anxious to have that second baby arrive! The estimated due date came and left without a childbirth, so when approximately two weeks later, very early on September 5, I was pleased to have started labor. I entered Long Beach Osteopathic Hospital at 5 AM and endured labor (on Labor Day) until 5 PM with my male obstetrician, part of the time, holding my hand and encouraging me. It was another happy natural childbirth, with a warm welcome to our second beautiful daughter, Patricia Ann! She had a darker, more olive complexion than anyone on my side of the family, so we decided she was like the Romanian side, perhaps taking after one of Johnny's grandmothers. Again, Johnny wasn't allowed in the delivery room.

I started the nursing process in the hospital, and then looked forward to going home the usual time until I was told I had to go back to bed instead of continuing the post childbirth walking. The reason was that I told the doctor I had a pinched feeling in a vein near the surface of my skin near my right knee, and that it was pink and warm to the touch. The diagnosis was thrombophlebitis. I was given a blood thinner for a couple of days until it cleared up. Besides, the doctors (two by this time) said they had to discontinue the medication because it would be like rat poison to my baby when I nursed. I went home soon afterward after the admonition from the doctors that I would have to have vein surgery some time that year. They said I had no choice in the matter, because I could be sitting, as in an airplane, and have a clot that could go to a lung and kill me.

Well, here we were, rather anxious about the situation. We trusted the doctors' advice, and since we now had two young children we would go ahead with what seemed to be the responsible thing to do—have the surgery—but not immediately.

The other recommendation from the doctors while I was in the hospital was not to have any more children, just to enjoy the two we had. And I was not to take "The Pill" (new in 1960) because of the possible risk of clots. The latter was easy, I thought, and I wondered if they could pose other risks to women's bodies, as well. However, the earlier advice of having no more children was harder to take.

Patti was baptized, and took to the nursing easily, so mother and baby were content. Since I was also aware of some of the negative cultural opinions toward nursing as being primitive or crude, we did it mostly at home.

Because Johnny needed to help me a little after the surgery, we opted to have it done over Thanksgiving weekend. The surgery was a breeze for me, even though they ligated (tied) and removed veins in both legs! (Why both legs when I had the phlebitis in only one? Did I really have a deep vein thrombosis? It looked like it was in a superficial vein, not an artery.) I wish we would have thought to ask these questions before the surgery! Besides, we were told that to compensate, my body would generate more veins. When I woke up I had only two massive bandages on my thighs, and the doctors had me walking soon afterward to get the circulation going, which was easy.

Then, the unexpected happened. When I nursed Patti, there wasn't any milk. Why didn't the doctors tell me the shock of the surgery and anesthetic could do that? Maybe they didn't know? If we had, I would have waited longer to have the surgery. We quickly had to buy baby formula, so she had that while I worked at getting my milk going again. She eventually had both, but my milk supply was never as good again because of the supplemental feeding. Fortunately, Johnny was home with me one evening soon afterward when Patti, on her back, threw up a lot of formula and immediately turned purple because she couldn't breathe from some caught in her throat. Johnny grabbed her, turned her upside down, stuck his finger down her throat and got the rest out! Thank God, and Johnny, she was fine after that.

17. TRAVELING—AGAIN!

WE DIDN'T KNOW UNTIL we were in Long Beach in 1960 that Mom and Dad had been buying property in Arizona. Their eventual goal was to live there and until that time, they would be traveling back and forth in their new camper truck which provided them with lodging until they could settle permanently. It was adventurous for them.

While teaching at Starr King, Johnny went in the fall with his class to sixth grade science camp at Lake Arrowhead and science nature lover that he was, enjoyed every minute of it! During Christmas vacation he drove the four of us up there for a day's excursion. There was snow on the ground, so John even went ice skating.

At 1961 spring vacation time Johnny announced, "It is time to pack up the girls and hit the road." We loaded what we needed into our white "gypsy" station wagon and began a trip from Long Beach through California as far north as Shasta Dam and Lake.

It was another fascinating, scenic journey that only California could provide! We were not only experiencing spring, but also at various times, it seemed we were in fall and winter yet. We traveled north through the middle of the state, aiming for Yosemite. As we approached cooler, higher elevations, we found some gold and copper colored fall leaves—the last— still tenaciously hanging onto the branches of deciduous trees beside a gurgling, rocky creek. Those leaves, together with others already on the ground, brightened an otherwise overcast, but lovely scene. The higher we drove, the mistier it became, until there were gently falling snowflakes. By the time night was approaching, we were fortunate that we had a room reservation at the historic Ahwahnee Hotel in the valley. After a great dinner in the dining room and carrying a sleeping baby, we sat for a little while in the expansive lounge near the great stone fireplace, basking in the warmth of the fire. We surveyed the scale of the architectural features of that pleasant interior environment: massive wooden ceiling beams, high ceilings and huge windows. Always interested in Native American crafts, the artistry of their baskets adorning the room also caught my attention.

After breakfast and seeing the almost unbelievable views of Glacier Point and Half Dome from the hotel, we left to continue our trip, and for Johnny to take photos along the way. Even in the mists, the overcast scenes in the snow were impressive, held his keen interest, and reaped some worthwhile pictures.

Entering spring again as we descended the mountains, we drove by sun filled grassy meadows on our way into the Gold Country. It was cloudy in the riparian areas, but that didn't detract from the dramatic beauty which we saw at Sutter Mill near Placerville, where gold was discovered in the 1800's. Nor did it affect the even more incredible American River scene that we viewed near Auburn, where the meandering confluence of the North and Middle Forks takes place, carving its way over rocks, through verdant canyons and forested ridges.

Once we arrived at the northernmost part of our trip at Shasta Dam, we stayed a short while and then started south toward home, taking the ocean route when we came into the Monterey Peninsula area. We bypassed the city to take the 17 Mile Drive through Pebble Beach, stopping to photograph our girls. We took Highway 1 from Carmel, through the coastal part of Big Sur. Golden poppies, with rugged mountain/ocean views, where at times the mountains rise abruptly at the sea have to be some of the most stunning in the world! The Monterey Cypress trees are testimony not only to their beauty, but also to their tenacity and strength, buffeted for many years by harsh, cold ocean winds, fog, sun, and, then yet, remain green. After these experiences, the rest of the way home was a bit anti-climactic, and we arrived in Long Beach safe and sound.

18. HAPPINESS IN TEACHING

WITH SCENES STILL FRESH in his mind of that last unforgettable journey, Johnny thought he would like to live and work in northern California again, this time near the Sierra Mountains. He was so enthralled with the American River area that he applied for a teaching position there. I don't remember which school system it was, but when he received a letter back and found out the pay was $4,000 yearly we decided he couldn't support our family on it, so we didn't consider it any longer.

At first, I probably would have been willing to go there, if he had found the right job, but after thinking about it some more, I don't think I would have been satisfied living there very long. I love nature, but I need to live in more of an urban area that supports the many kinds of educational and cultural activities that I think are important for me and my family. The American River area is great for outdoor vacations and round year living for some people, with hiking, whitewater rafting, camping, and fishing activities, but we didn't do a lot of that anyway. And, I know Johnny wouldn't have been fishing, for he knew that eating fish (or even any kind of seafood) was repulsive to him! (That was one of my pet peeves because he had never tasted it!)

Meanwhile, summer and vacation from school was fast approaching, and the relatives in Ohio were interested in seeing our latest family addition. That's all the motivation my "King of the Road" needed to plan another trip so he could enjoy showing off Patti! So, our "Roma wagon" took off again for Ohio in July with must-see chances to visit Zion National Park in Utah, and Rocky Mountain National Park in Colorado.

Once in Ohio, we stayed at Mom and Dad's while we enjoyed visiting with friends and relatives. One of those relatives was cousin John Hedrick, who was at that time teaching public high school in Plain Township. He was interested in hearing my hubby's dissatisfaction with teaching sixth grade, even though his Long Beach job had been satisfying as far as the students and administration were concerned. He wanted to be in the higher grades where he would be concentrating more in his teaching specialty, the social sciences. Hedrick knew Dr. Drage, Superintendent of the Plain Local Schools and suggested that Johnny get an appointment with him, which he did.

When he came in the door after his appointment, he had a slight grin and a pleased look in his eyes.

"Hi—I have a job!"

"You're kidding!"

"No, I'm not. Dr. Drage hired me to teach world history to ninth graders, and I think I'm going to like it."

"What about our love of living in California?"

"It looks like it's going to take a while to get what I want in California, and with this opportunity of a job I'll probably like, I don't want to refuse it."

Disappointed one way, but pleased about the job, I reluctantly accepted the idea of moving back to Ohio. As it turned out, I continued to have some of the happiest years of my life there.

So, while the girls and I stayed with Mom and Dad, Johnny drove back to Long Beach, rented a trailer, and came back with our few belongings (books—including two new encyclopedias, clothing, radio-phonograph, Mom's paintings, our wedding gift refrigerator and new, Scandinavian styled rocking chair). For the rest, it was good that we had used furniture, which was easy to leave.

We rented part of a nice duplex with two bedrooms in middle class suburban North Canton, only several miles from his work. There was also a permanent swing and teeter-totter in the yard for the girls and a clothes line for me. After Johnny started getting teaching checks in September, we bought necessary furniture, and moved in. He also bought the recently published, comprehensive history of Nazi Germany, William Shirer's *The Rise and Fall of the Third Reich.*

He had taken a cut in pay, because urban school systems in California in the sixties generally paid better than those in Ohio. Warren, who was out of the military, found work in California that he loved with the private sector, and which also paid better than teaching. When Johnny and I decided to be teachers, we were both naïve about the pay and lack of respect by many for the profession. But by this point in our lives, we were still ready to accommodate ourselves to it and he shared, "This time I want to stay here until retirement, and not borrow from that fund like we did to move to California." We were fortunate in that we weren't in debt for either move. In a note to my Mom and Dad, he wrote that since he was teaching world history, he was enjoying his work very much.

19. INCLUSIVENESS

ONCE WE SETTLED IN, John and I joined St. Paul's Catholic Church in North Canton. During our previous time in Canton, we had met so many good people—a lot of them relatives in my husband's family. The new friends we made, beginning with that initial endeavor at St. Paul's and continuing through the wider Canton community, were also some of the finest people we've ever known, affecting us often in profound ways.

Tom (Corky) and Sally Corrigan were two of those. So were Gene and Joanne Buffo, and Roy and Doris Richards—all at St. Paul's. It was Sally and Tom who introduced us to the Catholic Interracial Council of Stark County (CICSC) and Percy and Norma Marcere. Sally, born in Romania, had lost family members to the Holocaust while Norma and Percy were dealing with the problems of racism in the United States. Therefore, they felt a special empathetic connection.

On February 18, 1962 we attended a day-long human relations workshop at Central Catholic High School. The theme was "Human Dignity and Christian Responsibility." It was sponsored by the CICSC (associated with the National Catholic Conference for Interracial Justice) and The Eucharistic Fraternity of The Third Order of St. Francis (a laypersons organization). Non-Catholic sponsors were The Greater Canton AFL-CIO Council and The Penguin Men's Club of Canton. At the end of the workshops, there was a Mass, then a banquet with speaker Matthew Ahmann, Executive Director of the National Catholic Council for Interracial Justice (NCCIJ) in Chicago, introduced by Norma, President of CICSC.

In the early sixties, it was our impression that the American Catholic Church was coming out in solidarity against racism. There were no church teachings condoning it; in fact, it was just the opposite, based on the social teachings of the Church. More than a decade before, Francis Cardinal Spellman had been quoted as saying: "It is impossible for any good Catholic not to be on the side of and in the forefront in the struggle for interracial justice, for all men are brothers."

We learned that there was an entire weekend, June 15-17 1962, devoted to an interracial justice conference at John Carroll University, a Jesuit institution in Cleveland, sponsored by the Ohio Catholic Conference for Interracial Justice. Along with workshops and masses, they included a banquet at the Pick-Carter Hotel with speaker Jackie Robinson, first black baseball player in the major leagues.

In reference to the Canton workshop, there were seven priests taking an active part, including The Reverend Mark Zwick, panel leader for "Right

60

Conscience-Religious Responsibility" and a black priest, The Reverend Allen Simpson, a participant on that panel, who was also the celebrant for the evening Mass. The keynote speaker was Brother Thomas Farrell, FIC (Brother of Christian Instruction), President of Walsh College (now University) in North Canton, Ohio. Brother Ferrell's address was entitled, "Christ-Likeness", which if practiced, was inclusive of all people through love, excluding racism and all other forms of hatred.

There was also excellent cooperation from the community-at-large, involving more people than I can list here. They were black and white, Catholic, Protestant and Jewish. The topics also encompassed employment, housing and urban renewal, legislation, sit-ins and boycotts. It was a day of high inspiration, so we became members of CICSC!

Father Zwick visited us a couple of times at our residence, and we found him to be such an interesting conversationalist, and so dedicated to his work. We respected him highly. He was chaplain for the Catholic Action and Information Center in Warren, Ohio (our Youngstown Diocese) at that time and was known as a professional social worker-priest. He told us that everyone (ordinary people like us) should strive for sainthood, which meant what exactly? It was living with courage according to the Christian Gospel, where Jesus taught us to feed the hungry, clothe the naked, give drink to the thirsty, care for the sick and homeless, visit prisoners and perform other works of mercy. In other words, especially help the poor, for they have no power and often suffer because of it. Work against injustices. Practice non-violence and love. When we did these, Jesus said we were doing them for Him.

20. TUMULTUOUS TIMES

AFTER THOSE BRIEF TIMES with Mark in 1962, we often wondered what he was doing later because we had lost contact with him. Eventually we learned from other Catholics in our area that he had been transferred to work that year at St. Columba Cathedral in Youngstown, the center of our diocese.

At the time Mark was teaching classes to possible converts he met Louise, a Protestant Youngstown University student who wanted to learn more about Catholicism. She had been looking for him on the recommendation of some nuns, and found him accidently on the steps of the cathedral. She then took classes from him and became a convert in 1963. After her graduation, she worked for Catholic Social Services and then for Gilead House, an inner-city community center near the cathedral which she and Mark established to address problems of poverty and violence. As their lives revolved around the liturgy and Gospel teachings of Matthew 25, the scope of their Christian work through love included resistance to injustices and war. They realized, as friends, how much they had in common, fell in love and married in the church in 1967, after Mark had been laicized.

After having been inspired by Dorothy Day's life, they established a Catholic Worker House of Hospitality in Houston, Texas to serve the destitute and working poor with works of mercy, without a salary for Mark. It is named Casa Juan Diego, after the poor, indigenous saint of Mexico. They opened it within months of Archbishop Oscar Romero's assassination in El Salvador and Day's death in November, 1980. Louise had been hired in October at the Houston Public Library as a children's librarian, so they would have an income to support their family.

This was after a circuitous journey which included a brief time in Central America. Prior to that, they had moved from Youngstown to Chicago, then, northern California, obtained masters' degrees for both of them, and gave birth to their children, Jennifer and Joachim. They were living a comfortable middle class lifestyle in California with Mark as a psychiatric social worker, when, after praying and meditating about their next possible move the four of them left the United States in 1977. Their primary goals in doing so were to learn Spanish and participate in the life of the Latin American church while living among the poor in San Salvador, the capital of El Salvador. Mark and Louise were unaware, until they arrived, what a growing horrendously violent situation it was against the poor and those who were working to help them with better education and working conditions, non-violently.

The fourteen families in control together with business leaders, the government and military labeled everyone accomplishing those goals as Communists. That included teachers, labor leaders, lay catechists, nuns, and Roman Catholic priests. It included Mark and Louise. Our American government was providing funds and guns to the Salvadoran military and government in their zeal to "fight Communism", and as Mark said, "my taxes are helping to fund this and could kill me as well!"

There was no respect for human life. Thousands were slaughtered—many tossed into mass graves and garbage dumps. At the beginning and through the civil war the Salvadoran army and guerrillas were forcing recruitments and ordering young men to kill or be killed. El Salvador is Spanish for *The Savior* and in a Christian mystical way He was being crucified again and again.

Louise and Mark fled by car with their children through Guatemala and Mexico, arriving back in the U.S. through Brownsville, Texas. In less than two years after working for Catholic educational and social services in McAllen, and St. Theresa's in Houston, their ministry at Casa Juan Diego began. Huge numbers of refugees poured in from El Salvador, Guatemala and Nicaragua. Young men were fleeing the forced recruitments.

The Zwicks continue to help many desperate men and women today who suffer various other hardships, which include sickness, injuries, and those fleeing economic disasters because of unjust global economies. Most of the refugees have been from Latin America, but some have been from Africa, Europe and Asia. Food, clothing, English classes and help with employment have also been provided, and some families have been reunited. They get calls for help day and night from hospitals, Immigration and other services.

John started our subscription to the Houston Catholic Worker (English and Spanish) newspaper in the early 1990's as soon as we learned about its existence. We already had a subscription to the New York Catholic Worker paper since 1955. They both kept us informed by sharing the thoughts and works of Day, the Catholic Worker (CW) and Catholic social teachings as a way to live the Gospel through works of mercy instead of wars and nuclear destruction. That's love in action.

We donated to the CW in New York and Houston. They were such small drops in the bucket of huge needs, but they were always appreciated by those contemporary saints. The Worker writings did much more for us than what we could ever accomplish for them as they wrote much of what it means to be Christian in the real world.

21. POPE JOHN XXIII AND JOHN BIRCH SOCIETY

AS MUCH AS WE respected how the CW people were living, Johnny and I believed it was important also for us personally to take active roles in understanding how governments operated, since they determine many aspects of their citizens' lives, whether positively or negatively. It included our belief that separation of church and state was necessary, holding the leaders of both accountable and responsible for their decisions. Protection of democratic ideals non-violently through the rule of constitutions and ongoing humane, non-repressing laws which benefit all citizens such as the right to vote was critical, as were the rights of freedom of expression.

As a social studies teacher, he believed he had a special responsibility to include the actions of our country and others during the 20th Century. During the early 60's we respected the strong leadership of John Kennedy and Pope John XXIII. The discussion of Catholic Church reforms of Vatican II in 1962 was still continuing in April, 1963 (Easter Week) when the Pope released his encyclical (papal letter) to the world, "Peace on Earth", only two months before his death. We were pleasantly surprised when we read it.

Written through his Christian moral lens of respect for the human family created as he said "in the image and likeness of God", it meant therefore, "that all people were endowed with intelligence and freedom." Flowing from that nature were rights and responsibilities that were "universal, inviolable, and inalienable". It was addressed to Christian and non-Christian clergy and to all men (terminology for all used at that time) of good will. It was considered relevant and praised, not only by Catholics, but also non-Catholics because it dealt with key issues facing everyone in the modern world. They were presented to, and involved, both individuals and groups.

He said with deep personal sorrow that there were countries continuing in the buildup of war armaments and stockpiling them. He wrote that it was very important for justice, right reason and responsibility to humanity that those practices should stop, nuclear weapons should be banned and nuclear testing should be discontinued.

He wrote of the importance of the United Nations in helping to work toward peace among nations and agreed with the U.N. Declaration of Human Rights and the resulting, respective liberties.

There were more rights and liberties mentioned for the benefit of the common good than I can express in this chapter, so I highly recommend reading the whole document. Pope John also concluded that there can be no peace among men unless there is peace within, and quoted from the Prince of Peace: "Peace be to you".

Catholics John Kennedy and his Attorney General brother Bobby were peace builders, striving to work for all American citizens, as in working for civil rights legislation. The Peace Corps became a permanently funded government agency in 1961 to help the poor developing nations become more self-sufficient. In 1962 the President helped the whole world avoid nuclear war by diffusing the Cuban Missile Crises with the Soviet Union.

However, not all Christians were in agreement with John XXIII and the Kennedys. They couldn't make the connection between Christianity and the peace and life building efforts of Pope John, Kennedys and Martin Luther King Jr. Even some Catholics at St. Paul's didn't like this letter from the Bishop of Rome, and didn't respect the Kennedys or Dr. Martin Luther King, Jr.

Johnny and I found that even within our Christian Family Movement discussion classes, which we led, and where the encyclical was up for consideration, the other members refused to discuss it. We couldn't get any agreements or even declarations of their own viewpoints. We were getting nowhere so we had to drop out. Due to our other responsibilities with family (including our third child) and his teaching, we just didn't have the time necessary for the struggle. Our pastor was no help! He was an elderly, staunch anti-Communist who had been influenced by parishioners in the John Birch Society (JBS). He had a history of name calling and criticism even of his own bishop from the pulpit, particularly about reforming the Mass.

Christmas of 1962 we had received a JBS Christmas card which contained a note that it was from Catholics! Easter 1963 was a disaster. Our Easter message that was given to all the parishioners as we left the sanctuary after Mass was a leaflet entitled "Straight Talk" from the Birch Society, stapled to a drawing of a woman in a large hat with the words "Happy Easter", with no mention of the Resurrection. Also, one of the Birch infiltrators, a prominent banker, had the gall to say the Catholic Interracial Council was a Communist front because it was associated with the NAACP! That wasn't surprising, though. The organization also branded Christian Baptist minister Dr. King and former President Dwight Eisenhower as part of the worldwide Communist conspiracy for world domination.

The JBS was a relatively new organization at the time, having been founded in 1958 by retired candy manufacturer Robert Welch Jr. in Indianapolis. He named it after John Birch, a Baptist missionary and U.S. military intelligence officer who had been killed by Chinese Communists in 1945. Welch was deeply affected by it emotionally, so became strongly committed against anything he determined was evidence of or related to Communism and its influence. The dozen people who helped establish the Society and joined him as board members included brothers Lynde and Harry Bradley, owners of the Allen-Bradley Company, and Fred Koch, head of Koch Industries and father of four boys, including Charles and David Koch. JBS picked up on anti-Communist campaigning, originally spear-headed by Catholic Senator Joseph McCarthy in the '50's. They were highly organized, under the tight control of Welch, and had established Birch chapters around the country where they promoted anti-Communist hysteria, labeling American social and economic structures that didn't agree with their laissez-faire economic policies as Communist. (On the plus side, they pioneered grass roots lobbying, petition drives, and letter writing for issues.)

In the 70's they campaigned against diplomatic relations with China and continued into the 80's opposing the U.S. membership in the United Nations because of a conspiracy belief, and fear of a one world government. Robert Welch died in 1985, and by that time the membership had largely declined. The fall of Communism in Europe also took some of the wind out of their anti-Communist rhetoric.

Fast forward to the 2000's, and we find the JBS still in existence, having become more prominent again opposing President Barack Obama, his political and economic policies, and cooperation with the United Nations. According to the Southern Poverty Law Center of Montgomery, Alabama in 2014, there were JBS chapters in all four geographical regions of our country, with only about 11 states and the District of Columbia without them.

22. CAROLYN

MY BROTHER WARREN AND Byrle were married in a small but beautiful wedding in Long Beach early in '62, but unfortunately we couldn't attend due to our recent California trips and another pregnancy for me. While we were still in Long Beach and Warren was dating Byrle, I thought she was one of the most beautiful girls I had ever seen! Evidently, Warren felt the same.

We were looking forward to the child we said would be the last addition to our family, because of economics and especially my leg problems. I was pleased to find Dr. Brumbaugh, who would allow me to deliver without anesthetic, and encouraged me to breast feed. As far as Johnny's presence at the childbirth, that was iffy.

So it was, because Carolyn Christine arrived at a time when no other childbirth was taking place in the adjoining delivery room on August 18, her dad was allowed to be present— but in a limited fashion. As another beautiful, healthy daughter entered the world her father experienced the awesome event at 2:00 A.M. He stood behind a window in a small enclosed area between the two delivery rooms, looking like a doctor wearing a surgical mask, head covering, and scrub clothes. The medical thinking at the time was that the mother and child had to be protected from germs. Another concern was that fathers might pass out from the blood or the whole experience. But he did just fine, and had been so pleased to have been there!

I didn't do as fine as I hoped because the pesky problem of phlebitis surfaced on one of my legs again, so I was in the hospital a couple additional days. When we arrived home, Patti, Barbara and their Grandma Mary welcomed Carolyn with open arms and much excitement. When my paternal grandmother Sophia Carolina learned of the name, she was so pleased, thinking we had named Carolyn after her, but we had never known her middle name until then! It was a happy family phenomenon. Soon after, Carolyn was baptized on September 2, pleasing her Finnish Lutheran great grandmother again.

Diapers—cloth diapers! A few weeks after Carolyn was born, we celebrated Patti's second birthday, which meant, in our family at least, there were two children in diapers. Fortunately (or unfortunately), there was a permanent clothes line in our yard. Our neighbor lady next door said, "Either you're the dirtiest or the cleanest gal in town!" I was spending an inordinate amount of daily time on that chore in addition to all the other tasks I had as mother and wife.

"Johnny, I need a dryer! No questioning—I need a dryer!"

I got one soon from my husband who wouldn't even change a diaper, let alone wash them. What a situation that would have been, if I had gone on strike, which I didn't even have to threaten.

Hooray! As far as nursing was concerned, mama and baby were finally successful longer than the previous two times. I was so proud when I reached four months and had not had to use any supplementation. But patience carried me only through the ninth month. I should have gone on longer; and still, no one I knew was nursing a baby. They were too "modern" for that.

The neighborhood was lovely, and an added bonus was the remnants of a farm. I took the girls on walks almost daily, weather permitting. At the farmhouse yard I would take them to the duck pond, and across the street to play in the sand pile. We couldn't get very close to the picturesque old gray barn, but could gaze at it from the country slab wooden fence.

That colorful fall I took them up the hill to watch and listen to the high school marching band. Back down the hill the older girls could play in our yard, and Barbara played a lot with Johnny, a good friend and neighbor boy her age on the other side of our place.

By the time the children were in bed, their father would be preparing lessons for his classes, and I was usually cleaning up, which often meant dishes at midnight. Often, by the time I hit the bed I was too tired. One night as he started making love to me, I was falling asleep at the same time. Poor guy, he said, "Some lover I am!" Which, of course, wasn't his fault, and I didn't let it happen again.

I was fortunate in that I was healthy enough to do all that I did at home. However, I arrived at the point of thinking, in terms of chores, "Is this all there is to life?" Joining the Interracial Council helped, giving us purpose outside the house and social life with great people.

By December we welcomed by long distance another new life into the family, Warren and Byrle's first child, Dawn.

23. RACE IN AMERICA -
FORWARD AND BACKWARD

ON A SUNDAY MORNING we attended Mass at St. Paul's in North Canton with friends who were also members of the Catholic Interracial Council and had them and their two children at our place for brunch. After we ate, we noticed our next door neighbors to the side of us seemed to have a larger group of guests at their place. Barbara, who was five, took her sister Patti and new friends outside to play. It wasn't long until they came back in, and Barbara said, "Mr. (So and So) said Patti and I couldn't play in his yard anymore because of what you and Daddy have done." There were no fences between the yards and both families of children had always felt free to go back and forth to one another's grassy turfs to play. We didn't know why the neighbor told her what he did, but we told Barbara to abide by what he said because he had a right to say who he wanted on his property.

While we were eating, mutual friends of us all invited us to come over that afternoon. We had such a delightful time we stayed until dark and then returned to our respective homes.

In a couple of days Johnny and I received a note in the mail from our landlord that our rent was being increased by $30.00 a month, and that it was due immediately, with no further information. So we met with the landlord to find out why. He told us that a number of neighbors called and hysterically told him that we had moved carload after carload of Negroes into the neighborhood to picket and march! Therefore, they said we were ruining property values! After we discussed the trumped up fear and hysteria to get us out, we told him what *really* happened: that we had invited only one Negro couple and their two children over for a meal, and that the children had been having fun playing together outside. He then dropped the rent increase and said we could entertain anyone we wished, as long as we didn't abuse the property.

Seeing the neighbor about it was totally different. The next day, while holding baby Carolyn in my arms, I walked over to the neighbor's house to talk with the lady who lived there. She "greeted" me at the door by walking outside and saying, "We won't associate with filthy people like you, so we had to do something about your living next door to us! We're fed up seeing "niggers" in your house. My friends won't come to my house if they see those friends of yours in your house. And you're ruining property values! It's only you Catholics and Communists who are forcing "niggers" rights!"

"We can't be ruining property values, because we're only renting!"

"If you owned a house, you'd think differently about it!"

69

"No I wouldn't, because people are more important than money, and if we buy and sell a house again, it will be sold on a non-discriminatory basis! Also, if we had been abusing the property, guilty of lewd, malicious, violent or noisy conduct, then you would have a right to complain! But, for us to be denied our rights to living quarters and the right to entertain guests on the basis of skin color is unreasonable, unfair and meant to humiliate our friends!"

Treating Negroes as social equals was also part of the problem. "Would you have been enraged if there were uniforms on my friends, and the relationship had been one of employer-employees instead?"

"No, there are other people in this area who employ them, and I haven't objected to that."

This was a neighbor with whom I had always been on friendly terms before this incident. We had chatted many times in our yards as our children played together. Occasionally we would walk together with our children to the duck pond. So, having had good times in the past, I was able to reason with her enough to have her drop her antagonism and listen to me explain our membership in the Catholic Interracial Council and what we stood for, based on social justice, civil rights and love of neighbor, which meant having friends of all kinds. We seemed to have parted with a little bit better understanding between us.

The next morning I was very emotionally touched and surprised when she came over to apologize. In tears, she said she couldn't sleep the night before, and didn't think money was more important than people. She said she didn't feel about Negroes as I did, but that we should have the right to invite any of our friends to our house. All I could do was thank God quietly, thank her for her courage and accept her apology. I rejoiced after she left that here had been a change of heart, and that recognizing an injustice against another human being was a step closer to tolerance and acceptance of that individual.

Not everyone in the neighborhood had protested to our landlord. Dorothy, an Episcopalian, and mother of Barbara's friend Johnny backed us up completely in what we did with our Negro friends. She was appalled at what had happened. So were the Carpinellis, who lived upstairs.

When President Kennedy delivered his TV speech on civil rights in June, describing it as a moral as well as legislative issue, and proposed a 1964 Civil Rights Act for Congress, we cheered. We were going forward! Then when NAACP leader Medgar Evers in Mississippi was assassinated the next day, we mourned him, his wife, and three children who were left behind and the movement which was going backward again. The murder of the four little girls who were in their Baptist church on that horrific September day also spawned our angry frustration over how the corrupt police system behaved that day. I eventually penned a poem:

Birmingham "Justice" 1963

Black mothers cry. Where were your little ones --
Safe in the church singing hymns?

Yes!

Great was the peace since God's love was present

Then

Hate bomb exploded and in
Rushed police for fast white protection lest
We become troublesome with
White sinful slaughter of our precious girls

Dr. Martin Luther King, Jr. delivered the eulogy with a heavy heart at the scene of the crime, which was the Sixteenth Street Baptist Church. The more we learned of the struggles and accomplishments of Dr. King the more we and the rest of our friends in the Interracial Council drew inspiration from him, to continue his work.

Justice for the Klu Klux Klan members who were responsible for the children's deaths finally took place when three of the four went to prison in 1979, 2001 and 2002. The fourth died in 1994 before any sentencing.

My mother said that if anyone had killed her children, she thought she would go insane.

Yet in 21st century America many African American families are still losing unarmed children and young men to gun violence, due to the poison of racism which still exists.

24. BELDEN LIVING, MORE CHALLENGES

"YOU KNOW, HON, IT won't be long until I'll have to go back to Kent State for my master's. It'll help me with my teaching, and also give me more pay. "

"Uh-huh, you're right."

"Do you remember the little Monzione grocery store on Belden Avenue near where we used to live on 4th Street?"

"Yes."

"Well, I just learned that the Monziones have a nice apartment where they used to live available for rent, and it's less cost than our current place, so it'll help with school expenses."

"Oh, no! Except for our recent neighborhood flare-up, I'm really enjoying North Canton, and it's close to your work. Where is it?"

"On Belden Avenue, across the street from their store on one side, and facing Belden Elementary, where I used to go to school."

"Well, going back to Kent really makes a move an imperative. We've lived in the area before, and were happy there, but this location isn't as good as our prior one. What's the inside of the apartment look like? Besides, there's more traffic, and Barbara is starting kindergarten. Is there one at Belden?"

"I think so, but we'd better check, to be sure."

So it was, in the middle of summer 1963, that we moved into that nice apartment with a large, grassy lawn and paved area for their tricycles shortly before Barbara's first adventure in school.

The first day of kindergarten for Barbara was triumphant for her, and for a brief moment a bit melancholy for her mother, as my daughter stated she didn't want me to go. I was slightly stunned as I watched her walk by herself across the street between the traffic guards, and into the school. We had visited her room together and had met her teacher, whom we both liked, giving her more confidence than I realized for getting to her classroom. I was so proud of her, since everything worked out well, and both of us were happy to greet each other outside our apartment when class was done. To this day and throughout her life, she has maintained her wonderful, independent spirit, mostly in beneficial ways.

It would have been helpful to have paid a person to assist me with some of the household and child care chores, but that wasn't as much of a financial priority as Johnny's professional quest. There were no nursery or Montessori schools yet in Canton, and I didn't know about the Canton

Art Institute's excellent program in the arts, the only local program at that time for preschoolers, until Patti and Carolyn were available for it. The only possible option, which wasn't acceptable to me for the children, was to hire unskilled, uneducated adult baby sitters who would mostly watch the girls play with each other and put the children in front of the TV for much of the time. If outside, they would have to be careful that the girls didn't get too near the auto traffic since our yard wasn't fenced.

So, the girls and I had so much fun that year, reading and hearing stories, singing, playing games, baking and creating paint, crayon, or clay masterpieces. We didn't always keep up with the constant need for paper, so some masterpieces were even on the backs of old mimeographed tests that their daddy would bring home from school. Learning to help with cleanup was also part of the activities, and at their ages, they often thought it was fun! After we celebrated Carolyn's first birthday in August on that beautiful lawn, we learned shortly thereafter that Warren and Byrle's second daughter, Lisa, was born.

Since John had the car, he would do the main grocery shopping at Fisher Foods super market near work, but sometimes we had a need to buy some items at Monzione's Market across the street, which I could incorporate into my walks with the girls. Then, for our meals, I cooked everything from scratch, believing that would be healthier than using packaged, processed meals.

John and I drove to London, Ontario, Canada—less than a full day's journey— to keep my appointment with Dr. Evan Shute, medical director at the Shute Medical Institute for an exam and prescription for vitamin E. This is where Evan and Wilfred Shute, medical doctors and brothers did their valuable landmark research, development, and successful treatment of the nutrient starting in the 1940's. I'd had enough with phlebitis, since it surfaced a second time after Carolyn's birth. I had some hope for assistance after having read encouraging literature on the effectiveness of the natural d-alpha form of the vitamin for cardiovascular problems, including phlebitis, because of its anti-coagulant and anti-oxidant properties. After receiving an exam and the recommended dosage of 1200 I.U., we returned home satisfied.

We had a black male kitty named Midnight with us in our North Canton duplex which we brought with us in the move to Belden, but sometimes cats take a while to adjust to their new environments. We tried keeping him indoors, but one time he darted out into the night, and we couldn't catch him! We spent weeks hunting for him, and then we finally found him—a little different looking, but still charming to us with those beautiful green eyes.

Well, Midnight really wasn't Male Midnight as "he" was Lady Midnight and she presented us with four beautiful babies behind the clothes dryer. The girls (especially Patti) were delighted with the change by having gained more playmates.

I joined the Belden School PTA and became the Parent Education chair as a way of contributing something to Barbara's school. It was through this volunteer job that I met Betty Givens. She came to our apartment one day to explain the chair position because she had held it the year before, and we became good friends.

Disappointing to some in Canton was the exodus soon afterward of Betty, her husband Hoyt and their three children to Madison, Wisconsin. He had accepted the position of associate executive of a new million-dollar Northside YMCA. I liked him and Betty a lot, so I wished them happy years in Madison. I could understand their frustration due to their exclusion from neighborhoods in Canton because they were Negro. It didn't matter that they were college-educated, good parents to their children and good citizens. Betty's ancestors, Negro and native American, had been in this country far longer than mine and yet I was the privileged one when it came to housing. It just didn't make sense.

Racism never makes sense.

* * * *

After our North Canton incident we learned that our former neighborhood to which we had returned was more racially integrated than when we left it in 1960. Johnny consented to assist with child care some evenings so I could be more active in the Interracial Council. I was asked to chair an all day workshop on racism especially for educators but open to the public at Central Catholic High School on Sunday, November 24.

I accepted, and it was a great team project. Norma played a major role as program chair. The goal was to spotlight and study some of the interracial problems so that we as teachers and educator parents could do something about them. The hope was for better understanding and improved relationships.

Friday afternoon November 22 a neighbor lady knocked on our door to find out if I knew the unthinkable national news yet that President Kennedy had been shot! No, I had not, and responding to it first in brief disbelief, I then hoped and prayed for his life. When we learned that he had died, I wished it was a nightmare from which we would all wake up and know everything was alright. Instead, it was a real life emotional black hole for me.

After Johnny came home we sat in a stunned stupor glued for a while to the TV. But since we had young children, we had to eventually explain, with difficulty, the multi-dimensional tragedy in ways they might understand while we performed, in tears, the simple tasks of eating and putting them to bed.

And the workshop—should we, and were we even able to go ahead with it? Would anyone even come? So, the phones buzzed constantly and we leaders had an impromptu emergency meeting as we struggled over what to do. Then we came to a common consensus that we should go ahead. All of the presenters, including the main speaker, were still planning to participate. However, out of respect for the President's death, we cancelled the gala banquet.

It was encouraging to see how many people were being registered that Sunday! However, the amount of people there added to my discomfort as I stressed out over the welcome greeting I had to give on the microphone as chairperson. I didn't feel like speaking on it. Having functioned that morning in a subdued mourning mood, my confidence had suffered from it. Then Brother Farrell, one of our council members and moderator for all three panel sessions, said, "Dolores, you can do this."

So, before more than 300 attendees I said, "Welcome. This week we have all seen to what extent hatred can lead. I hope this tragic event will inspire us to strive even more for the love of God and neighbor so our late President will not have died in vain. We of the committee are going ahead with the workshop because we feel this is in accordance with his wishes as a promoter of civil rights and social justice. As chairman, I dedicate the entire workshop, including Holy Mass, to the memory of our late President John F. Kennedy." I felt relieved and better after I finished. Listening to the musical selections helped also.

There were three main sessions with four different categories and speakers for each. Session I was titled "Giving the Stereotype His Human Qualities". Following that, the morning concluded with the Mass celebrated by Negro Father Alan Simpson. It was a moving Requiem for President Kennedy.

After lunch, Session II began with "Cry in the Night", a playlet relating to the theme of "Sore Spots in Human Relations" with an actor, followed by the speakers and their topics.

Session III's theme was "The Ghetto Game" , showing the vicious cycle of the economic, educational, and sociological effects on the community resulting from discrimination. Our extensive resource bibliography was passed out to all.

The conclusion and featured speaker was Father Philip Berrigan, SSJ, a Josephite Missionary, with a background in race relations as a teacher, a white leader working with low income adults on race, education and housing problems. In Father Berrigan's address, he said the President's death would force people to analyze the forces of extremism and that those who support racism by action or inaction betray Christ. "The white debt to the Negro is one of love and the guilt is that of the white. The Negro now is offering humanity to the white."

It was back to heartbreak on Monday watching the funeral on TV.

December was better. We received a beautiful Christmas card from Father Berrigan, with a personal note to me and John in response to my thanking him for speaking on November 24. The card was published by the Fellowship of Reconciliation and has on the cover a pen and ink nativity drawing by artist Fritz Eichenberg, which I kept.

25. GUILFORD

WHILE AT BELDEN AVENUE, we were able to pay our bills, but we were struggling. After Mom and Dad Tate learned about it, they walked down the few blocks from their house to visit us one evening.

Dad asked, "Why don't you try to get a job at Ford?" (Dad worked there).

John replied, "I appreciate your concern, and I like building things with wood, but I wouldn't be happy working with steel and building cars. I think it's great that you've been happy there. It's a good thing you belong to such a great union too. We want to stick it out, at least for now, because I love working with people, ideas, and education. But, thanks for thinking of us."

Our interest in Pope John XXIII's encyclical *Pacem in Terris (Peace on Earth)* was revived in February of 1965 when the Center for the Study of Democratic Institutions in Santa Barbara sponsored an International Convocation on the Requirements of Peace, based on ideas from the encyclical. Included was encouragement for cooperating with the United Nations and discussions of the political and economic problems with which nations struggled for implementation of the ideas. Robert Hutchins, president of the Center, was Chairman of the Convocation.

John had a lot of respect for him in the past and what he represented, so he trusted that the convocation was worthwhile. By that time we were also proud owners of the *Great Books of the Western World*, with Robert Hutchins as Editor, Encyclopedia Britannica as Publishers and University of Chicago faculty contributing editorial advice. We owned a Britannica Encyclopedia Britannica and John also subscribed to the Santa Barbara Center Magazine.

And then, there was me and my relatively small world of ideas and activities. That included taking care of our daughters. Sometimes it was a bit much doing what I did outside our home while I still had young children. In one twenty-four hour period I had no sleep—too busy. It caught up with me the next day as I functioned in a semi-zombie condition. John said I needed to take better care of myself, and if I didn't take good enough care of our girls, they could grow up and do things to destroy the world that I was trying so hard to improve! What he said hit home with me. He was right and I had to work in such a way as to do only what I could reasonably handle along with my family care from that time on.

Soon afterward, John learned that because he was a veteran he could qualify for assistance to buy a house. There was a new brick, three bedroom house for sale across the street from Taft Junior High, where he taught. Oh, did we want to try for it! He wouldn't have to drive to work and do the grocery shopping anymore, freeing up more time for him to pursue his graduate work. Even though having the car would give me another shopping chore, it would also give me and the girls more options away from home.

Yes—we did it! We moved to our new house on Guilford Avenue in April. After that was accomplished, John enrolled in the master's program at Kent State that same month. He had the opportunity to become a principal, but he declined it, saying, "I want to be where the action is—in the classroom." He found that more fulfilling, so he enrolled in the Master Teacher Program.

Barbara transferred to William Day Public School, which was next door to Taft. She did just fine, receiving outstanding grades, as she had at Belden.

As a non-Jewish, white family, we were able to move to the neighborhood of our choice—no restrictive covenants. The only restriction for location was cost. That's why we wouldn't have been able to live in beautiful Avondale, which was only a block from where we bought. It was probably the second most affluent place to live after Hills and Dales. We were in a nice middle class neighborhood — full of many advantages — which included a swimming pool where our girls could get swimming lessons, and Arboretum, one of our city's loveliest public parks. We became enthusiasts over the extended nature near our house: bunnies, birds, butterflies, fireflies, and raccoons. The girls reveled in constantly bringing me beautiful bouquets of wildflowers—especially white Queen Ann's Lace and blue chicory. We even accidently uncovered fossils with seashell imprints in our back yard while digging for a garden.

Other new beginnings were taking place that wonder-filled spring. Somehow I learned about the preschool art and movement classes at the Canton Art Institute, located at that time in the former, beautiful Case Mansion. It was the only preschool program in the city, and an excellent one, led by Judi Hertzi for art and Blossom Perkins for musical movement. Barbara was too old for it, but it gave Patti and Carolyn holistically joyous foundations for all their future learnings. They had such fun as they expressed their ideas visually and romped with Blossom across the third floor ballroom's polished wooden floor to the pianist's tunes on the grand piano.

I took Barbara by herself with me there through the art galleries on a Sunday so she could experience the child and adult masterpieces. She was attentive, and then when we arrived home, I asked her to tell her daddy what she had seen, and what she liked the best. To our surprise she said, "Daddy, they have the most beautiful bathroom!" Then I recalled the restroom and that it looked like it had original early 1900's decorative white small tiles with black tile trim. Currently she is an interior home designer.

26. SATISFACTIONS

FEBRUARY 1965 WAS BIRTHDAY month for Dad. So after John, the girls (seven, four, and two years old) and I watched a Young People's concert with Leonard Bernstein together, John was excited to share.

Sat. Feb. 20

Dear Dad,

The whole family watched the children's concert from N.Y. with Leonard Bernstein last night. Very beautiful — the entire thing was dedicated to Sibelius and his works. The selections were Finlandia, Symphony no. 2 in D major, and a violin concerto (brilliantly played by a native born Romanian!) Did you get a chance to see it on TV? Dolores and I thought it was an appropriate time to show it — the birthday month of another Finlander! Happy Birthday! Have a great time this year.

Love.

John

Canton, Ohio 1965

79

* * * *

I was asked in February 1965 by Barbara Saltsman to be a panelist for a local branch of the Panel of American Women, a national organization started in 1956. My volunteer work with the Interracial Council and PTA was less intense, so I wanted to consider it. Also, it wasn't long before the Catholic Interracial Council joined together with other community members to form the Human Relations Council of Greater Canton. Barbara, (who I didn't know), read about the Panel in her Methodist Journal and had been inspired by its goals. Those were to have four local women at a time in various cities speak to the public about their experiences with prejudice and discrimination: a Jew, a Catholic, a Negro, and a white Protestant. Orthodox women in Canton were invited but they declined. It was established by Esther Brown, a Jewish woman in Kansas City, Missouri.

That original Canton Panel consisted of Betty Givens, a Negro; Blanche Feiman, a Jew; myself, a white Roman Catholic; and Yvonne Cave, a white Protestant as panelists and Barbara, another white Protestant as moderator. Since Betty moved soon after it had formed, Paralee Compton took her place. Susie Burnett, chair of the Canton Urban League's Religious Resource Committee had also recently read articles on the Panel, and decided to join as one of the white Protestant panelists.

One of the first organizations to hear us was Malone College's faculty women's group. As we received more requests to speak in Canton and other area communities we increased the size of the Panel: Joanne Buffo, Catholic; Harriet Narens, Jewish; Mary Dennison, white Protestant; and Lillian Barnes, Protestant Negro. Everyone serving had felt the effects of discrimination and prejudice as violations against their democratic principles and religious beliefs. Each was given five minutes for her talk, and then there were questions from the audience. As the list of volunteers continued, Norma Marcere, the Negro Catholic, decided to speak in the role of a Negro, because that's how she had suffered the most discrimination. It was such a privilege for me to serve with such outstanding, conscientious women. Also, as Norma eventually said, "We became a loving, understanding support group." My gallant husband was a big emotional supporter and took care of our girls when needed.

27. MORE ON MARCERE

IN ORDER TO AVOID confusion about the different descriptions used for African Americans in the twentieth century Norma had pointed out to us that the term colored was commonly used until the mid-1930s. The various degrees of Caucasian-African mixtures, including the term mulatto, were included.

Negro, which means black in Latin, became widespread until the Civil Rights movement in the mid-1960s. At that time there was a growing awareness in the English word black as a term of pride in African roots and identified themselves with such phrases as "Black is beautiful". Norma shared that not until Dr. Martin Luther King Jr. showed an appreciation for it were some of her friends willing to use it for themselves. It then became their identity as well as an adjective (black) and as a noun (Blacks).

It was during the period of using Negro that John and I met Norma in 1962. Initially, we noticed a gracefulness and strength of spirit that exhibited a strong positive attitude. It was this that had been helping her through the tough times of racism and discrimination.

Later that year in an October publication of Community magazine she shared the illuminating story of her recent trip to Rome to attend the canonization of Martin de Porres. Upon arrival she expected personal discrimination due to her conditioning in the United States. She was stunned when she experienced none of it anytime she was in Europe.

She felt "unspeakable joy" in St. Peter's as Pope John XXIII celebrated the beautiful service at the altar. The good monastic brother himself was celebrated for his saintliness in helping the sick and poor and for the miracles attributed to him. She was overcome with emotion as the painting of Martin was held high in the procession, the Sistine Choir performed and thousands of others spontaneously broke into song. All of this for a man of color seemed almost unreal to her—"too much to believe it was actually happening!"

Born of a white Spanish father and a Negro Panamanian mother, Martin's father had abandoned the woman and their two children because the children were, in his opinion, too dark. Though Martin lived in Peru in the sixteenth and seventeenth centuries, she felt a personal bond with him for a parallel in her own life. At the time of her 1908 birth in Canton, Ohio, she had been a disappointment also to her father Norman because he had wanted her to look like her mother, and she didn't. Ida was of mixed ancestry and was lighter in color than he was. Instead, his first child was dark like he was and they named her after him.

Norma empathized with all who suffer personal rejections and needs for acceptance as well as patience to endure and serve such as de Porres from Peru. Another inspiration for her was Dr. Martin Luther King, Jr. "The two Martins made me very proud of my dark skin. I was ready to scale the highest fence!"

Norma also credited her mother for giving her children the love, discipline, sense of security and self-worth in their early childhood that lasted all of Norma's life, giving her the confidence to excel. By the time she was at McKinley High School she had hopes of going to Oberlin College, which was only 75 miles from Canton. Though not an African-American college, it started accepting them in 1835 and had been active with the Underground Railroad in freeing slaves soon afterward.

However, Oberlin was too expensive for Norma so she worked as a cook and maid during the 1920's so she could attend Kent Normal School in Kent, Ohio with the goal of becoming a teacher. After graduation she couldn't get regular work as a teacher during the depression, so she, in her own words, "became the most educated cook in town!" She also took care of children in affluent homes. Finally, Norma worked in Judge Hunter's office as a receptionist and then at the Tuberculosis Association for twelve years from 1944 to 1956.

By the time she acquired her master's degree Kent Normal was Kent State University. She became the first tenured black teacher and first black counselor in the Massillon, Ohio, City Schools. After obtaining her doctorate at Akron University Marcere became the first black high school guidance counselor and the first black psychologist for the Akron, Ohio, City Schools. Through the years she received numerous recognitions for her human relations work, including that with the Catholic Interracial Council. In 1973 she was named Woman of the Year by the Junior League.

In 1980 it was because of Norma's introduction of Mr. Pridgen to me that I successfully finished my college degree. In 1996 on a visit back to Ohio, John and I attended a reunion with our Catholic Interracial Council friends that Norma organized. The attendees included her son Al and her daughter Norma Jean, and was a happy affair though we were missing Norma's husband Percy, Brother Farrell and Bernie Schario who had died previously. In 2004 Norma passed away. We've always remembered her as a very special friend, for her courage and many accomplishments. She is greatly missed.

28. APPRECIATIONS

IN JUNE OF 1965 my husband was surprised and grateful to receive such a nice note from one of his seventh grade students:

Dear Mr. Tate, I would just like to thank you for devoting your time and efforts to educate and interest me in spelling, reading, and social studies. I know the knowledge gained in class will be useful to me later on as well as now. Since social studies and English are my favorite subjects, I appreciate the fact that we covered them in more detail. Thank you again.

Sincerely yours, Ann

He started in the fall as a student teacher classroom supervisor for KSU students in the social sciences. Now that he was working with university students, he wanted to be known only as *John*. Since he had always been my Rock, upon whom I could count for strength of mind, body and spirit, I found that the word resonated even better with John.

One of John's first KSU students was Bill Paulus. A retired teacher from Taft, he remembers meeting John with fondness. He said that his supervising teacher was "tall in stature, dark haired, very trim, conservatively dressed, almost to a point of being stereotypical! His manner was quite reserved, quiet, but had a strong but not loud or obnoxious voice. He was quite bright of mind, articulate, extremely well versed in his subject, having depth of understanding in what he taught and how he supervised."

As a fellow teacher, Paulus said of John, "His lesson plans were works of art, hand printed in neatly drawn small symbols/letters, done with great precision. His study guides/assignment sheets were ingeniously executed with diagrams and activities, cleverly designed on that ditto paper we all used then. As far as his brown bagged lunches from home were concerned, he ate healthy long *before green was vogue*."

*　*　*　*

With the move to a new neighborhood, we were within the boundaries of a new church. We checked it out and also the school. They seemed excellent at the time, so we thought they would be good influences on our children, and helpful in raising them. The nuns were Sisters of Notre Dame, a teaching order, who had a superior rating and reputation. Added to that was the fact that it was an affluent parish, with adequate financial resources for the school.

So in the fall Barbara entered second grade with Sister Mary Teran, and did well that whole school year with grades of A's and B's. On Thanksgiving

Day we were giving thanks for Barbara's First Communion, and wrote to her these sentiments:

To our lovely Barbara,

May this great and generous spirit of love that you give so happily to God now, remain with you the rest of your life.

Love from your Mommy and Daddy who are very proud of you, on this, your First Communion Day, Thanksgiving, 1965."

So began another faith tradition in our family that we carried on with the rest of our children.

On the first of November, Moshu had died. He was John's paternal grandfather, as the term of endearment in Romanian meant that. George (Gheorghe) was his first name, and his last name? Well, since Transylvania, Romania, where he originated was under Hungarian rule in 1913 when he came to the United States, he was bilingual. His Hungarian name was Czicz (pronounced Zeets). In Romanian, it was Tit (with marks under the t's that in English look like commas, and would make it sound similar to the former spelling and pronounced as Tzeetz). Fortunately for our family and my in-laws, it became Tate in English! In another Romanian variant it could be Titu with the same markings under the 'ts'. His education had been limited in his Romanian village but was able to get employment as a steel worker in Indiana and Ohio.

He was fortunate to have lived until 86 years old, for his wife died in Canton in her fifties. A colorful character, he sometimes drank a bit too much of his home made red wine, was formerly a cantor in his Romanian Byzantine Catholic Church, and played a folk flute all his life. After Aunt Vickie, his youngest child, and Uncle John moved near St. Benedict's Roman Catholic Church, George lived with them and their sons and also attended St. Benedict's. As was traditional in the Roman Church, he would periodically go to the sacrament of confession, which was more often than in his previous church. After he was a bit hard of hearing, he would speak a bit too loud in the confessional and everyone could hear his confession! For his own welfare, the priest eventually moved him to a room where no one else would hear him. One of the family relatives recalled hearing him at least once say, "Damn it Father, I tried to be so good, but here I am!" When he couldn't navigate a car anymore due to a change to one way streets, he visited friends and relatives (including us) by walking a lot with a cane he created for himself out of a tree branch, which he then decorated with a wood burning tool, and which I still have. He would take a train trip once a year to Hot Springs, Arkansas where he visited friends and relaxed in the hot springs. He had a zest for life, as well as raw garlic—three times a day! He was missed a lot; not so much the garlic.

We decided to take our children to the funeral. My parents never took Warren and me to funerals, but in John's family it was an important thing to do. It was done out of respect and a coming together of family in support of one another through the grieving process and closure. It meant a lot to our new family then, too — another tradition worth preserving.

29. NAM

JOHN HAD EVOLVED FROM a seventh grader excitedly posting Allied WWII victories with colored pins on a large world wall map, to accomplishing the necessary paper work for processing troops to and from Korea, to eventually being appalled with war on a conscientious level.

On October 31, 1966, John wrote a letter to my parents:

Dear Mom and Dad,

Let me first thank you for remembering my birthday. I'm collecting quite a few now. Time passes so rapidly when you spend so much time doing all the things you want to do. I enjoyed your pictures of the desert and boating. Hope you will be able to finish that desert dream of yours soon. It's a splendid idea.

I have been very disturbed by the Vietnam War since it first began. Not having any first-hand knowledge of events, I, of course, must rely on the reporting of others and their honesty. This has sometimes been confusing. I tend to see the situation somewhat as Sen. Morse does. We are mistaken for being there and ought to make use of the United Nations to settle grievances. One of the best articles on the subject I have read was in the Sept. 24th issue of Saturday Review. Edward Keating, editor of Ramparts Magazine, wrote a guest article. He rather expresses my political philosophy and Vietnam views to a 'T'. ...I'd also feel better with Johnson OUT. I find it hard to trust or believe him.....I wish I had the article from Saturday Review to send you, but I don't. If you haven't read it or any of Keating's other writings, I'd certainly recommend getting it from the library. (That's where I got it.)

With Love, John

Even though Morse had helped create humane legislation in such areas such as civil rights, education, and health care for the elderly before Medicare, this constitutional law professor's other strong efforts toward peace eventually consumed most of his time. He led a national outcry against the war and was dubbed "Mr. Peace". He continued through the end of his time in Congress, which was 1969.

Edward Keating said, "The end sought is not a new system. Our ultimate goal is peace, and this is impossible without justice—social, economic, and political."

As a lawyer and also publisher of Ramparts Magazine, Mr. Keating's opinion on the American political scene was one of several points of view in 1966 that was published by Saturday Review, a literary magazine.

He believed that the American system had all the built-in aids necessary to arrive at justice for all people. Most important of all was the elective system of government. That is why, rather than replacing the system, he thought it better to work within it and try to understand the national and international contexts in which all Americans were involved.

He thought that as a nation we didn't understand the enormous complexities of the rest of the world. These included varying political systems, religions, ethnicities, climates, geographies and huge disparities in standards of living. Keating thought that we had a rather simplistic approach to all of that.

Keating continued, "If anything marks American political orientation and direction, it is this paranoia over Communism. ...On April 20, 1966, while testifying before the Senate Foreign Relations Committee, Secretary of Defense Robert McNamara said, *'During 1966, 638,000 tons of bombs will be used in Vietnam. This amounts to 91 percent of the total dropped in Korea over thirty-seven months, and to 48 percent of all the bombs used against the Nazis by United States forces in World War II.'"*

Keating argued, "You cannot bomb Communism to death; you must feed it to death, clothe it to death, and heal it to death. Where there is ignorance you must bring knowledge, where there is poverty, you must bring relief, and most important, where there is oppression you must bring justice.

"We talk of foreign aid, but it goes into the pockets of dictators, domineering oligarchs, and a few land owners. Scarcely anything trickles down to the people, and even when it does, it carries a high price in monetary and political terms. The cry of the people is for land reform, and nothing is done. The cry of the people is for peace, and we give them war. There exists in Vietnam an entire generation that has not known one day free from war, yet our policymakers insist we are only interested in the good of the Vietnamese people. ...We talk of reconstructing the Vietnamese countryside with schools, hospitals, and hydroelectric plants, but how can we do all that when all the while we are dropping napalm, phosphorus, and anti-personnel bombs on that very countryside."

Keating explained, "The historical truism that 'might makes right' has been the basis of all international relations down through the centuries. Whenever a vital interest, such as pride or treasure, is at stake, the merits of the case are set aside; the issue is decided by force of arms. But war can no longer be the ultimate sport of men and states; *we possess the power to end life on this planet.*

"It has been said that the first victim of war is truth. It could be added that the second victim is compassion." Keating's understanding also included what he said was universal to all Mankind—inner peace.

30. PRIORITIES

ON JANUARY 4, 1967 I wrote to my parents:

"In the November ('66) election, the school bond issue for our school district was defeated, so it was voted on again in a special election in December, and soundly defeated again! That meant the teachers' raises went out the window, too. Plain has dropped to the lowest paying district in this area because it has continued to vote down bonds while the surrounding districts have passed them. Even though we live among one of the most affluent Canton housing areas, many of the people are reluctant to pay higher taxes. The burden on the individual school districts is high, because the state has not kept up with its obligations. The legislature has begun to move on university aid but how long it will take to get it going on all levels of education is hard to tell. When John came to Plain, it was the highest paying district. Now the administration fears the loss of many teachers (especially men) if something isn't done fast about the salaries. John could look elsewhere, but his seniority in experience would drop, meaning not a raise, but a loss in salary, and he enjoys the job he has right now. After he gets his master's degree, we hope our financial status will be changed for the better, and he should have a better chance for changing jobs if he desires. Who knows? Unless Ohio's educational policies change, we may move again outside the state—but only if it means an improvement job-wise, and a place we like."

Male teachers all around us kept leaving their jobs for better pay in industry and the YMCA. We couldn't blame them, but thought it was scandalous and stupid, when good teachers were so needed for the kids. The cultural and legislative values were screwed; not enough value was being placed on public education.

When it came time for Patti to go to kindergarten, there were no public ones in Plain Township. "How archaic," I thought, when I attended one in Minneapolis in the 1940's! Except for cost, though, the negative turned into a great positive! Not too many miles from where we lived we were able to enroll her into a private one operated by excellent teaching nuns. John and I were so pleased that among other important learnings, they worked with pre-reading with the children, which at that time disgruntled some first grade teachers because they weren't quite ready yet for the speed at which these young ones were eventually reading compared to others who had not attended there. Pre-reading and reading were not usually taught in kindergartens!

There were bonuses galore! The building was a beautiful, large Tudor style, former mansion on a high plateau which was reached by a mile long, tall, deciduous tree studded driveway.

When the weather was inclement the children could peer out of the clear, small geometric windows to marvel at the raindrops and snowflakes, sometimes while seated on cushioned window seats. While outdoors, they sometimes took walks to a lovely farm. Since we lost that last black kitty in the move to Guilford Avenue after finding homes for her kittens, Patti was given another kitten from people who owned the farm and had a child in Patti's class. To say the least, all of our girls were delighted, and for Patti this was a very special happening! She was full of pride when she named him "Whiskers". He was quite a character, a beloved member of our family for many years after that.

In 1966, after Patti "graduated", Carolyn followed two years later.

31. POWER MAN AND FAMILY CULTURE

I HATED THE FACT that John, my worker scholar man was a cement company laborer even before school was out in spring of 1967. He was teaching daily at Taft 8 AM to 4 PM and at Diamond-Portland from 4:30 PM to 12:30 A.M., wielding a 100 pound air hammer on top of a cement tower to break up an overflow of cement! Never afraid of heights, he may have thought it wasn't much worse than running the rototiller. He did that every spring for my vegetable garden, but that was only during the day and on the ground. I was worried about his safety and the stress on his health. He did it for five weeks until school was out. By then he was exhausted. On weekends he relaxed as much as he could at home.

On June 22 I wrote to my parents:

I resent his having to work so hard at two jobs, and hope that this will be the last summer job for this kind of work. He makes about as much as a laborer as he does teaching! This is really a scandal, after having spent four years in college preparing for his profession. He will have five years when he gets his master's degree. He will then have better job opportunities.

For now, we hope to get rid of our Penney's charge account this summer, and save for his graduate studies and Carolyn's kindergarten. Fortunately, he will be getting two raises in teaching pay this coming year. We hope it will be enough so he can go to night school this winter and summer school all next summer.

It's only because John likes and believes in the importance of his profession so much that he burdens himself to stay in teaching.

I have a wonderful husband and am proud of him for living by his ideals, for his intellectual abilities, and for his humility in taking jobs that an arrogant man would reject. Also, we both have a great deal of respect for the men and women who labor hard with their hands.

After Carolyn is in school full-time, then I can consider employment, if the budget demands it. Until then neither of us wants me to work."

By mid-June John was working only days, five days a week! We reveled in it and were able to relax one night with the girls for some "free culture" on the downtown plaza. We were treated to a band concert and an international bazaar, sponsored by the downtown merchants. We zipped past the new, attractively designed KSU branch in Jackson Township, which was close to our home, and almost ready to open for students. John and I discussed Canton's plans for building a new Cultural Center, which would provide a new art institute and Players Guild Theater, as well as a symphony hall. The orchestra had been, for years, practicing at the YMCA and performing at the Timken High School auditorium. For its size, Canton had been doing well in providing the arts to the community, and we looked forward to benefitting even more from them.

32. POSITIVE HUMAN RELATIONS
AMIDST THE PAINS

BEFORE JOHN STARTED HIS Diamond-Portland job in the spring of '67, we celebrated Passover Seder at panelist Blanche Feiman and Rabbi Paul Gorin's Temple Israel. In doing so, we heard some of the most moving, relevant ideas about various forms of individual and collective freedom versus tyranny that we had ever heard. One of John's students at Taft was Rabbi and Mrs. Gorin's son David, so we had the additional opportunity of attending his Bar Mitzvah a few weeks after that. It was the first time we had attended both Jewish celebrations. We were favorably impressed with both.

Sometime after our Panel of American Women had begun in 1965, the greater Canton area had established a human relations council, which encompassed a more diverse population than our local Catholic Interracial Council, and that the council supported. So did the Panel, and other organizations, such as the Canton Urban League and members of the Jewish community.

In June I assumed chairmanship for the Panel. By summer we panelists included our families in a picnic gathering at Doris and Roy Richards' place in North Canton. In 1966 we had celebrated Paralee's graduation from college at her reception.

By 2003, Paralee's alma mater KSU bestowed upon her the President's Award for Social Responsibility at their 15th Annual Diversity Scholarship Dinner. In 2004 at a special dedication ceremony in Canton, her hometown, Lathrop School was renamed in her honor as Paralee Watkins Compton School. Upon reading the list of her accomplishments for Canton Public Schools, it's understandable why there was a school named after her. She had become a teacher, principal of Martin Elementary School, Director of Human Relations, School/Community Liaison, Director of Elementary Education, Director of Instruction and Staff Development K-12 and the district's first woman and first African-American assistant superintendent. She involved herself in education reforms and teaching methods. She is an original lady, whom I am pleased to have known, and grateful to have been one of the panelists with her.

By Thanksgiving of '67 we celebrated Patti's First Communion as part of our annual gathering with John's family.

Earlier in the fall, the Human Relations Council of Greater Canton was working hard to establish fair housing in the area. Mrs. Nathanial Roberts said, "We were helping a few blacks find homes, but we felt we weren't doing enough. Ohio's fair housing law doesn't cover individual housing—only multiple dwellings." When approached about discrimination in housing, real estate dealers said they couldn't show houses to minorities in certain areas unless people there wanted them as neighbors. So the idea came up to have a "good neighbor" campaign where residents could sign pledge cards stating they were willing to welcome minorities into their neighborhoods. It stated: "I will welcome into my neighborhood any responsible person of whatever race, religion, or national origin and I will work with him and other neighbors to create a desirable community for all."

Mrs. Roberts and Albert Getman were co-chairs of the pledges, working with James Meacham who was chairman of the Fair Housing Committee of Greater Canton. John was pleased to learn that Jim, also a teacher, was in charge. He remembered that they had played together as young kids in their Northeast Canton neighborhood. Jim was one of the children of a black minister.

The Fair Housing Committee members were committed to registering homes and apartments available to minority groups and would aid persons seeking homes by contacting owners and brokers.

Letters were sent to Christian clergy in Canton, North Canton and Louisville, asking for their cooperation in preaching about housing and were asked to distribute the cards. December 3, 1967 was designated as Good Neighbor Sunday and a sermon suggestion was included in the correspondence. The story of the Good Samaritan was part of it, as well as the statement that Jesus of Nazareth would not be able, at that time, to live in some parts of the communities because he was a Jew.

Also supporting this effort was the Protestant Greater Council of Churches; Ecumenical Association; Inner City Ministry board; Catholic Interracial Council and 45 individual churches. However, there was nothing being done, collectively or individually, by the Catholic churches, including my St. Michael's Catholic Church. I was part of a group of Catholic women who were dissatisfied with that. We were members of the National Council of Catholic Women (NCCW), Stark (County) Deanery for our diocese. I was also representing, as chair, the Dialogue and Fellowship Committee of the Canton Human Relations Council and Panel of American Women. Most of us decided, then, to take a trip to Youngstown to meet with our bishop early in 1968. We were a small band of women, probably less than ten, and the names of those that I remember were Ruth Kling, Deanery president, Grace Noon, and Florence Zwick, Mark's mother. We were able to get an appointment with the auxiliary bishop, Rev. James Malone. He was kind and hospitable, and listened respectfully to us.

Our list of concerns was long. We stated that there was a lack of leadership from Catholic clergymen in Canton. There had been no action in working with ghetto blacks in inner-city programs, as Protestant clergymen had been requesting, and no education from the pulpits or classrooms on the formation of moral character in regard to racism. There was no support for fair housing and the Good Neighbor Pledge Card Campaign. In fact the comments from clergy were awful! Some examples:

"You're only trying to build fires under people—the less said about this the better!"

"You won't get cooperation on this from any of the pastors."

"But who is teaching the social teachings of the Church?"

"I'm afraid the financial contributions would drop."

The final results of the campaign were embarrassing as far as the Catholic clergy were concerned. To their credit, one Catholic pastor from a small Canton area parish and one assistant priest said they would help. We received only nine cards from Catholic homeowners because of the lack of promotion by the leadership. There were 80 Protestant churches participating.

Out of the 12 panelists in our interracial, interfaith Panel of American Women, only the Catholic women did not have their pastors participate. All of us panelists promoted fair housing in the community.

When we were done, Bishop Malone revealed to us that he was going to be appointed as the main bishop in 1968 and he would, at that time, dedicate himself to interracial justice, involving our endeavors and any else that were related to it.

"Thank you, Bishop Malone!" We went home grateful and looking forward to some better times. He was installed May 2, 1968 as Bishop of Youngstown by Pope Paul VI, following the death of his predecessor, Emmett Walsh, and shortly before that on April 11, President Lyndon Johnson signed into federal law the Fair Housing Act!

Even before May 2, on April 26, the Youngstown Diocese had scheduled a meeting in Canton with the urgent declaration that inner-city problems in the Canton area were part of a nationwide urban crisis. It was held at the Catholic Action Center with five selected priests of the downtown Canton area and our representatives of the Stark Deanery NCCW. In addition, there were the Executive Secretary of the Catholic Community League of Canton, Inc. (a layman) and the priest who was Director of Catholic Charities.

Helpful to our agenda were further statements coming from the bishop's office:

The American Bishops, in a statement of April 25, 1968, have dedicated themselves to increased social action programs. It is their intention to devote the Church's manpower and financial resources to solving housing, education, and employment problems of the urban poor.

These programs are to be professional, and are also to include maximum use of present Church parochial and educational structures, in their own right and in cooperation with other community agencies.

The clergy and laity of the inner-city parishes, together with board and staff of the Community League of Canton, Inc., the diocesan Catholic Charities office, and other interested parties, should seek and make specific suggestions for action, on both a Catholic and ecumenical basis, on housing, education, and employment problems in Canton.

Preaching against racism in the churches was added, and included in our handouts were two maps published by the Canton City Planning Department: the Washington School Rehabilitation area project and poverty statistics showing the concentrations of poor families generally, and what proportion of non-white families were within that. These actions accelerated after the death of Dr. King on April 4.

One of the first things we Catholic women did was to plan a day care center for working mothers in the inner-city. Ruth Kling asked if I would assist by making it a project of the Community Commission of the Stark Deanery, of which I was recently appointed chairperson. I was vitally interested, so I enthusiastically said yes!

However, with family obligations also expanding, I couldn't do both that and continue as Panel chair, too. So having served as chair for only a year, I resigned after our speaking engagement for the Kent State-Stark Recognition Dinner for outstanding students and their faculty advisors. I didn't want to resign, but having Glenna Reynolds, former Rhodes Scholar and Protestant panelist assume the position made me feel better.

Our day care center program was designed to help develop the learning potential in each preschool child, as was Head Start, which had been set up by the federal government in 1965 for poor children who would eventually be attending public schools. Besides learning programs, the children also received medical care from HS. As good as that was, it was originally only a summer program, for only part of the day but was gradually increased through the years to longer times. Our facility was open from 7:30 AM to 5:30 PM Monday through Friday, ten months of the year with quality care, but not medical.

Our teaching personnel took care to teach material that would not be repeated in HS or kindergarten classes. Our structured learning also had an emphasis on language development, art and music, and identifying and tasting foods. There was also outdoor play, hot lunches, snacks, crafts time and cots with blankets for napping.

It was a great cooperative effort that made the Allen Community Day Care Center a success. The need had first been identified and suggested to Ruth by Arvis Averette of the federal Office of Economic Opportunity (OEO) neighborhood center. As the planning progressed, the primary resource director for the Canton Public Schools and the resource teacher for the city's kindergarten program assisted in the designing of the learning activities. A director for the day care center was hired and two VISTA (Volunteers In Service To America) workers were provided by the OEO to be assistants. Volunteers were women and high school girls from Catholic churches in the area. The funding was provided by OEO and parish affiliates of the NCCW. Canton Public Schools provided the facilities and equipment at Allen Elementary. The principal at Allen worked with the OEO director in the selection of the children and a permanent board was chosen.

I served as chairperson for the project until it was off and running in September and then resigned, since I had been getting chronic sore throats for months. Jane, chair of the board, graciously consented to chair the maintenance of it in my place. I was very grateful, both to her and to her co-chair on the board, Audrey, for all they were doing.

As far as the diocesan leadership was concerned, Bishop James Malone continued until 1995. He had led well. Even as an auxiliary bishop, he had attended all the Vatican II sessions in Rome (1962-65) with his predecessor Bishop Emmett Walsh. From 1983-86 he served as president of the National Conference of Catholic Bishops, (the first prelate to do so who was not an archbishop or cardinal.) Malone implemented the Vatican II reforms and as a group, the other bishops supported the same. They issued a letter on commitment to work for the poor, issued a major policy statement condemning nuclear weapons stockpiles and disarmament, and contacted President Reagan about them, but he escalated them instead. The NCCB's position was that funds spent on defense should be invested instead in domestic programs. Ecumenism was encouraged from Rome and Malone was prominent in leading as president of the Ohio Council of Churches, a mostly Protestant organization, and was also co-chair of a national Catholic-Methodist dialogue group.

33. TRANSPORTATIONS AND TRANSITIONS

I WAS NEVER A soccer mom. Like so many other have-car-will-travel mothers, I was a scout mom, a take-them-to-schools-and-church mom, as well as take-them-to-creative arts lessons-and-concerts mom. Except for Girl Scouts, which started with the Brownies at the beginning of elementary school, this chauffeuring began in the girls' preschool years and continued to expand as they grew older. Almost always someone was taking music or art, and eventually we added drama for Carolyn. John and I felt blessed that Canton offered so much for the children's holistic development.

Though I couldn't keep up with my chairmanship commitments, I decided I would do once-in-a-while volunteering, such as panelist, music and movement teacher twice a month with the children at the day care center, and continue as assistant to Patti's Brownie leader. Another reason to curtail my activities was to assist the family with the serious health problems of my mother-in-law Mary.

And there was my family out west and keeping up with what was happening with them. My dad had a history of asthma, as far back as his childhood. Fortunately for him, it didn't seem to be constant and chronic. I only remember him having a severe attack once when I was in junior high.

March 9, 1968 he seemed to be doing okay, and wrote a thank you letter for our remembering his 54th birthday, which had been in February.

Dear Dolores and John—

Thanks for remembering me on my birth date. I've acquired so many years now, I think I'll stay with Jack Benny—39 from now on!

I like Vegas in comparison with Southern Cal. The air is smog free and working conditions are better in construction. So—it looks like I'm making another transition.

Besides, it's only 2 hours from our property near Kingman.

I love these wide open spaces! It does something for me personally, emotionally, etc.

In reference to John's mother and her condition: She must be a very sensitive person to have suffered so over the years. I have a great compassion for her.

What we are doing in Viet Nam is an example of man's inhumanity to man.

Greet John's folks and the children.

So long for now, Ol' Daddio.

P.S. I'm flying back to Long Beach next weekend. Warren and I will haul our furniture, etc. to Vegas. Byrle and Mother will drive out in Warren's car.

34. OHIO AND MINNESOTA BENEFITS

1968: CAROLYN FINISHED KINDERGARTEN with a great day at the nearby farm with her class for a picnic and hayrides. John was working his last summer at Diamond-Portland as well as taking two of his graduate courses. In August I was teaching seven year old Patti how to type and the whole family enjoyed a concert at Blossom Music Center for its grand opening season. The place is a gem for concertgoers in the greater Cleveland area, both for music and its location, nestled in the gently rolling green wooded hills of Cuyahoga Falls between Akron and Cleveland.

John and I had been taking turns with the girls to classical musical concerts in Canton since they were preschoolers. Now we were embarking upon new musical adventures to hear the famous Cleveland Orchestra, known to be one of the best in the country. This was the new summer home of the Orchestra, under the direction of George Szell. The pavilion, a contemporary amphitheater with slanted roof, could seat over 5,000 people. There were many natural wood and colorful seats within, adding to the beauty. It was more expensive than the lawn area, so when we took the children we would sit on the sloped lawn and eat a picnic dinner. It was quite an all-around bargain, complete with soul satisfying sights and sounds! During the musical masterpieces during daylight we would survey the outdoor beauty and pavilion below us and when walking, we would check out the large sculptures along paths near the trees. After dark we would stargaze to the music. At that summer opening season there were also other concerts, such as folk, a jazz night and The New York City Ballet. Eventually they added pop and rock concerts as well, and our girls attended some of those too as teenagers.

September had marked a grand achievement—the Marceres moved into their dream home in North Canton! The latter was a kind of victory for all of us who had been striving for fair housing. Our whole family celebrated with friends and family of Percy and Norma at their Open House in October.

That same month Barbara, now ten, was allowed to take a week off from school to fly to Minneapolis with me. The reason was to see her great grandmother Sophia Carolina, who was eighty-four and had suffered a bout of uterine cancer. We couldn't afford to have the whole family go, but I wanted to see her very much because we didn't know how much longer she would live. Also I didn't want to miss seeing her while she was still alive, like I did with my Grandma Ida.

Sophia was in a stable condition, still able to get around and still do some of her housework and cooking, but shockingly thinner than I had ever seen her. And she looked like a little dried fruit. According to her, she was dry and wrinkled from excessive radiation. The day we arrived, she had home baked treats for us—pie, bread and biscuits which she had prepared the day before, even though she had been diagnosed with a weak heart condition. (Fortunately, Alex was looking out for her.) Soon after we arrived, she amazed me again by having organized a luncheon with Aunt Lil, her stepdaughter-in-law, to be held at her and Uncle John's house at Lake Nikomis. We were joined by three more of the older half siblings of Dad's, plus one of the adult daughters.

We spent every night at Grandma and Alex's, in a lovely, single-story house, smaller than their previous one, except one night that we spent at Uncle Carl and Aunt Bernyce's, our Swedish side of the family. The hospitality continued as we visited more cousins on both sides of our family. Sunday we celebrated church with Grandma and Alex at their Finnish Lutheran Church.

It was very good to have taken the trip, and Grandma lived to be 88. Blessed life. She passed away peacefully in her sleep at home. Blessed death. Thanks be to God.

35. MARTIN, MERTON, AND BOBBY

I CANNOT LEAVE 1968 without further mentioning Dr. Martin Luther King, Jr. and Robert Kennedy. Thomas Merton was the third person of a trio that had inspired us greatly, and there were a few connections concerning the three that I share now. Unfortunately all three died that year too young.

When I had my chance to see and hear Dr. King it was in Canton for our City Wide Freedom Rally held at the Fawcett athletic complex on March 20, 1964. The large ecumenical group of local clergy who worked on it helped make his appearance possible. The AFL-CIO supported it, and there also seemed to be citywide support for equality of opportunity. Mayor Stanley Cmich welcomed him, and Hoyt Givens gave the statement of reasons for the occasion as local residents were called upon to face the issue of civil rights. Neither Norma nor I had been a part of the planning, but we went together, and were pleased with the turnout. With us were some of her Negro lady friends. As we walked together toward the stadium in the colorful crowd, I smiled and said,

"This is the first time in my life that I'm in the minority!"

Norma grinned and said, "Don't let it bug you!"

"Absolutely not—I'm enjoying it!"

To hear his eloquent, inspirational preaching *in person* of non-violent resistance with active love that pursues it was just what we needed for continued sustenance.

His rare, tremendously courageous Christian example was primary, but he also impressed John, me, people worldwide and the Scandinavian Nobel Peace Prize Commission with his intelligence, determined actions for justice, grace, gifted oratory, compassionate openness and selfless love to all kinds of people, even to those who hated him. He was justifiably recognized for it on December 10, 1964 when he became a Nobel Peace Prize awardee.

When a hate filled, ignorant racist murdered him April 4, 1968, it was a fulfillment of the happy desires of many other racists in American society who promoted hatred through speech, writings and violent actions. The killing was done from a *hidden* nearby spot with a gun, after the unarmed minister was seen on the Lorraine Hotel porch in Memphis, Tennessee. In Dr. King's own words, "It doesn't take courage to be violent." I don't know if this cowardly man's self-image was that of strength and toughness because he used a gun, but he was in reality stupid if he thought so, because the power was in the weapon, not him. In my view, it diminished his manhood.

It was a horrible force that cut off a good life and caused so much suffering. Many rejoiced at his death; others like us, turned to deep mourning, were stunned and depressed. Carolyn, only five at the time, remembers how I burst into sobbing with John holding me for support. Then there were hundreds of riots in American cities from frustrated rage in black ghettos.

In a mystical way it was a crucifixion of Christ again. Martin died on Thursday of Holy Week before Easter. He seemed to sense the possibility of his demise the night before when he was delivering his *I've Been to the Mountaintop* speech to Memphis recently unionized sanitation workers. He left us the next day at the young age of 39, after a powerful life well lived as he preached against racism, poverty, and war. While he was on the motel porch, some of his last words before he was killed were *Precious Lord*. It was a request to his musician friend Ben to play the black Gospel piece at a concert Martin was planning to attend that night. It had been his favorite song, and Mahalia Jackson sang it soulfully at his funeral, since he had requested her to do it earlier whenever he died.

For a while and also that last night of his life, his commitment to nonviolence was being challenged by some, including some Memphis blacks who were stressing black power—advocating the use of violence because they were fed up with the attacks still being used against them by white racists. He could understand their feelings but he didn't agree with their philosophy and actions. He was still in solidarity with the Memphis workers and striking non-violently, but he just didn't feel like having to go out in the raging thunder and lightning rain storm to talk to them. He was exhausted. However, he was talked into it and went anyway. Consider some of the words in that favorite song with which he could especially be associated with that night:

I am tired, I am weak, I am worn

Through the storm, through the night

Lead me on to the light

Take my hand, Precious Lord, lead me home.

    Thomas Andrew Dorsey 1932

Soon after the shooting, I was speaking to young Sunday school children in Ernest and Janyce Newborn's black Cherry Avenue Christian church about Dr. King, at their request. He was the minister, and I had met Janyce as one of our Protestant black women on our Panel of American Women. At first I was a little stunned, especially since the other minister had been killed by a white person. I was humbly moved and touched that they could be so generous with their (agape) love.

What was I going to say to the children? Live good lives so you can be killed while you are young, like Jesus and Dr. King? It was a tough situation for me. The best I could do was to share how Dr. Martin Luther King Jr. had loved Jesus and people, especially children, and that he was the father of four children. I told them that he and his wife, Mrs. King, had been strong and very brave, living peacefully like Jesus, even as they were threatened by bombs and guns as he courageously worked for fair treatment of all people, especially black people, which would help them, too. I said further that we, with Jesus's help and like Dr. King, must also love all people, be strong and brave for peace and fairness (justice), even if people are mean and hateful to us. I told them that I believed Dr. King was a great and good man that they could be proud of, and that it was important to educate people about his ideas, which should help our country and the world to have less violence. I indicated that I was so pleased that I had seen him speak in Canton. We ended our meeting together with prayers for the children, the Newborns, the King family, all the people in our country, me, and for healing from this sad occasion to become happy again. I shared that I thought Dr. King would be pleased and happy with our being together.

It was no accident that it was after King's death and the rioting in numerous cities that the Fair Housing Act was passed and signed into law April 10th, after having been stalled in Congress since 1966. Also, the Gun Control Act was signed by President Johnson on October 22, 1968, after five years of debate.

* * * *

Robert Kennedy was another rarity. Born into the wealthy Joseph Kennedy Catholic family, he had the privilege of attaining a Harvard University education and law degree at the University of Virginia. Since his father stressed service to others the younger Kennedy had chosen at first to serve in legal battles against corruption in unions and businesses. He worked for a while with Senator Joseph McCarthy of Wisconsin, attempting to prosecute those within the federal government that they believed were Communists. He had helped his brother John win elections to the U.S. Senate and Presidency. They could have been content to protect the privileges of only their class, but decided to expand their scope of influence to be more inclusive.

Having been raised in a rather insular world where the Kennedys hadn't been exposed to the realities of blacks living in dire living conditions, John and Robert's life education about poverty developed as they became politically active. Once John became President and Robert became Attorney

General, they began to make changes. His and President Kennedy's gradual involvement with civil rights came as a matter of justice. Robert knew racism was deep within the national American psyche, but once he found out how bad the common life situations were for blacks in the south, he was appalled at the violence against them for such activities as non-violent resistance against segregation and attempts to vote. At first, he and his brother weren't always in favor of the demonstrations because they thought some progress could be made without them and the accompanying violence that erupted against the demonstrators. But they were propelled into the volatile situation without a choice. They met with black leaders, including Dr. Martin Luther King, Jr. for solutions. As they continued to deal with the volatile movement and the violence against blacks, including the murder of NAACP civil rights leader Medgar Evers in June of 1963, the more they were coming to realize that it was a moral imperative to lead in this area. Compassion was happening. Bobby, as the Attorney General was called by his siblings, sat with Medgar's brother Charles during the funeral and consoled him. After the funeral, President Kennedy took the Evers family to the White House for the rest of the day. When the President was assassinated in November, and the Attorney General was emotionally devastated at the violent loss of his brother, he still looked after his sister-in-law Jackie and the children, Carolyn and John Junior.

Through his love of children, he became involved with fighting poverty after visiting children living with such inhumane conditions as hunger and disease in rat infested housing. Those children were white as well as black, and also included Native Americans and Hispanics.

He also strongly supported the quest for decent living conditions through unionization of farm workers under the leadership of Cesar Chavez. Bobby first visited Chavez in 1966 and kept contact through March 10, 1968. Farm worker union members were asked to commit themselves to non-violence. Kennedy wrote to a constituent after the trip that "His (Chavez') non-violent struggle for the rights of the migrant worker is a great achievement..."

When Dr. King was assassinated in April, it tore Bobby apart emotionally, too, as he ministered to Coretta King, another widow of civil rights murders. He sent a plane to Atlanta to take her to Memphis for retrieval of her husband's body and back to Atlanta for the funeral and burial, which he attended.

After our initial introductions to the Kennedys we developed high hopes for what we thought were their intelligent political leadership and accomplishments toward an improved American Society. There was sophistication, sense of style and beauty, appreciation for science, arts and education, and human rights which we thought was great and exciting for everyone! But then, with John Kennedy's murder, many of our hopes were dashed.

When it came to Viet Nam, and the fact that it was still raging under President Johnson and tearing our country's citizens apart emotionally by the loss of lives and important social programs, we were seeking a president we felt we could trust again. When intellectual professor Eugene McCarthy became a candidate against the war, we were interested in him for a while. Our support for him lasted until Bobby Kennedy entered the anti-war race on March 16. Because of Kennedy's record on civil rights and his personal investigations into the social problems related to poverty, we felt he could lead the country better domestically because he understood those issues better than McCarthy. His experiences in co-leading with President Kennedy in solving the Cuban Missile crises and his own influence against apartheid during his South African visit stood him well with us on international leadership too.

He had become a people person with folks in need, and with those who worked with him. His speeches took strong stands toward non-violence and gave us hope again. We were ready to vote for him. And then it happened—another nightmare in the American psyche for those who cared about him and the violence issue itself. It was another Golgotha. *Another gun death!* What were we to think? It's so easy to shoot people in our country! Why were we killing some of our best leaders? There was more faith in guns than in the inspirational power of non-violence.

* * * *

Merton the Monk was not the usual monk, either, as his future activities were to illustrate. In 1941 Thomas Merton entered Gethsemani Monastery in Kentucky where he found peace for his restless spirit. An order of Cistercians, better known as Trappists, devoted their lives to contemplative prayer and self-sustenance, still at that time, through farming. Vocalization was mostly performed as singing in the chapel and further communication among themselves mostly with sign language. They followed a Benedictine Rule for their daily rituals and routines. Merton was ordained a priest in 1949 and given the name of Father Louis.

Earlier, he was a convert to Catholicism while a student at Columbia University in the 1930's. Among his other subjects he had studied Christian saints as well as Christian and Asian mysticism, which had influenced him in his decision to convert.

I don't know how long my John thought he wanted to be a Catholic priest, but by his senior year in high school (1948-1949) he was strongly interested. I wouldn't be surprised if Father Louis had been an influence on his religious choice. I didn't think to ask him if that was so, but maybe I did and just don't remember it. John had read Merton's spiritual autobiography *Seven Storey Mountain*, which was first published in 1948. All I know was that he told me of his enthusiasm for it early in our relationship.

By the time I met John in 1951 he was a fan of Merton and remained so until the monk's death. Following our 1954 marriage and move to Ohio, our home library began to expand with Merton's writings in the 50's: *Seeds of Contemplation, No Man Is an Island, The Living Bread* (Holy Eucharist)), *Thoughts in Solitude* and *The Secular Journal of Thomas Merton*. In *Thoughts in Solitude, in the second of two sections entitled The Love of Solitude*, Merton wrote:

When I am liberated by silence...my whole life becomes a prayer.

John could relate to contemplative prayer and a way of life in silence better than I. For John, growing up in the Eastern (Byzantine) Catholic Church, there was more of a sense of mysticism in its Liturgy and Eucharist (Communion). Growing up as a Protestant, there wasn't any avenue for me in the churches I attended regularly to experience that same sense since religious retreats and services were less structured and prayer was vocal, directed to God, and toward other people in getting them to accept Jesus as their Savior. Communion was not central to every worship service as it was, and still is, in the Catholic Mass. The central part of the service was usually preaching. In the Biblical story of Jesus' visit with sisters Martha and Mary, I was more the Martha, always busy, helping and providing for others and John took more time out for spiritual quiet attentiveness, as Mary did with Jesus.

While we were living in Ohio, John had wanted to make a spiritual retreat sometime at Gethsemani with Father Louis, especially since it was within easy driving distance just south of our state in Kentucky. However, that opportunity never came.

In 1958, while on an editorial outing to Louisville, Thomas Merton had a spiritual awakening experience as he stood on a street corner (the iconic "4th and Walnut", now "4th and Muhammad Ali"), watching people go by. He suddenly realized that the silent, solitary and secluded life that he was living and writing about at the monastery was not enough for him. He had an overwhelming feeling of compassion for people, realizing that he loved all anywhere and everywhere, not only inside the walls of the monastery, but also outside those walls. Since the religious, social and economic issues of the modern world affected the whole human race, he soon felt the need to be more involved with them in his writings.

Like Merton, John and I loved people, books, nature, music and art. We were spiritually inclined, and connected with the intellectual Merton, as he had written so well in *No Man Is an Island, "...without a life of the spirit, our whole existence becomes unsubstantial and illusory."* Neither of us was pious or "wore our faith on our sleeves", but we held spiritual beliefs and actions that came from deep within, hoping with God's help to live committed, responsible lives. Thomas Merton was able to articulate what we thought were foundational, relevant Christian principles and practices of compassion, love, forgiveness and social justice, which translated into lifestyles of inclusiveness of everyone, including the poor and non-Christians. Love of God and neighbor was primary in his writings and hopeful for our commitments. As he wrote about racism, violence, war, nuclear disarmament and peace as part of Christian spirituality and responsibility, he was an important guide for us.

In the sixties John acquired more of Merton's books, one of which was *The New Man*, which contained meditations on the nature of the soul's identity. Also at that time the monk created a flurry of writings on peace and war, starting with articles in magazines and the *Catholic Worker* (*CW*) newspaper. The first was in October 1961 in the "The Root of War", which I still have. In 1962 he wrote the poem "Original Child Bomb" which was about the atomic bomb dropped on Hiroshima. Articles in other publications followed: "Red or Dead: Anatomy of a Cliché" in *Fellowship;* "Nuclear War and Christian Responsibility" in *Commonweal*, followed by controversy and rewritten in the *CW* as "We Have to Make Ourselves Heard", which I also have; "Christian Action in World Crisis" in Blackfriars. "Christian Ethics and Nuclear War" was published in the March *CW* with a "footnote" about it from Merton in the April issue with further clarification. I have both newspapers. A rewrite of this was published as "Religion and the Bomb" in *Jubilee*. Like Dr. King and Robert Kennedy he came out against the war in Viet Nam, and in the March, 1968 issue of the *CW* wrote "The Vietnam War: An Overwhelming Atrocity".

In spring, 1962 he was pleased that he had a book almost ready to be published by Macmillan with a lot of the ideas he had written in the various published articles. He entitled it *Peace in the Post-Christian Era*. However, he was censored by his French Abbot General Dom Gabriel Sortais, who forbade him to write any more about war and peace, thinking that it was not something a monk dedicated to a life of prayer should be doing.

When we learned of this we believed it was something his abbot should not have done—especially for being against something as Christian as nonviolence and peace, based on the spirituality of Christ. Merton defended his writings to Abbot Dom Gabriel hoping for a change in the decision, but could not get it. However, Merton was able to mail some mimeographed writings from the book out anyway to correspondents of his. This was with the approval of his current monastery abbot, Dom James Fox, who said because it wasn't being published by a commercial publisher for the general public, it was permitted. However, because Father Louis had taken the vow of obedience and did what his Abbot General ordered, the book in full form was not published commercially until 42 years later posthumously, by Orbis Books in 2004. Much of what he wrote then still applies today. In 1963 he was the editor and wrote the Introduction for the book, *Breakthrough to Peace*, which contained views of twelve other rather famous people in addition to his own on the threat of thermonuclear extermination. By 1967 Macmillan published the small book *Seeds of Destruction*, which included issues of war and peace, without censorship. John bought it and I still have it.

According to associate history professor Thomas Spencer of Indiana University, South Bend, the controversial monk didn't know Robert or John Kennedy personally but had become acquainted with Robert's wife Ethel and her mother Ann Skakel through their mutual friend, Professor Dan Walsh. Ethel, a graduate of Manhattanville College near New York City had taken philosophy from the professor there and Merton was introduced to Walsh when he taught some classes at Columbia in the 1930's. It was also Walsh who had originally introduced Merton to Gethsemani Monastery and in 1960 had become head of the philosophy department there. He also helped keep Merton informed of world events.

His huge amount of correspondence included people who were not famous, as well as those who were. Besides Ethel Kennedy, another famous one was Pope John XXIII, with whom he started writing letters in 1958, soon after John's election to the papacy. Father Louis thought that this new pope was positively engaged in pastoring his people, writing seven encyclicals (papal letters) to the groups of bishops and laity within the Catholic Church. Then, his eighth and final one was published shortly before his death in 1963. *Pacem in Terris (Peace on Earth)* was addressed not only to Catholics, but also to other clergies, laities, and all people of good will. It was famously praised by many outside, as well as inside, the Catholic Church, including Merton, who had been censored for writing some of the pope's same concerns about human rights, war and the nuclear arms buildup.

Another with whom he corresponded was Boris Pasternak, the Russian writer/poet/musician. In Merton's book Disputed *Questions* (Ferrar, Strauss and Cudahy), which was one from John's collection, we learned that though both loved music, what excited them the most about each other were their ideas expressed as writers and poets. Having excellent rapport with each other, Merton respected the other highly for his courageous writings in a cultural climate of Soviet leadership that opposed Pasternak's ideas because they didn't endorse Communism. (According to Merton, they also did not promote the Western world's materialism.) It was especially true with the Russian's epic novel, *Doctor Zhivago*. He tried to get it published in his own country with the magazine *Novy Mir* but when the editors denied it, he smuggled the manuscript to Milan, Italy where it was accepted by the publisher *Feltrinelli*. Merton could also identify with that because of his own defiance of censorship.

The two poets wrote to each other for approximately two years, soon after Zhivago was published in English and Merton had read it. There were two letters exchanged before the awarding of Pasternak's Nobel Prize. On September 27, 1958, which was identified by the Russian as Holy Cross Day, he wrote to the monk:

Dear and reverend friend

Thank you from all my heart for your warm congenial letter. It also (like my writings to you) seems to me wonderfully filled with kindred thoughts as having been written half by myself...

I thank you from the bottom of my soul for your prayers and wish you health and forces enough for your good life and deeds.

I don't sign the letter for the better sureness of its reaching you.

Peredelkino near Moscow (his residence at the writers' colony)

The culmination of outrageous rejection by the Soviet political leaders and some fellow writers against author Pasternak became internationally known upon the publication of *Dr. Zhivago* and the awarding of the Nobel Prize.

After Pasternak's death from heart disease and lung cancer in May 1960, Merton learned that near the time of his death, Pasternak requested and received the last Rights of the Orthodox Church from an Orthodox priest.

Pasternak, an artist, whose parents were visual and musical artists (like Merton) was apolitical, but spiritual in his writings. Merton, as well as many others, considered him to be one of the greatest writers of the twentieth century.

My John's favorite book of fiction was *Dr. Zhivago*. Today his paperback 1958 publication has lightly browned pages that are constantly falling out as anyone reads the still legible words! His Merton "Disputed Questions" is still on my bookshelf. In 1965, the film *Dr. Zhivago* was released in the States. It was a collaboration of Metro-Goldwyn-Mayer Films, Producer Carlo Ponti, and David Lean, Director, who had also directed other epic films. The love story of Yuri and Lara was the main focus. John and I both enjoyed seeing it together once, and then he continued to see it some more, without me—I don't know how many times!

There could have been several reasons for his love of both the book and film. First, as a child with his father, he had spent years participating in the Byzantine Catholic Liturgy, which was identical to the Russian and Greek Orthodox Divine Liturgy with Romanian variations of choral music. All was in the Romanian language. Second, in his undergraduate work at the university, he pursued a comprehensive social studies curriculum which included not only American histories, governments and geographies, but also similar courses on Europe, which included Russia. With his secondary school teaching he thought it was imperative that his students be informed of issues in democracy, government roles, freedom, human rights/responsibilities and totalitarianisms. Third, there was Yuri, the story's noncombatant both in physicality and will who helped heal the wounded, and with whom John could agree. And then there was Lara and the hauntingly beautiful music, especially *Lara's Theme*. Of course, all three main characters in the movie, Yuri, Tonia, his wife, and Lara, his extra-marital lover, are good looking. Lara, played by the gorgeous Julie Christie, in my observation, could be seductive even with just her eyes when lights were shining on them—in tears as well as dry!

* * * *

Early in 1968 a spiritual retreat was being arranged for Dr. King after he had tentatively agreed to go to Gethsemani Monastery and meet Thomas Merton, according to retired Professor of Religion William Apel at Linfield College in Oregon. Unfortunately, Martin was assassinated that spring, shortly before that meeting. June Yungblut, a doctoral student at Emory University in Atlanta was a friend of Coretta Scott King and correspondent with Merton. After the student and monk learned of the murder, both were horrified and renewed their commitments to justice and peace. She was with Coretta shortly after it happened and wrote to Merton of her great admiration for Coretta's great courage in the face of such overwhelming grief. When she was with Mrs. King and the children, the two young King sons, Martin and Dexter, said they would not hate anybody since they had been taught this at home and church. Thomas Merton did the only thing he could do at the time. He sent a note of faith, courage, hope, and love to the outstanding Christian family who, in the midst of sorrow, were united in love, even of enemy—an *agape* love and an inspiration to others.

Professor and Merton scholar Cristobal Serran-Pagan y Fuentes has pointed out that both King and Merton agreed and practiced *agape*, a Christ-like love that can transform people to actions of redemption, reconciliation and renewal in society.

That unconditional *agape* love, in King's own words, "is not a weak, passive, love. It is love in action...Non-violence is a powerful and just weapon. It is a weapon unique in history, which cuts without wounding and ennobles the man who wields it. It is a sword that heals."

Merton agreed with King, and both believed love of enemies was part of this non-violent way of life. In Serran-Pagan's words, "Neither one claimed originality. They were simply trying to recover the old prophets' message in the religion of Jesus. Both King and Merton followed Jesus' commandment of loving God and loving neighbor as well as enemies."

Both died in the same year, King in April, and Merton on December 10, the date he entered Gethsemani in 1941, and the fourth anniversary of King's reception of the Nobel Peace Prize. Both died violently but Merton didn't die from an assassin's bullet, he died from electric shock from a malfunctioning fan in Bangkok, Thailand while attending a monastic conference of Christians and Buddhists.

It's noteworthy that as time passes, more people around the world are learning about these twentieth century American spiritual giants whose writings and films about them are still causing positive changes in individuals and organizations. Primary sources for learning more are the Martin Luther King Center in Atlanta, Georgia, and The Thomas Merton Center at Bellarmine University in Louisville, Kentucky.

36. EXPECTATIONS

JANUARY, 1969 AND TIME for our Christmas gift notes of appreciation:

Whether
    summer outdoors or
    winter indoors
    our sleeping bags will be greatly used...
    regardless the
Weather...

Many thanks and love
John and Dolores

(We required our daughters to write their own notes of appreciation.)

Economically, we were still living an almost hand to mouth existence, but we were excited about the hopeful prospects of the new year. The girls were still going to get music, movement and art in addition to Girl Scouts and swimming outside of their regular elementary education. The highest point for John and me would be the attainment in August of his master's degree in education, Master Teacher Program. The excellence of all that made me so proud of him, and satisfied him, that he would be an even better equipped teacher.

The girls were excelling in school, and they were all there now *full-time!* With the extra time for me and the increase in John's salary, we both felt that I could now consider taking university courses toward my elementary education degree. I also had a keen interest in Maria Montessori, the Italian medical doctor. I read some of her books and respected her research on child development as she worked with young children, both normal and mentally challenged ones.

We hoped I might get part-time work at a Montessori school, so in January I observed a Montessori preschool class all morning and was very pleased. Afterwards, at their invitation, I had lunch with the director and her assistant—a bonus for me as I was able to ask questions about what I observed in their classroom. By spring I was offered a paid assistantship there starting in the fall. It was just the kind of work I would love, so I enthusiastically accepted!

* * * *

I was still going out with the Panel occasionally, and on the morning of April 22 Barbara, Norma, Blanche, Nora and I were the featured speakers as part of a special day for the Akron, Ohio Hadassah Jewish Women's organization. The title for it was Haskalah Day—Day of Enlightenment.

Our Canton Panel of American Women had grown annually in numbers and this particular engagement was its eighty-ninth in its three and a half year existence. Not only had we increased our numbers, but each of us had also grown in respect and insights as we heard other panelists' talks for the first time. These personal stories of experiences with various forms of prejudice and the discussions that followed were riveting to members of the audience as well.

After our Akron engagement Nora and I were looking forward to April 29 when her husband Rick was to be ordained into the deaconate of the Episcopalian Church. This was a change in his faith journey as he had been a minister in the United Church of Christ denomination.

The special Divine Service at St. Paul's in Canton that Tuesday was beautiful with special music for the Litany for Ordination. It was celebrated by three priests, including the Episcopal Bishop of Ohio and the rector of St. Paul's—Reverend B. Whitman Dennison.

Reverend Dennison's wife Mary, one of the Panel of American Women panelists, sat with Lisa and me. It was such a celebratory day, complete with a reception afterwards. None of us were prepared for the emotional plunge that we all experienced in the traumatic tragedy soon to happen.

37. BOARDS AND PILLS

SINCE I HAD ACCEPTED the job at the Montessori School for fall, I had visited a vein specialist in the spring because I knew I would be on my feet a lot. I had noticed a protruding vein near the front of my left ankle and wondered if it could ulcerate, as was the case on one of my father's legs. He recommended surgery and I naively accepted the proposition, thinking it would not be much of a job, and would put me in good shape before I started working.

The family went into quick planning mode so I could enter Aultman Hospital on May 4. Mom Tate was out of the hospital, and Dad would be caring for her. I got all the washing and ironing caught up before I went so the family would have enough clothes to last until I got back home. The only exceptions were play clothes and underwear which would be good enough from the dryer. I learned that I would have a phone in my semi-private room so I could keep touch.

I believed John and the girls would manage beautifully. The girls were already used to making their own beds, washing and drying the dishes, and helping with school lunches. Barbara was to babysit her sisters for an hour after school every day until their father would return from teaching, which was just across the street. Homework would be done via phone with me or with John when he wasn't attending his grad school course two nights per week. Saturday the 10th John would be taking a field trip with his university geology class, so Mary Jean agreed to watch them during that time.

When John took me to the hospital the girls attended a Canton Civic Ballet performance with a family friend and enjoyed it very much. Or, to put it into Barbara's terminology, she said it was really "tough"!

I had the top Aultman vascular surgeon, so I trusted his judgment on what had to be done. It was to be more than I requested, and on both legs. My third pregnancy had caused more varicosities. Since the first surgery in 1960 had been so easy, relatively quick, and had me walking the next day with only one large bandage on each thigh, I expected this procedure to be about the same. But I was wrong. I had not been told the details ahead of time and I trusted my doctor's judgment.

The first surgery was performed on my right leg May 7. The procedure involved stripping (removal) and ligation (tying) again as in the '60 surgery, with the difference having been to make many more incisions in segments because of the prior one. It was more work and it was longer—about 1-1/2 hours. According to the doctor's report, I tolerated the operation well, and there were no complications. I awoke from the anesthetic on my back with a full length wooden board on both sides of my leg, so as to hold it in place and keep me from lying on my side. The only problem was that I couldn't sleep that way. It was the first time I had to use sleeping pills.

The more difficult surgery on the left leg took place on May 13. The procedure remained the same, with stripping and ligation, only this time it took three hours and 20 incisions to accomplish what he wanted. Many of the incisions on both legs were small, but there were a few that were 2 and 3 inches long. I did well with the surgery again—there were no complications. All the veins operated on in '60 and '69 were superficial—no main arteries, and I was told by the doctor that I had good circulation otherwise. In my room bed though—it was still boards and pills for sleep and pain.

My spirit was boosted by beautiful flowers and many cards and notes, including my sister-in-law Byrle's beautiful handmade card, and darling ones from her daughters Dawn and Lisa.

The boards were taken off for inch by inch measurements of my legs from below the ankles and up as far as my waist to customize the size and correct pressure of a heavy Jobst leotard. The incisions healed well, the boards were removed, and the stitches were taken out from the right leg before I left the hospital on May 18. Four days after I was discharged, the stitches were removed from the left leg in the doctor's office. I had noticed the same small, protruding vein that caused me to see him in the first place, so I pointed it out to him and asked about it at that time.

"Dolores," he said, "I couldn't do any more. After those three hours, I was exhausted!"

The stitch removals were slightly painful, but the worst of all was when I had to stand on my feet the first times after the surgeries and the blood rushed down into the newly agitated areas and the nerve endings reacted like multiple tiny knives on the 32 incisions. I couldn't hold back the brief yelling! The pain gradually subsided as I started walking around. Before I left he said, "By the way, you'll have to wear a Jobst leotard whenever you're on your feet much for the rest of your life!" (I said to myself, "How depressing—I'll feel handicapped the rest of my life!") What I couldn't do for years afterwards was play the piano because sitting on the bench would cut the circulation in my legs.

When I came home from the hospital, it was to a very appreciative family and a cleaner house than I had expected. As a surprise for me, Nora came over on the Friday before I came home and scrubbed the kitchen floor, dusted the house, washed a load of clothes, and baked us a chocolate cake! What a great friend—I called and told her so. Now I could slowly get back to taking care of the family. In the beginning, I could be up some, but to avoid swelling, I was off my feet more than I was on. Soon I was wearing my thick, tight, miserably uncomfortable leotard when I was up and was able to start driving. Eventually I was able to shed my leotard as I took enough d-alpha tocopherol vitamin E to make my legs feel normal again, without pain, and it was wonderful.

Poor John and my in-laws—as soon as I got home, Mom Tate went back into the hospital with a blockage near her heart. Because she was in the intensive care unit, John was there daily for the brief times he was allowed. Fortunately for him that spring he was a teacher supervisor for a Kent State education major doing her student teaching. It was she who had to prepare and teach most of his classes, so that possibly kept him from a breakdown of his health as he coped with his graduate studies and all that was going on with his family.

38. HEARTACHE TURNED TO JOY

SUMMERTIME ACTIVITIES WERE GOING well, with Barbara and Patti at different times enjoying scout camp, even though the skunk visitors into their tents caused some anxieties to flare until they were able to get them out! Letters were exchanged between them, us and their grandparents in Las Vegas.

It was a great time for reading, too, since we were making trips to the library to get books I had chosen from the huge New York Times children's books' list. Carolyn, having just completed first grade, was off to a great start that began in her class. She was reading well orally, and understanding what she read, whether orally or silently. She and another girl tied for first place for reading the most school library books in their class. Her printing had not been the best, however, and her teacher thought it was sloppy because she was more interested in cursive writing. Months before, she had copied her sisters' names and her own whenever she saw them at home. So, she eventually became our cursive name writer for their school lunch bags. She was so proud of her accomplishments and pleased that I thought they were good enough to put on the bags. My mom, the stamp collector, often sent the girls first day covers for their stamp collections, which they enjoyed seeing at home and using them also for scout badges.

John was attending summer school taking the last classes he needed before graduation and working for the last time at Diamond-Portland Cement. He was lucky to be doing some drafting and surveying for the engineering department when he wasn't working as a laborer, which was so tedious and boring for him.

I attended an intense workshop in July, 1969 for members of our Panel of American Women. It was important for us, because it was led by Esther Brown, the founder, who was dying from cancer, and yet was helping us to improve. The organization had mushroomed to 61 panels. Our local newspaper, the Canton Repository printed an article about her while she was in town. She was called the "Pied Piper of Non-Prejudice", citing the many ways she had influenced peoples' lives by inspiring the many personal stories of discrimination given by panelists of various creeds, races, and religions.

Things were good at home, except when I realized something was missing.

"John, I need to talk to you about something important."

"Okay, what is it?"

"I haven't had a period since before my surgery."

"What? You mean you might be pregnant?"

"Maybe."

"Man, that's all we need at this time! Have you made a doctor appointment?"

"No, I wanted to talk to you about this first."

"Well, do it!"

"Of course!"

I went to Dr. D, an obstetrician, and he confirmed that, indeed, I was pregnant!

I was not only stunned when he told me, I was speechless with frustration. I thanked him and told him I would be in touch after I told my husband. Before I arrived home, I stopped in the city park near our place as I burst into tears over the mixed emotions of worry and disappointment. I was disappointed two ways—sorry I would not fulfill my career ambitions again, and sorry that I couldn't feel joyful over bringing another child into the world. Since the pregnancy was so near in time to the stressful surgeries, I worried about being healthy enough to bear a healthy child and wondered what effect it would have on my legs. I also worried about finances. I prayed for help and drove home.

"By the look on your face, I bet you're probably pregnant!"

"I am—are you angry at me?"

"How can I be? Upset, yes, but we're both responsible for this, so you could be angry at me too."

"That's true, but I'm not. The timing, though, on this is awful. I've been crying over it. Abortion? It's not even a consideration. It's not the child's fault—so how could I destroy that innocent life?"

"I agree with you!"

"Because of our love and joy this new life is coming into being and deserves to be greeted with the same. But right now I'm having a struggle with the joy part!"

"Me, too."

"I'm going to have to give up that job opportunity and postpone my university classes—again! I'll have to drop all my church and community commitments, even the Panel! I can't handle them during this pregnancy—I'm just not up to it! The doctor said I would have to be off my legs and in bed a lot to save my legs."

"We'll just hope and pray for the best as you take good care of yourself as you have with the other pregnancies. By the way, what happened with the birth control? It was working so well."

"You know, I probably should have thought about that more. Now that I have been thinking about what went wrong, I remember what happened to my milk supply for Patti immediately after the first leg surgeries. The stress dried it up, remember? The only possible theory I have now is that the stress of the surgeries this time, which was even more severe, caused the timing of my periods, which had been consistent, to change."

"We'll make the best of the result now, and look forward happily to welcoming our baby with joy, as we have with the others and those others will be delighted to know of the good news!"

"I love you so much, thank you!"

"I love you, Dolores, and together with God's help we'll get through this new adventure."

There was such strength in his graciousness. My Rock had turned my anxiety to peace and my heartache to joy.

39. SUBTLE CELEBRATIONS

THIS TIME JOHN WENT to his graduation, taking four eager girls (daughters plus wife) with him. I told our three children that this was an important event for our family, especially their father — that this was a high accomplishment for their father after spending years studying for it. This was why he was gone attending a lot of classes at night while he taught students during the days, I explained.

John was the first in his immediate family to attain a master's degree, the first to graduate with a bachelor degree — even the first to graduate from high school. Near the end of his graduate studies, his academic advisor, Dr. D., thought John would be a good candidate for a doctorate degree. He respected Dr. D. highly and he appreciated the advice, but politely refused. "Thank you, but it won't mean much more money, and I have to concentrate on spending more time and resources on my growing brood at home."

He was handsome for graduation day in his academic regalia with the light blue and yellow parts of his hood starting from his chest and cascading down his back, representing his master's degree in education. They contrasted nicely with his black robe and cap, as observed by us four at home before the day of the ceremony, humorously giving him our stamp of approval.

August 30 was a hot, muggy day in the 90's and the ceremonies were at the Kent State stadium. The program was of interest to John and me, but not for our grade school girls. It was understandably long and boring for them. They were uncomfortable but endured quietly. After the affair we commended them for it and rewarded them with lunch, complete with ice cream in a lovely air-conditioned restaurant!

When we left after the morning ceremony, I was emotionally happy but physically, I was absolutely miserable. The heat, humidity and hard, wooden bleachers had caused my legs and ankles to swell in that miserably hot, constricting leotard. It was awful to be on my feet in that condition. Fortunately, I was so relieved that we had decided before the graduation to go to the restaurant to eat. I was in no condition to cook and unfortunately, before the graduation I decided I could not have a party for John, nixing any celebration with others. I felt badly because of it.

After we arrived home, we all had a wonderful sense of relief, relaxation and appreciation of John's accomplishment. Because Mom was recuperating from her heart attack, she and Dad could not celebrate the day with us either, so though our celebration was very small, it was happy and better than only having the degree mailed, as it had been with his first graduation.

* * * *

Excitement was high as we made plans for Barbara's entry into Canton Country Day School (CCDS), a private school, grades 1-8 recently relocated near Avondale, less than a mile from our home, so during nice weather, she would be able to ride her bike.

This happened because I had gone there in the spring to apply for an office job before I was hired for the Montessori School. While there, I learned that teachers' children were eligible for scholarships because of their financial need. I spoke to the headmaster, Al Getman, with whom I had worked on fair housing, of our concerns and he told me that their students represented a cultural variety (more than St. Michael's): religiously, racially, and economically, since some of whom were also on scholarship. His own children attended there and he also didn't want them to associate only with the country club set. John and I observed classes before we decided to let Barbara take the exams for eligibility, and we found definite advantages.

Barbara passed and was accepted for sixth grade! At St. Michael's, she had already been in good math, science, social studies, English and reading programs, and those would continue at CCDS, but she would lose faith formation classes. We thought the family involvement on faith would suffice. During the summer we had to buy her a long list of required books to read, which she began reading before school started. She would also be taking French, gym every day (more often than she had been getting), and choir.

Her fifth grade teacher, Sister Mary Lucinda, said she was artistic and would benefit more from specialized art instruction. Barbara had taken classes at the Canton Art Institute prior to fifth grade and now she had the opportunity to study with Judi Hertzi, who was the art teacher at CCDS. Judi was an excellent teacher (I had seen her interact with children) and she had two of her own. As mentioned before, she had Patti and Carolyn in her preschool classes with Blossom, and was an active artist who sold her beautiful paintings. She was also the wife of Joe Hertzi, artist and Director of the Canton Art Institute. At CCDS there would be a great variety of art projects in the special art room, which also had a kiln for firing pottery.

Barbara was more interested in art and better at that than in music, so we allowed her to quit her piano lessons, which she had wanted to do for a while. The money spent on music lessons and St. Michael's was transferred to our share of costs at CCDS. The school was extremely expensive, so we told her how fortunate she was that she was receiving most of her payments from the school in terms of scholarships and anonymous donations. We told her she needed an attitude of gratitude and had a responsibility to do the very best she could while there. We hoped it would sink in, as she was excited to go.

She had already become so ambitious that summer! She loved to bake and cook, so she made some chocolate cakes, and worked two hours one day scrubbing and polishing the car to earn money for my birthday present (her own idea.) She combined that with some change from her sisters, and then John took them to a florist shop where they bought a beautiful bouquet. What a proud and wonderful experience it was for us all!

40. NOVEMBER NEGATIVES

NORA GAVE US A high chair and bathinette which she didn't need anymore. They were more than welcome since we had given all our baby items away years before...

Sunday, November 16, 1969: I received a call from a friend. Nora was gone! Not only was she gone, but so were her three children: Becky, 11, Joey 10, and Josh four. Yes, they were on a trip, but this was much more than that. They were in Pennsylvania going to a wedding, but they didn't arrive. There was a nightmarish nighttime car accident on Friday during which they all suffered sudden deaths on a highway, ten miles short of their goal.

The loss to all who had appreciated them in life was staggering. My brain wanted to brush away any more thoughts about their deaths, but more had to be known. The small Toyota, which Lisa had been driving, crossed the divider lines and without slowing, slammed into, and rolled under, a huge tractor trailer truck, crushing the car and all within. The truck driver tried to avoid the car, but because it happened so suddenly, couldn't do so.

The autopsy performed on Nora proved she had not been drinking alcohol, and had no drugs in her system. She had fallen asleep.

Anyone driving late at night can be susceptible to falling asleep. But there were significant stress factors involving her. We knew she had been too emotionally drained and physically exhausted since August when Rick had asked her for a divorce and had abandoned the family.

He had stopped supporting them financially for a couple of months when we found out about her dilemma. She didn't share with us why. By then, she as a nurse during weekdays had taken another job on weekends at a nursing home, just to survive. Then she started having periods that were more severe from increased blood flow. Since the children were suffering emotionally with their loss, she had to help them with that. Because of our own circumstances, the only things we could do at that time were help with groceries, emotional support and a birthday gift for Becky.

John and I had known Rick and Nora only three years, but in that time had enjoyed their friendship as we shared a number of common interests, such as music, art, nature, spirituality, education, and the Panel. Our children had played together and I had taken Becky and Barbara together to their piano lessons. Nora had been such a good person and friend in so many ways. I miss her a lot.

I and other members of our Panel attended a memorial service at St. Paul's Episcopal and contributed to the United Nations International Children's Emergency Fund (UNICEF) in her memory, for she, like I, was on the local committee. I decided then that I would also like donations to UNICEF in my behalf when I die.

* * * *

Two days before Thanksgiving John was on a first time, two day teacher's strike. There was a long list of grievances. For one, the Plain Township school board and superintendent at that time were anti-teacher and probably anti-union as well. The teachers were never considered in any educational decisions and didn't have respect. They were back in the classrooms while negotiations continued. The financial loss was hard on us, but we thought the sacrifice was a necessary negative, considering the circumstances. Eventually there were some improvements, affecting teachers, students, and quality of education.

That year Canton City Schools didn't even open until November for a second time because voters rejected a school levy. According to John, the state hadn't done enough of its share, either.

41. PEACEFULNESS

THANKSGIVING AND ADVENT GAVE us sweet respite. Our family started with Carolyn's First Communion and proceeded to celebrate afterward at Mary Jean and John's with Tom, Steve, Randy, Dad Tate and Mom with the traditional turkey dinner. Soon after Thanksgiving the girls and I took turns lighting the candles on the Advent wreath at home in preparation for the coming of The Child of Bethlehem. At least the girls were civilized about it. We had to put it away the previous year because they fought over who would light and who would blow, causing family warfare! This time they were even attentive to the readings.

We were looking forward to our own baby too.

John went to our teachers' credit union and took out a loan. That was an unusual act for us, but we felt justified because it was for such good reasons. Two years prior we had bought a reel to reel tape recorder; now he was able to buy speakers, plus an LP phonograph and radio receiver. We were delighted! We started recording the children, and since I was home most of the time I found the radio and phonograph music soothing for my soul.

The older girls were quite independent with their Christmas cards for their grandparents out west. They told us about them after they had already made them. In fact, Patti even sealed the envelope before we could see hers! Barbara's was unpolished, but full of love. Carolyn sent her own little poem at the top of her picture.

We always decorated a Christmas tree, and that year we added some new decorations. They were white paper ornaments which John and the girls made of their own cutout designs, stapled together to give added dimensions, and then hung on various lengths of strings from the ceiling. They looked beautiful against our aqua dining area walls.

John took the girls to a holiday production of the *Nutcracker* by the Canton Youth Symphony and Canton Civic Ballet. He also took them to his cousin Bob's wedding with a small reception there and then picked me up so we could all go to more celebrating with Romanian foods at Bob's parents' home. Climaxing all that was attending Christmas Eve Mass and then to John and Mary Jean's for Christmas Day. Family life was good in many ways.

42. CHRISTINA

THERE WASN'T A LOT I could do out of bed in January, 1970. Standing to do some cooking and using the bathroom were major endeavors for me, even though neither the kitchen nor bathroom was far from our bedroom. It was excruciatingly painful to go bare legged (which I had tried), so had to wear that custom thick, heavily elastic maternity Jobst leotard for the support and less pain every time I was up. I was fortunate to have it, but the process of getting it on was such a struggle that it left me briefly breathless every time at the finish. No one else could help me, due to the physical awkwardness of the situation. I had to lie on my back, and after the toeless feet were on, had to pull each leg on quickly to avoid tourniquets if stopped before the leotard legs were fully extended on my legs. Only then could I pull it over my big belly which was in the way! It is a humorous scene to visualize now, but then it was no laughing matter.

On the bed *sans* the leotard there usually was enough comfort to accomplish some of my tasks, such as folding the laundry that John would wash, and oversee the girls' homework. By then John was also doing the grocery shopping again as well as supervising all the household chores. Patti, Carolyn, and Barbara helped as much as they could with dishes, meals, and other small household tasks, which included feeding Whiskers. They all had so much patience; I wished I didn't have to give them so much to do.

Since I interrupted work and college again, my frustrated spirit wondered if I would *ever reach those goals*. I took naps, read, prayed, did a lot of soul searching and had *no* exercise. After being used to so many meaningful activities with friends in the community, I was lonely a lot while in bed when the family members were at their schools. The only visits from friends were Panel members Doris and Blanche. But at least Doris would bring her guitar and the two of us sang with joy and humor, and Blanche brought a delicious casserole that she had made: comfort food. When we didn't know what to do about a crib for Christina, John's Aunt Leona came over with a lovely used one.

I liked my obstetrician Dr. D. and at my exams he boosted my morale. My mother Peggy was good at that too:

Dear Dolores, John, Barbara, Patricia, Carolyn and Wee One on the way:

Salutations are getting longer these days! This last event does affect others besides your immediate family, as you know. We are concerned for your welfare. We hope everything will go just fine and you will give us another beautiful and wonderful grandchild as all the others are.

Love, Mom and Dad

125

On the last day that Doris came over with her guitar during my pregnancy I don't remember what songs we sang, but we had so much relaxing fun singing in unison and harmonies. By the time she left, I was in a state of joyful peacefulness, not unlike a meditative state of mind. Then, I experienced a clear awareness, a discovery of a change for my teaching vocation: rather than stay with my plan for becoming an elementary school teacher, I should teach in the arts, for there were fewer of us who could do that than those who could teach the other subjects in the classrooms. It was my own epiphany, and it made a lasting and deep impression upon me. It was also a curious and somewhat puzzling challenge, for I had no idea how that would happen, given the life circumstances I was in at that time and my limited arts education so far. All I could do was hope and pray that since this experience was so illuminating for me, the value and truth of it might be demonstrated someday when I would become an arts educator.

My February due date for childbirth came and went. "Here I go again—I wonder if I'm going to be two weeks later than the estimated due date like it was with all three of my prior childbirths. Right now I feel as though I'm going to be permanently pregnant!" I so wanted to have it happen *soon*, but I also wanted it to be the right time for the child. It would be a joy to have a boy, but thought it would be easier in many ways to raise another girl.

Less than a week later, I was so thankful when my labor started at home on the evening of February 25. By the time the doctor said to go to the hospital, we had to leave quickly with neighbors assisting with care for the girls until John could make it back home. It was dark and heavy snow was falling furiously. Driving there was intense as well as wonder-filled as John and I watched out the clogged windows the largest, most beautiful dime-sized clumps of snowflakes that we had ever seen. At the same time we were hoping that we would continue to navigate the roads, not stop, and get to the hospital so Baby Boo would not be born in our "snow sculpture" on wheels! For both of us it was unthinkable for John to deliver our baby under such circumstances, and in 1970 the idea that we could call for help, from the car, of course never crossed our minds.

Thankfully, we greatly relieved, snow-covered travelers arrived at the maternity ward of Timken Mercy Hospital safely. As the labor pains intensified, I felt, for the first time, like all my organs were going to burst! Mercifully, after I received the saddle block for the brief delivery it was easier. My legs were wrapped in elastic bandages and I was hooked up to an intravenous anti-coagulant as soon as I was put on the delivery table. Thankfully, everything went well, meaning I had a normal childbirth, and saw, from the moment she appeared, that we had another beautiful, healthy daughter at 12:59 AM February 26, a special birthday gift for my father since his birthday was on the 28th. Again John was not allowed to be present for the big event, which was a disappointment. After he learned about it and we were allowed to be together again, we decided to name our newborn, Christina Dolores. After he saw our latest masterwork, he left to be back with the rest of our brood and I contemplated that she would be our last great creation, since my body would not be able to bear another child.

I was a few days longer at the hospital again and frustrated because of a mild case of phlebitis in my leg, even though I had taken natural vitamin E to prevent it during my pregnancy and I was on intravenous anti-coagulant during the delivery. After I left the hospital I learned that the prenatal inorganic iron I was taking during pregnancy negated the effects of the vitamin E. If I took the iron, I was supposed to take it at a different time than the E, with 8 or 9 hours between the two, and I didn't know that. (Natural iron from foods doesn't affect the E.)

When John picked up Christina and me from the hospital a week later, we also picked up Barbara from CCDS, who was waiting by the curb with several of her girlfriends who were also excited to greet the tiny creature in the car!

The girls were crazy about Christina. Carolyn was seven at the time, and in remembering the welcome at home later said, "I never had any jealousy of Christina, at all! Guess that jealousy just isn't in my nature, even as a little kid. I adored her! I considered her like my sweet little baby. Still do in some ways. I was glad not to be the youngest anymore, didn't want to be the baby of the family. I figured I wouldn't be teased so much anymore!"

We were overwhelmed by the many kindnesses shown before and after Christina's birth, even by people we hardly knew. Everyone was in a celebratory mood. Taft teachers and students were part of that. While I was still in the hospital, one of the teachers, Mrs. Born, sent me a beautiful plant and had John and our girls over for dinner one evening. John even had a baby shower given by the students in one of his classes! Three other teachers provided us with dinner the day Baby and I came home from the hospital. A neighbor and a former neighbor—one with ten, and the other with eight children—provided meals. All those food preparations were such a help, since I wasn't up to cooking for a little while.

My parents sent greetings and money. When my sister-in-law Mary Jean and brother-in-law John came to the house, they brought a chocolate cake, made by super baker Mary Jean. John's parents came too and we all recognized the fact that with our four, we were specialists in girls, which John called his "Little Women", and John and Mary Jean were specialists in boys, having had three.

Little by little, John was being relieved of the many house and child care chores he had assumed for almost a year, without complaining. Out of gratefulness, I couldn't praise him enough for it.

Christina was baptized soon like the other girls and we had a similar small celebration with family and godparents. She was nursing well, so content, and a joy to have around. Though I was tired off and on, I was feeling so much better than during my pregnancy, and was told by the doctor that I could go back to my regular work routine gradually. I volunteered as assistant Brownie leader of Carolyn's troop at St. Michael's and took Christina with us. I helped them create animal puppets and puppet shows with a large cutout cardboard box for the theater stage. It was so much fun and it looked like even Christina enjoyed it!

Since Carolyn enjoyed the puppet shows so much we enrolled her in children's theater courses through the Canton Players Guild. Her teacher whose name I can't recall was a lady member of the Guild and worked well with the children. *Family life was good again.*

43. KENT STATE AND PANEL LOSSES

WHILE WE WERE BUSY enjoying life and especially the new life in our midst, we were shocked by the killings in Kent. It was the loss of more innocent people— four unarmed students at Kent State on May 4, 1970 by the Ohio National Guard called out by Governor James Rhodes. Besides the deaths there were serious injuries to other students from the shots. There had been protests over expanding the war in Viet Nam into Cambodia. Rhodes was responding to a heightened atmosphere of fear after an ROTC building had been burned on Saturday and there were mob reactions, trying to keep firemen and police from extinguishing the fire. On Monday, some students were onlookers, others were protesters, and some of those were hurling rocks. We could understand the tensions and fears. There had been tear gas, but why bullets? While I hadn't been, John had been paying attention to the protests which had started in 1969 with a bannered march down the street in Kent shortly after he had received his master's degree at KSU. Suddenly we were both attentive to all that was taking place.

* * * *

Amidst the turmoil, outrage and sorrow reported in the press about Kent, we received the news that Esther Brown, founder of the Panel of American Women, succumbed to her cancer before the end of May. This beautiful woman, spiritually as well as physically, had died with courage, consistent with the way she had lived. Her compassion for people was boundless as she volunteered her time to work against the barriers that kept them apart from one another: racism, poverty, and religious bigotry. Even cancer didn't keep her from working from her hospital bed!

The loss of Esther was felt deeply by the panelists and many others around our country. The eulogies given by men and women who knew her within her own Jewish faith and who served on the national Panel board reflected beautifully how she had lived for others, and also how she believed people could change for the better. She was another beacon of light for me.

The five years I worked on the Panel of American Women had been so gratifying and educational for me. In addition to the audiences, we panelists also benefited from each panelist's personal stories. Some of the points that I emphasized in my own presentations were:

Prejudicial attitudes of stereotyping based on ignorance leads to serious barriers between people religiously, racially, and politically.

The need for dialogue between Catholics and Protestants was great.

Be prepared to be called Communists when working for social justice, even when you're not.

By giving our children positive human relations experiences, hopefully they will accomplish even more than previous generations.

Love is social and active, or it ceases to be love.

44. ELGIN AND GUILFORD

WORKING IN THE BUILDING and decorating trades usually involves times when there are no jobs. That's why Mom worked also through many years of their marriage in Minnesota, California, Nevada and Arizona. When living in California, Dad was rarely unemployed. After moving to a Las Vegas apartment in 1968 as a transition to an eventual move to Arizona, he had painting jobs there steadily early in the year. By May, he started working about 65 miles from Las Vegas at the Nevada Test Site (NTS) near Mercury, Nevada, where the pay was considered very good; he remained there until November 1969. As 1970 began, he was working in Las Vegas and Henderson until March, when he went back to the NTS. Soon he found himself out of work there and in Las Vegas due to strikes, so he found employment in Boulder City, 25 miles from Las Vegas. However, that meant driving 150 miles a day because they had just bought their Arizona desert home in July. He was wearing himself out with that plus working at his own house on weekends. By the time the strike was over in Las Vegas, he was getting up at 2:30 AM to be at work there by 6 and worrying Mom excessively because he was driving 200 miles a day. By the end of September the strike had ended at the test site too, so he started working there again. Like many of the workers, he stayed there week nights and went home on weekends. It was helpful to have medical care there, for he soon had the flu and bronchial asthma.

The reason their housing dream for living on their land opposite picturesque little "Steamboat Mountain" had been changed was because they couldn't afford the costly drilling for the well. It had been such a disappointment! What they did then instead was to buy a partially built two bedroom home on Elgin Road that dad finished building and then painted. It wasn't as charming as the first place was to be, but it was comfortable and nice. Mom was ecstatic that they finally had a place of their own! Since she loved growing plants she proceeded to plant 52 of them: trees, bushes and flowers, even though they had to pay to have water trucked in to water them and provide their other water needs. Eventually she was hired to work in a judge's office, in Kingman, approximately 25 miles from home.

* * * *

After July of '70, John did not work anymore that summer. Except for the loss of income, we gained some real bonuses. Our house on Guilford Avenue lacked enough places for storage of our books and music items, so he designed, constructed, and painted built-in bookshelves and cabinets on our living room wall, which helped some. We were so excited over it. Then, with the help of Mom Tate and Aunt Leona, he and I canned 36 quarts of dill pickles with Mom's recipe, complete with cucumbers, Hungarian hot peppers, celery and carrots—our family's favorite dills.

He was able to join us at Burrshire swimming pool, which was only a block from our house. Our family held our collective breath the first day we watched Christina, four months old, get her first swimming "lesson". Our little Pisces performed marvelously, keeping her eyes open the whole time, above, and even below the water! I had been a bit nervous about it when the opportunity was first offered until we checked it all out. The teacher from the YWCA was an expert with infant swimming and set our minds at ease after that first day. We all celebrated Patti's 10th birthday with a party there at the end of summer.

At summer's start, Carolyn had finished second grade with straight A's and had blossomed into a great little artist, too. Her drawings and beautiful cursive writing were outstanding for her age of seven. With the warm weather she was spending a good amount of time outdoors. Sometimes she would come into the house complaining of a stomach ache; she'd say she was sleepy and wanted to take a little nap. She always felt better afterwards so I didn't suspect anything more was involved. But when this behavior became chronic, I took her to the doctor and he diagnosed her with a bladder infection. She went on a regime of medication therapy, would get better, eventually was declared okay, and then, before long it would happen again. Even that routine became chronic, and included a stay in the hospital by fall. Even her doctors there were puzzled by this pattern. The children and teacher, Miss Gustin, in her third grade classroom missed her, so they sent her their handmade cards which cheered her and helped her boredom. I was getting concerned that maybe the infections would lead to worse problems if we couldn't get to the cause and cure. We also explored the possibility of taking her to the Cleveland Clinic. As it turned out, we didn't have to.

Finally! We had a breakthrough when our cat Whiskers was caught urinating in the sandbox, (using it for a litter box) where Carolyn still spent some playtime. John destroyed it, and Whiskers was banished from sitting on the couch, chairs, or lying on the beds. Even in the future with any other family cats the policy was the same. I gave her megavitamin therapy for a short while, especially vitamin A, lots of water, and the problem was solved.

By the end of summer, 1970, Barbara received the disappointing news that she would not be attending CCDS in the fall. She had loved it there.

All her school life, she had always been an A/B student and was known for being a hard worker. She continued this way at CCDS, excelled also in choir and art, but by spring she received three C's and in science, a couple of D's. By the end of the year she was mostly excelling again. As part of her English class, she received an outstanding rating on a movie and commentary that she and a classmate produced on pollution. Her teacher's comments: "A superb project! Excellent in every respect! It reflected a considerable amount of work." Science was not so great, with a C for the year. She received the D's because she didn't like the teacher's methods and was bored both with him and the material! We don't know all the reasons, but the teacher's contract was not renewed. She did well on her paper work with French, but had a difficult time with pronunciation. Her teacher had always written on her report cards that she worked very hard, but by June it was different. On her last report card the teacher's comments were that she had not been working as hard as usual because she was too interested in boys. (Welcome to puberty!)

Al Getman was leaving the headmaster post and the new headmaster didn't have the contacts that Al had for scholarships and besides, Barbara wasn't excelling enough anymore. We were asked to pay half of Barbara's tuition plus supplies, which was too much for us.

As far as public education in Ohio that year, the commitments from state funding were woefully inadequate and unjust. In reaction, the Ohio Education Association put sanctions against the state, explaining to out-of-staters that it was not the place for teachers to apply!

Meanwhile, in John's classroom that fall, he was getting a new student that he knew already—his own daughter! We thought she was old enough to help make the decision where to attend school—St. Michael's through eighth grade, or Taft Junior High through the ninth. She chose Taft and wanted to be in her dad's class. Fortunately, the school allowed it. John was pleased; she was pleased, but he also cautioned her that she would be treated the same as her classmates. She would not be getting any special treatment because she was the teacher's daughter. She understood. She was ready for that. After she was in the class, she said she thought it was the most interesting of all her classes. (She may have been prejudiced, but we were pleased with her comment.)

Preparing her clothes for school after the easy task I had with the girls in uniforms was a bit of a "wrinkle" for me, but a delight for Barbara. She could express herself more fully through her clothes and developed a keen interest in clothes fashions which has stayed with her yet.

45. WESTERN ADVENTURES AND
MISADVENTURES

BY MAY 1971 WE were able to give the whole family a great gift—
a green Ford club wagon—which made traveling out west possible! It could
seat 12, so we had plenty of room for our brood plus luggage and other paraphernalia in the back. It was a rarity for families at that time, and a joy for
us. In July we were ready for our other great gift—the trip to Arizona and
California.

For John and me it was a return trip to our grand, favorite canyon. Since
Barbara was too little to remember the first, her dad and I were anxious to
share the awesome experience with as much of our family as we could this
time around. Only Christina, at one and a half years old, would not be able
to remember it. Since Barbara was the oldest, the experience made the biggest impression on her. She felt breathless at first sight and said it was the
most beautiful scene she had ever seen.

After the visitor center and meals, we were lucky to have been one of
the last groups into the crowded campground for spending the night. That
van was wonderful for car camping! There was room for all the girls to lie
down inside, and John and I camped out on the ground with sleeping bags.
Once all the girls were asleep, and no one else was around, the two of us
had a chance to relax and enjoy ourselves surveying our little dimly lit spot
on what seemed to be hallowed ground, rich with Native American and
geological history. As we settled down the slight little night breeze gently
rustling the tree leaves flickered the muted moonlight as beautifully as any
candlelight, creating just the right ambience for romance. Sleeping under
the sparkling stars meant more than sleep alone as we made love "sparks"
in our "bag bed". With our children nearby and John's and my "treats" for
each other, it was one of my happiest nights ever...the eventual sweet sleep
was just a bonus.

The next day we drove to the Painted Desert where Patti, our "Rock
Hound" purchased a couple of small petrified wood rocks which she still
has today. We had already seen a lot of beauty in Arizona, and we went on
to experience more by passing through the San Francisco Peaks—Sunset
Crater—Flagstaff area on our way to recreation at Oak Creek Canyon. We
didn't see much of the Colorado River at the Grand Canyon, but playing in
the water at this smaller picturesque canyon was great fun! There was a
section called "Slippery Rock Slide" where the momentum of the rollicking,
rolling water would carry each person onto the rocks and down to the end
of the slide area. Everyone there wore cut-off jeans because swimsuits were

too fragile. John, Patti, Carolyn, and Barbara had a hilarious time with it! I had fun watching them from my perch above on a huge, flat rock where Christina took her nap. By evening we settled down for sleep on the outskirts of beautiful red rock Sedona.

Traveling on the low elevations of desert was always challenging during the days, particularly since our van didn't have air conditioning. On those treks we made sure we had plenty of water for people and van, and didn't stop unless it was for gas, food, or restrooms. On the road we had open windows for circulating hot air, drank lots of water and chewed ice.

Next destination on our trip was Mom and Dad's, and finding their place wasn't easy. By the time we were in their area, it was dark, making it even harder to find them. Out in the country pole lights were few and far between. We were driving slowly on bumpy desert dirt roads which seemed akin to old fashioned washboards. They were not far from Highway 68 in Golden Valley, but to get to their place, lots of turns on other little roads were necessary. By the time we arrived, we six were tired, but then revived somewhat upon seeing Mom and Dad.

The next morning was an adventure. We checked out all the wonderful space around their place. No neighbors were close, but acres away, and across the road in front of the house, there were no other houses, but a view of hills. There were rock formations, cacti, creosotes, chaparrals, and beautiful yuccas nearby plus the landscaping Mom had done in the yard. The house had a small patio, across from Christina's favorite haunt—the dog's house! She loved walking in and out of that small doorway, which she probably thought was perfect size for her. We could take walks, but the children couldn't romp on their own because of rattlesnakes in the area. The expansive back yard and sunset views were especially beautiful.

We visited Davis Dam and went swimming in Lake Mohave with Mom and Dad. Days were fun, but evenings, we discovered, were not so much. John had always liked to relax on visits by having long talks on politics and current events with Dad. But Dad seemed more subdued this time and by Sunday night things really fell apart! After dinner we were on the patio where Dad was smoking and having some beer with John. We couldn't have Christina out there very long because she kept picking up dad's cigarette butts off the floor and putting them in her mouth. I brought all the girls in to play, while dad kept drinking after John had quit. The conversation between the men had ceased to be interesting because Dad was getting drunk and antagonistic, so John came into the house too and then the phone rang. I answered it, and it was Grandma. She asked to speak to Dad so she could tell him that his older half-sister, Hilda had died. Oh no! She had been my favorite of the older members of the Hill clan, the one I was most acquainted with, so it was a considerable loss to me, as well. I was mortified, as I couldn't let Grandma speak to Dad at such an important time! I told her he wasn't there, and that I would give him and Mom the message. Dad truly wasn't there—in mind. He was drunk, still on the patio and screaming about everything that was bothering him. We didn't have a clue why he was like that. We put the children to bed and hoped they would sleep. I had to talk to John. It was the first time I had ever seen my Dad drunk, and I hated it. It was the first serious emotional trauma I had ever experienced. I was hoping Dad's problem was just a fluke, not something chronic. If the latter, we agreed he needed help even if he wouldn't get it himself. There would have to be more information and possibly action about this. I was so upset I don't even remember where Mom was at that time.

The next day Dad apologized to Christina for yelling at her when she was picking up his cigarette butts. I don't know if Mom told him to do that or not, since he didn't seem to know what else had happened. He may have had a blackout, but who knows? John and I had a talk with him, but how much good it did, I don't know. Family doesn't always make a positive impression on people with this problem. When I offered to help him, he said he didn't need any preaching!

Mom didn't talk with us about it and went to work at the judge's office the next day. Dad was off work so we took him with us on a trip over the border to Lake Mead in Nevada to swim. Unfortunately, probably because it was *the day after*, he didn't swim, was quiet, not cheerful, and sat alone. He wasn't the dad I remembered.

He had been anything but a loner in the past that I recalled—he was funny, good at impersonations, liked people, and most people liked him after meeting him. Dad loved music and the joy it gave him. When Warren and I were little in Minnesota he would play his concertina and sing. He had a beautiful voice, had been a Lutheran choir boy as a kid, went with his friend Carl to symphony concerts in Minneapolis as a youth, and liked dancing. Our parents paid for lessons—violin for Warren, piano and dance for me— even though they had not had the opportunity for lessons themselves. Dad and I used to have fun taking turns at harmonizing old 1930's pop music when I was a young kid. When Warren and I were in grade school living in the East Bay, he and Mom took us to symphony pops concerts and operettas in San Francisco. His favorite music was classical and he took me once to a chamber concert in Berkeley. He was a drummer in what had become a champion California drum and bugle corps and played in parades. Up to that time he had a lot of fun in life through music.

After moving to Southern California, the only active music he participated in was harmonizing songs with his brothers. He hadn't used his concertina for years, so he sold it to buy Mom a typewriter (his idea). However, going to occasional concerts was still an enjoyable activity for them. Moving to the desert, though, meant listening to music mostly on recordings. The culture of country music on radio wasn't particularly interesting to him. His work wasn't as interesting either as it had been in California, where he had worked at so many places requiring his excellent decorating skills, including businesses, schools, a housing project, expensive homes and Disneyland. He had pride in his work, but he had told us that working at the NTS for maintenance failed to motivate him very much. Also, he and Mom didn't like the week day separations, but were grateful he had work.

I think I may have hit upon at least some things that could have been making him unhappy. This drinking excessively was a temporary glitch, I hoped. It was the only downer of our journey. When we parted, we told them we would be back on our return trip home, and Warren and his family would be joining us.

We went to Santa Monica, where the kids had a great time swimming in the ocean. We continued on to Warren and Byrle's in Temple City, where we took Byrle, Dawn and Lisa with us to Disneyland. Warren had to work that day. It was the usual great Disney day for us except for the brief time when Barbara was separated from us in Tomorrowland and we were frantically looking for her. We had been busy talking and hadn't noticed that she had quickly darted away from us when she accidently saw a ninth grade boy she was slightly acquainted with at Taft. Impulsive, with that thought totally on her mind, she hadn't another thought to tell us that she was leaving to talk to him! Although we were greatly relieved when we finally found her, she then received our angry outbursts about her irresponsible behavior.

After recovering from Disneyland, we all drove to Arizona to spend a day with Mom, Dad, and Warren's family in Hualapai Mountain Park, near Kingman. Dad wasn't overly talkative, but this was a place he loved—mountain slopes, pine trees, and awesome views—a place he could share with his children and grandchildren that day. If there was compensation for living quietly in the country, this was part of it. The elevation of a few thousand feet didn't seem too high for his lungs, giving him the fresh air he craved.

Down in the valley he also enjoyed the various seasons of nature, especially the plants bursting into life in the spring and the dramatic summer storms where the lightening, thunder and rain created violent torrents of water rushing through the desert washes. Arnie and Peggy loved standing outside their house in the rain to experience the power of it all! Peggy often photographed sunsets—these were some of the most spectacular seen anywhere. Her landscape paintings—an art form that she had started in Long Beach—were now often beautiful desert scenes. Mom was content.

We felt better about dad by the time we left because there were no more "episodes". More national parks were on our list for the way home. Zion, with its beautiful red rock, green vegetation and "weeping rock" was an ideal place for lunch. Bryce Canyon, with its incredible towering pinnacle rocks was one of Patti's favorite places, but too huge for her rock collection. Rocky Mountain National Park in Colorado could not be outdone by anywhere else, with its spectacular peaks, elk and wildflowers in its alpine meadows. That was the high point of our trip before we descended and continued home. We had succeeded in at least introducing to our children our great legacy of beautiful American parks! It would also be an incentive to travel to some of those places and more by themselves someday.

* * * *

After we were home John took Barbara to College of Wooster for her first rock concert, featuring Emerson, Lake, and Palmer. They both enjoyed it, and John bought their *Pictures at an Exhibition* LP based on Russian classical composer Mussorgsky's music .We all enjoyed it for years at our place.

By the time school was in session for everyone I wrote a letter to Mom at her work explaining our concern about Dad's drinking, because it appeared that it was taking control of him. I had contacted counselors who were former alcoholics and specialized in alcoholism counseling, and gained some help from them. If Dad was displaying the behavior I described to them, then, they said without help he would get worse, physically and mentally. They recommended that Mom contact her boss, the judge, to give her resources in her area for help. There was only Alcoholics Anonymous and Dad would have nothing to do with them. The other advice was to not be embarrassed about asking the judge for help, but Mom was, and didn't. So John and I were left frustrated.

46. GUESTS

THE LIVING ROOM CURTAINS finally gave out completely, so we bought new ones and had the carpet cleaned, so then the room was dignified enough, not only for us, but also for guests. In April we had an unexpected one! When he arrived at the door, we didn't recognize him because he had grown a small beard and was wearing contact lenses instead of glasses. He had to identify himself to us, and it was Rick! However, he stayed with us only a matter of minutes as we arranged a dinner meeting with him to go three days later with us at Florian's European Restaurant. On the way there that night I was a bit apprehensive, remembering all that had happened to Nora and the children.

He was in New York when the accident happened, then went to Pennsylvania to take care of the funerals, burials of the children and Nora's cremation in Reading. Father Dennison and some of the parishioners from Canton's St. Paul's went there to help. The whole experience had been devastating for him so it was understandable that his health had gone way down because of it. By his time with us he had recuperated somewhat emotionally, and looked healthy. He didn't share why he had left the family. He clearly had suffered and had been changed enormously. When we parted we wished him well. It was the last time we saw him.

* * * *

During the last school year, John had numerous professional meetings, and had taught the new elective course for ninth graders, *Justice in Urban America*, in addition to his other classes. By June of '72 he received a Martha Holden Jennings Foundation grant to study in Chicago. This law course focused on what the teacher could do in the areas of curriculum development and design, and had been developed jointly by the Chicago Bar Association and Chicago Board of Education.

I was happy to take him to the Akron-Canton airport on June 25. As soon as he was gone, he was missed by all us girls, because we appreciated his constant, loving, strong presence and take-charge help with chores. We thought we were up to the laborious tasks that we needed to do without his assistance, but by a week later, the mischief had begun! The girls and I were taking turns cutting the grass, and could do it as long as our neighbor Roger was home. We were not able to start our temperamental lawn mower without his help. The weather was cooler than usual and one of the wettest ever, so beside the grass, the weeds in our larger-than-usual vegetable garden grew bigger and stronger than ever. (I have no idea why I wanted a larger one.) So, in between the rains, we were too busy on the lawns and in the dirt! Patti came home from scout camp just in time to help the day before John went to Chicago. She was very helpful in the garden then because she was interested in the several vegetables she had planted herself.

Then, the dryer decided to quit, and I had to take the heavy baskets of wet clothes to a Laundromat to dry until John could repair it, as he had done before. Shortly before John left, new neighbors moved into the duplex next door, and they had three dogs, two of which were huge German Shepherds who hated cats. So when they were out, we had to keep Whiskers in.

* * * *

I had been doing okay with my activities, but ever since Christina was born, I didn't seem to be quite as vibrant and energetic as I had been before my leg surgeries and pregnancy. Also, I couldn't run or jump anymore because I didn't feel good enough in my pelvic area. It had been a while since an exam, so I made an appointment when John was away.

What I learned was that I had a prolapsed uterus. That had also allowed my bladder to fall, so it created a pocket where urine could collect and breed infections. My gynecologist-obstetrician, Dr. D. advised a hysterectomy which would remove the uterus, but leave the ovaries. The bladder would be pulled up and sewn back in place. He had a wife and five children himself and would want the best for them, so I understood that he thought this was the best course for me to take. He also knew my health history, had taken care of me during my pregnancy and delivered Christina. In my mind then, upon my consent, he would be performing an act of mercy! Upon this diagnosis and treatment plan suggested, my mind also went back to my mother, who had a prolapsed uterus after two children and had surgery for it, and her mother, who gave birth to seven children with the seventh living only one day, had a prolapsed uterus. At what point that happened, I don't know. *My* body and legs were not built to have many babies. Besides genetics, my lack of exercise had been a negative also: two weeks in the hospital bed and post-op time for the leg surgeries, and lying in bed for months during my last pregnancy. Lifting Christina a lot could have contributed to it as well. Before I left his office I decided to have the surgery, and we scheduled it for September 25.

Meanwhile, John was favorably impressed with the law course. He also enjoyed taking in features of Chicago itself, including walks along Lake Michigan. He took photos from the top of the John Hancock building and loved touring the art museum and natural history museum.

He arrived home on July 21 and was given a week off before starting his half days' August job for his school system's Board of Education on the *Justice* social studies curriculum. He was rejuvenated after his trip and it was enjoyable to see him that way. He had enjoyed walking at night in that area of Chicago near where he stayed. He said it was lit up bright and beautiful and there were lots of activities going on. He was so impressed with the many cultural opportunities there that he wanted to share a day with me alone in Cleveland visiting University Circle, where he could share the pleasure of visiting museums again. And it *was* so much fun! The highest point was the Cleveland Museum of Art, one of the best art museums in the country. Second was the Garden Center. We had been to those places before with the children, but exhibits are often changing, and it was so relaxing and special with just the two of us.

I waited until he was working to tell him of my surgery so he could enjoy his little vacation.

"Well, it's not the best of news, but you need to have it done. Besides," he said, "we have great experience now in helping you recuperate!" I felt guilty because I hated being a burden to them, and so soon again. I was hoping it would be the last time they would have to do it.

No abdominal incision was necessary and the procedure was successful. My ovaries were left, and I had no phlebitis, so two days after the surgery I was walking. I was in the hospital one week. John visited me, and Christina, who was two and a half, went to her godparents' home. We didn't have to coax her. She was excited about going on "vacation" with her suitcase! Family activities at home and school were normal except for the meal preparations. Though John's Mom and Dad weren't in good enough health to take care of Christina, Mom made dinner for the family a couple of times. My mom had offered to come, but we preferred to have her come to us on a vacation. Instead, she and Dad sent cards and gifts.

Mary Jean watched Christina during the day when I was recuperating at home the following week. John and the other girls cared for her on evenings and weekends. Not everything went smoothly that first week home amidst five other somewhat noisy people, but with patience we did okay. By the second week we were doing better with the new routine at home and getting part-time help with Christina from Mary Jean and neighbors, including the one with ten children. Doris came with her guitar that week to sing with me and help with Chris. So all these generous, compassionate and musical endeavors helped me heal and I could slowly go back to normal activities. I was very blessed and grateful to all.

While I was in the hospital, Barbara, then fourteen, chose to go to a David Bowie concert Cleveland with friends, which she said was an epic experience for her, changing what she said was "my being a hippie to an artist". (Hippie? We hadn't thought of her being one— and we knew she was an artist since she was five years old.)

She met a nineteen year old there by the name of Mark and brought him to the hospital to meet me. He was described as a Kent State student who wanted to be a lawyer. What I wasn't told at the time was that he was intimately involved with rock artists and their concerts, which Barbara found to be glamorous, exciting events where she hoped for chances to meet musicians. She would never have the chance to meet Jimi Hendrix, who had already died in 1970, but, inspired by his musical reputation, created a stunning black, white and gray painting of his face with a tear in the corner of his right eye while she was still fourteen years old.

Almost immediately after meeting her, Mark wanted her to go steady with him, which she refused. She didn't feel ready for that, and she thought he was too old for her. We thought so, too, and said no. As time went on, we had to eventually deny him the chance to even be a guest at our house.

47. FROM FRUSTRATIONS TO HOLIDAY CHEER

BARBARA HAD BEEN A Candy Striper volunteer for several months at the House of Loreto, an assisted-living home served by dedicated Catholic nuns. But our fourteen-year-old found it difficult at her age to deal adequately with the daily problems of elderly people's incapacities. Instead, in the summer she directed her willingness to help by volunteering for office work in the local George McGovern presidential campaign headquarters. In between the political work she joined a group of teenagers supervised by adults to clean and paint a home for the blind.

She continued to help McGovern until after the election when it was disillusionment time! She had worked hard, and was optimistic that he would win. When he lost she cried for two days, even at school. She felt the pain of political defeat, part of the lessons of living in our democracy. After talking with other McGovern workers, her dad and me, as well as her school counselor, she learned how to work out her frustrations and disappointments.

Patti, our naturalist, Girl Scout, typist and artist, had turned twelve in 1972. Having finished sixth grade and Girl Scouts, which she had loved at St. Michael's, had also chosen to enter Taft Middle School. She was enjoying it, was excellent in her school work, and hadn't shown much interest in boys yet. She was always busy, so we thought she didn't want to make time for them!

Dear Grandma and Grandpa:

I polished another group of rocks this month; they turned out a bit better than the first. I have a lot of rocks on top of my dresser in boxes with plastic lids. They really look nice up there. I also have some under my desk, on top of my desk, and in the garage! I keep picking up new ones every day, it seems and add them to my collection. Our house will soon look like a rock quarry!

I made a skirt recently and now I am making a jumper. It is almost finished. I might make Chris a little dress, too.

How are you? I'm fine. I miss you.

Love, Patti

No matter what she created, she did excellently and beautifully with her gifted hands. Added to her printing, cursive writing, paintings and drawings was her sculpturing of Christmas gingerbread cookies by hand. She had been so good with clay creations, that after I found this great recipe and asked her if she would be interested in making them, she jumped at the chance! She decorated with red cinnamon candies, including the gingerbread man she made for Christina, and all were delicious, as well as charming. Some were even stuffers in the Christmas stockings.

I was pretty much back to normal with a short nap in the afternoon. I had energy and there were no more two days of suffering on the couch or bed the first two days of my period every month. I was taking vitamin E to keep me from getting clots and it helped the circulation in my legs so much that they felt normal. That meant I didn't have to wear the miserable leotard. It was good that I had resumed my regular responsibilities because John was going to "Zhivago Land" in December for a ten day trip!

Since this would be our first Christmas without him, he and I had been busy with the many preparations for us all prior to the trip. Less than a week before his departure, he and I finished the final interesting seminar of six at Kent State. They were designed to familiarize the travelers on various aspects of the Soviet Union life and language. He and other alumni, educators and some students were part of a group invited by President Glenn Olds of KSU to tour Soviet educational, economic, and cultural facilities during the 1972 Russian Winter Festival. Part of the expenses for each individual of the group of 143 guests was being met with a $200.00 scholarship.

We had an early family Christmas the weekend before his departure. We quickly bought and decorated a tree, exchanged gifts with the children, and visited relatives.

One of John's teacher friends helped me out by taking him to the airport so I could attend Carolyn's first leading role in a Christmas play at school that December 19 evening as "Mrs. Hurry-Up".

Our ten year old daughter surpassed my expectations by *all* that she did! She had absolutely no stage fright, even though the auditorium was completely filled! Barbara was so impressed that she sang her whole song on pitch. Besides that, I was also impressed with her acting ability. Her earlier course at the Players Guild Theater that year had prepared her well. At home I noticed she had the gifts for reading well and memorizing easily. Her talent needed to be nurtured and developed further.

For Christmas, Carolyn received money from us and my parents to take more drama courses at PGT in our beautiful, two year old Canton Cultural Center for the Arts. Her teacher was Professor Pike from Malone College in Canton. His excellent teaching showed in their performances in the professional disciplines he taught them. As she continued further she blossomed into a great performer and developed friendships. Classes were held during school years and performances were during the summers. Her first play was *Oliver Twist*; she continued with *Snow White and the Seven Dwarfs* and with *Peter Pan* as Wendy—"flying" through space (on wires)! In between the other performances, she learned about the World War II Holocaust by acting as a young Jewish girl in the Reader's Theater performance of *I Never Saw Another Butterfly*. Her last classes lasted through eighth grade, and according to Carolyn, "They were some of the happiest years of my life!"

48. TROIKA AND UNICEF

WHEN I KISSED HIM good-bye on the afternoon of December 19th he had "butterflies" in his stomach, even before he boarded the plane for his first trip to take him outside the United States. While we girls spent part of the 24th in church for the beautiful 1972 Christmas Eve Mass, John was briefly visiting each and all the cathedrals within the walls of the Kremlin, along with as many as he could see outside those walls in the brief time he had before leaving Moscow. It was the first day of sunshine and the last day of any bright festival posters and banners, as they were being taken down. Understandably, John was cramming in as many photos as possible!

By afternoon the Kent group was on a train for the eight hour ride from Moscow to Leningrad. John thought the panoramic views outside the passing windowed scenes were stunning, with forests of white and black trunked birch among the pines. They passed many small towns and villages and stopped at a few. There were colorful little houses with TV antennas and fences. Even though there was practically no snow, it was still quite cold: he saw many people skating or ice fishing.

There were many Russians on the train, including a few soldiers. Most were friendly and many were drinking. In the car where John was with Kent travelers, the only Russians were an elderly peasant man with his wife and two other adults. When the old man realized they had boarded a car with Americans, he wanted to share with one some gesture of friendship. He really didn't have any gift to give, but when he saw John he focused on him and insisted on his sharing his cigarette! John stood there while the man took out his supplies and rolled his tobacco onto a piece of newspaper. After the man puffed on it, he smiled and gave it to John, the non-smoker, who obliged the man by doing the same for the joint holiday spirit of friendship.

Before John went on his Soviet trip, he had prepared himself well for an overly frigid, stereotypical frozen Russian winter. Long underwear, wool turtle neck sweater and pants, heavy, lined winter jacket, gloves, boots, and newly purchased Russian fur hat would keep him warm for his imagined favorite outdoor activity over there—the troika sleigh ride.

Whether he was in the Moscow or later in the Leningrad areas, there simply was not an opportunity to feel the wind and flying snow with three galloping horses across the frozen land with laughing people in the open sleigh. It was the warmest winter in 200 years, so he had no opportunity to see a favorite Soviet sports event, troika racing!

After he arrived home, John organized what photos he had been able to take during the limited times of light, between 10 AM and 4 PM. And then, most of the days were overcast, with only a few days of sun. The movies didn't turn out at all, so they had to be discarded. He couldn't take any indoor photos with flash, so that was limited, and he was able to get only a few from others who also took the trip. He had been frustrated, but finally had enough decent ones for us and to present to others. He enjoyed sharing them with members of the local College Club:

February 23, 1973

Dear Mr. Tate,

Just a note to express our sincere thanks for your fine presentation and talk on Russia. From the many favorable comments I've received, you were much appreciated and thoroughly enjoyed by all.

Your talk was so much more 'in depth' than that of a casual traveler due to your knowledge of Russian history. This knowledge made the excellent films that much more interesting.

Especially enjoyed, also, were your comments on the schools and insights into the life style of the Russian people. Many thanks!

Sincerely yours,

M.B., Chairman

International Section, College Club

For our 24ᵗʰ of March party, we rented a large room in the beautiful, newly built North Canton YMCA, and John repeated for all 70 of us the same slide show, beginning with the large Intourist Hotel where he stayed in Moscow and finishing with scenes from Leningrad. The following are just highlights found in his much more extensive presentation.

"The amount of visual artistry in the cities throughout the trip was impressive. My first experience outside the Intourist was riding the immaculate and sleek Moscow subway. I stopped at several stations just so I could see their stunning works of art! Beginning with the mosaics, I had been smitten!

"I toured the iconic St. Basil's and had myself photographed outside it with its dark red and green exterior and multicolored 'onion' domes. Like many of the historical churches that were built as places of worship, St. Basil's became a museum under the anti-religious Soviet regime. Nevertheless, I was drawn to the beauty of so many and appreciated that they were originally built as sacred spaces.

"After I returned home, Barbara created her own unique and beautiful painted version of St. Basil's in pastel hues of greens, blues, and a hint of rose, outlined in black. The background was painted in gold leaf. We had it professionally framed in black and gold and hung it up.

"The government-run schools we visited in Moscow were traditional, free, formal and serious in style, where the impression was that the students had to pay great attention to the teachers and lessons given. All the schools in the country were uniform in how they operated. Like other European schools, history and geography were emphasized more than some in America. The students at one of the schools knew more American history and government than many of our own students and they wondered why American students didn't study Russian history. In a specialized English school, all the students, from grades one through ten, became fluent in the language. At the elegant House of Friendship, teachers were friendly, gave presentations and had musical entertainment by a couple of students from the English school. Sweet were picturesque little girls in black uniform dresses with white pinafores and large white puffy bows atop their heads.

"I found the Exhibition of Economic Achievement in Moscow, Pavilion of Space Achievement, and exhibits from all the Soviet Republics very interesting. The complex was so huge it also encompassed a museum, park, zoo, and amusement center. I wanted to see these but there wasn't time—it would take weeks to see it all.

"In Leningrad at the Museum of the Revolution our group saw a film on the 900 day siege of the city during World War II, a devastating, suffering part of their history. The film was also heavy with propaganda. Gold decorations were not only inside and outside many of the churches in Moscow and Leningrad but also in the huge tsars' palaces. When we viewed the gold onion domes, iconostases, and interiors of many decorated buildings, including the Hermitage Art Museum, we were all stunned by the extravagance as well as beauty. I loved being there to view one of the greatest art collections in the world. The whole place was fantastically beautiful! It was not possible to see very many of the exhibits, since there were more than two million exhibits housed in three hundred rooms.

"There was a bus tour of the city and a beautiful mosque. One of my favorite church visits of the trip was to St. Isaacs's Cathedral Museum, one of the largest churches in the world. It was 'unbelievably beautiful!' We found Leningrad a bit friendlier and more modern than Moscow. We stayed in the Leningrad Hotel, an ultramodern hotel built by a Finnish contractor. We were treated that holiday evening with a delicious steak and champagne dinner while a Cossack accordionist entertained us with his marvelous voice. A band playing American and Russian dance music concluded the evening."

At our party we had fantastic Russian folk music recordings that John brought back with him. We had food: homemade international breads and pastries donated by many. I made a Russian cylindrical sweet yeast bread with almonds and golden currents. I placed a candle in the curved white frosting top and surrounded it with fresh daisies.

We also had international dancing, which included a troika! True, it wasn't quite the same as the outdoor one, but it was great fun to have Blossom, our dance expert teach us all how to dance it, which took three partners in each group to imitate the trios of horses with sleighs.

In March we appreciated this gratifying note:

Dear Dolores and John,

Thank you for including us in your delightful gathering Saturday night. Your slides, John, were an eye opener to us on a facet of Russian life of which we were unaware. The degree of grandeur and the extreme wealth displayed in the churches was unbelievable. A revolution is more understandable to us now.

Dolores, the pastry table was like something out of Gourmet Magazine. What richness we have all around us!

And we have all enjoyed the Russian cake! We shared it at Eucharistic Celebration at Brunnerdale on Sunday at the close of an eighth grade CCD retreat Dave (their son) was attending. The remainder has been tasted and savored by everyone entering our front door!

We really enjoyed the folk dancing! Thank you for a memorable evening.

Warmly,

Gene and Joanne

* * * *

By fall 1973 I had my own international project. It was for UNICEF and was held at the Stark County branch of KSU. As a member of our local Interfaith UNICEF Committee, I was director of a UNICEF "Celebration of Life", educating while celebrating its scope in underserved areas of the world. Desiring to be open to the community-at-large, Mr. Morehart, Director of the Branch, and Ms. Wilson, Director of Group Affairs, enthusiastically endorsed the endeavor.

Students and some faculty members participated not only from KSU, but also from nearby Walsh and Malone Colleges. Many ladies from the area donated home baked international pastries. Exhibits included children's books from international cultures provided by the KSU professor of children's literature, African artifacts from another KSU professor, as well as teacher and young student resources. We showed UNICEF films and provided an American folk sing-along led by a KSU student guitarist from main campus.

There were easy international circle and line dances for all, led by various dance leaders, and so John jumped in. The dancing was accompanied by the Halkides Orchestra, which lent a festive cosmopolitan mood to the occasion. The music was paid for by a grant from the Recording Industries Trust Fund with the cooperation of Canton Local 111 of the American Federation of Musicians.

There were card sales at Malone's book store and Trick or Treat collections in the dorms for the first time prior to the celebration and also at KSU where it was decided to continue on an ongoing basis by the Office of Student Affairs. There was a college student who signed up for the UNICEF summer internship program. An internist from Cleveland made plans to come back to Kent-Stark for some follow-ups with student activities. Teachers took teaching resources and display photos, including John.

The activities leading up to the celebration and the celebration itself on the evening of November 7 proved to be an outstanding example of community cooperation.

49. THE DARK SIDE OF SOVIET LIFE

BECAUSE HE COULD NOT be a speaker there, Soviet writer Alexander Solzhenitsyn wrote a letter to the Fourth Congress of Soviet Writers dated May 16, 1967. It was an important gathering, because it included the Presidium and delegates, members of the Union of Soviet Writers, and editors of literary newspapers and magazines. It was a long letter, the heart of which is explained here.

At issue was the decades-long oppressive censorship of Soviet writers in a system that "gives people unversed in literature arbitrary control over writers." He said this was "not provided for in the Constitution" and therefore it was "illegal". Through most of the letter he spoke for various writers whose writings had been censored because they had been given such labels as "ideologically harmful", "depraved" and "counter-revolutionary". The writers "were not supposed to have the right to express their considered judgments about the moral life of man and society, or to explain in their own way the social problems and historical experience that have been so deeply felt in our country."

He continued by saying that many of the writers gave in to the censorship pressures, making changes to their work that distorted "them irremediably" so they could have them printed.

He proposed that the Congress of Soviet Writers adopt a resolution which would demand and ensure the abolition of all censorship and would release publishing houses from the obligation to obtain authorization for all publications.

He wrote of the abandonment, rather than support, of writers by the Union of Soviet Writers to persecution which they helped condone and perpetuate with exile, sentences in forced labor (prison) camps and death.

He brought up his own situation where he was being denied publication of his writing. One of his small books had been published with the approval of the government due to the intervention of Premier Nikita Khrushchev's de-Stalinization program after the death of Soviet dictator Joseph Stalin, which was in 1953. The one allowed was the fictional *One Day in the Life of Ivan Denisovich*, the story of the book's name and character as an inmate of a labor camp, published in 1962. He wrote from his own knowledge of such, after having spent eight years in various labor camps for casually criticizing Stalin to a friend, even though Solzhenitsyn had been a decorated soldier in WWII with the Russian army. After "One Day" he could not get further books published because the Soviet leadership had changed and his books were critical of the system.

Since he had no response to his protests to injustices and suggested solutions in his first letter—even though he had about a hundred other writers supporting him— he wrote again to the Writers' Union almost four months later. He cited slander to him and continued refusal of publication of his works.

He eventually had them published in other countries and was awarded the Nobel Prize for Literature in 1970. Especially potent were *The Gulag Archipelago* and *The Gulag Archipelago Two* published in 1973 and 1974. The Gulag was the huge system of forced labor camps that persisted from 1918 to 1956. In his own words he stated in the first publication that "...there are no fictitious persons, nor fictitious events. People and places are named with their own names." The Soviets expelled him in 1974 and took away his Soviet citizenship. He went first to West Germany, then Switzerland, then Vermont in the United States where he lived until the 1990's when he returned to Russia after the fall of Communism.

As knowledge about him and his writings became known in other countries, John bought seven books by the author in the Seventies. As much as John respected Soviet scientific achievements, assistance to the working class, free education and support for the folk and fine arts, he was also deeply opposed to tyranny, totalitarianism, suppression of truth, intellectual, spiritual and civil rights, wherever they existed in human history.

50. OHIO, WASHINGTON D.C. AND ARIZONA

WITH THE PUBLIC'S GROWING awareness of the ongoing political corruption and deception concerning the Watergate scandal, Barbara's idealism with politics was dealt another blow. The Viet Nam war was still raging, so shortly after her fifteenth birthday in January in 1973, with our permission, she traveled on a bus all night with a group from Kent State to demonstrate in the last large anti-Viet Nam peace rally in Washington D.C. It was held during Richard Nixon's second presidential inaugural ceremony. Her group protested by walking in black robes and painted white faces with large tears to mourn the deaths of Kent State students. Having been struggling with the frigid temperatures the whole time, even with bonfires, they returned to the bus that evening exhausted and bitterly cold. She slept all night again in her haven of rest until she was back on the campus.

Spring was better—at least for a little while. When John was in Moscow, he had attended a performance of the Bolshoi Ballet, composed of young people (7-17 years of age) and he said it was great, and done very professionally. He also enjoyed the Moscow Circus, which he was able to share with the rest of us when it came to Cleveland in April. The biggest hits for the girls were the horses and bears, and I enjoyed it all, especially the music.

On Mother's Day we all went to Cleveland again to see *The Emigrants*, based on famous Swedish author Vilhelm Moberg's classic fictional tale of Swedes who immigrated to the United States, to Minnesota. The time frame was the latter half of the nineteenth century through the early twentieth, which paralleled my own mother's family's arrival to the same state—first with my grandfather's two sisters, then his, and lastly my grandmother's in 1910 with their four little sons, the youngest only one year old. I was spellbound by the thought of similar hardship circumstances, believing that this was worthy of more family research for me in the future.

Just before Easter, one of Barbara's good friends died in a swimming accident and Barbara chose to attend her funeral, the first time she had to face the death of a friend. It helped her emotionally to continue with her art work then, and in the summer to spend time with her grandparents when they visited us.

For five days we crammed in as much as we could! There were picnics at Arboretum City Park under the sweeping, weeping willows five minutes from our house, and Blossom Music Center's tree lined, sloping lawn during an evening symphony concert. We swam at Burrshire swimming pool, half a block from our place, and had a Midwestern Corn-on-the-Cob Fest at our house afterwards, where we savored the sweet, picked-the-same-day freshness from a nearby farm.

We took them to The Wilderness Center, less than fifty miles from our place and one of our family's favorite Ohio places. A non-profit, the center was dedicated to wildlife conservation and natural history. There were prairies, a lake, a pond and an observation tower where we had a bird's eye view while surveying the scenes. The hiking trails were surrounded by all sizes of trees. Some of the best were huge old-growth beech from Native American days, and the sizes of some of their gray trunks rivaled Sierra sequoias. We had a light rain that accompanied us near the end of our trek and everyone enjoyed it. The girls still continued with their usual romping and skipping along the way and three year old Christina without coaching stopped occasionally to hug a tree!

When Mom and Dad left us for home, they took Patti with them for her first plane ride and full vacation in the desert. For her to be in rocky, sandy, picturesque Arizona was a dream trip! Not only did she collect rocks and seeds, she went swimming at Kathryn's Landing Lake, and explored the desert landscape area around Mom and Dad's. They took her to Oatman, the little town that has wild burros wandering the streets, a great place for photo-ops for an animal lover! Living in Golden Valley meant she rode with Grandma approximately 25 miles to Kingman to do their grocery and other purchases. The Mojave County Museum is also there, where she learned more about the area and viewed art, including Native American. Mom introduced her to a local artist, and she spent time back at the house, painting small canvases under Mom's supervision.

She celebrated her thirteenth birthday a little early, and also enjoyed playing with their dog Laddie and Smokey the cat. Then our brand-new teenager flew home by herself, refreshed and ready to get back into the swing of things. We framed her beautiful still life painting and she hung it on the wall of her room. She harvested the plants in her garden areas and watered her cacti. Besides the family and our cat Whiskers, also welcoming her back were her colorful zinnias, which had exploded with many more blooms.

Carolyn continued to "bloom" otherwise. She was earning some money baby-sitting and had saved her August birthday money, which helped pay for a part of her drama lessons and volunteered as an usher for one of the area high school's performances of Shakespeare's *Twelfth Night* at the Cultural Center. She loved nature (but not in all the same ways as Patti), reading, and lately, drawing—mostly people. She loved comedians, and was one herself!

* * * *

John received unexpected bonuses from his student teacher, which made him feel humble, appreciative, and that his work was worthwhile. There were gifts of wine and music, plus a heartfelt note written on the inside of a beautiful, long red greeting card, which on the outside had printed in bold, large, block letters—Thanks for the Red Carpet Treatment:

Mr. Tate,

I hope you'll enjoy your album and sip your wine while you're listening! It's very little in return for all you have given me!! I couldn't have been assigned to a finer teacher than yourself. Instead of giving me the seating chart and books the first day and leaving all up to me, you were very considerate and helped in any way that you could. After having talked to other students about their supervising teachers, I know mine was 'the best'. Because of all your help, aid, patience and comments, I know I'm starting on the right foot. You made me feel at ease, and encouraged rather than discouraged me.

I know I'll never be rich by being a teacher. I've always enjoyed working with children and pray I will never lose that gift.

I have learned more in the last ten weeks concerning my future than I have in my four years at Akron U. Studying in a classroom about teaching and doing your student teaching is very much different.

So again, I can't thank you enough for your influence and concern for me and my future. I'll never forget you and will keep in touch. Good luck to you and your family.

Thanks for everything,

Your Student Teacher—Taft '73

L. S. "

51. CONFLICTS

JUST MONTHS LATER, IT was no longer enough for Barbara and her best friend from high school to attend the rock concerts in Cleveland as just part of a group. Her friend decided she wanted to be Mark's girlfriend. Quickly, however, that changed.

Mark would visit our place occasionally, and we thought of him as a friend, not a boyfriend. Then, in November, 1973, Barbara attended a sold out Allman Brothers concert with him, which she said had about 10,000 people in attendance. Since Mark knew the musicians, he obtained stage passes for them. They both were on the stage during the whole concert, adding to the excitement. Of course, she reported that it was great, and I can understand that.

We weren't able to find out the details afterward when she said they went to a hotel after the concert to party with them. The full extent of any alcohol or drug use during or after the concerts she wouldn't reveal to us. She didn't manifest symptoms except laid back behaviors, such as one would get from marijuana. This concert however, had sparked a nightmare of events regarding her and Mark with activities often behind our backs.

The next time Mark was at our house I noticed strange behavior because he was paranoid about germs, especially on doorknobs. As Christmas approached, he had given her an expensive necklace, which seemed to us like another lure. Surprisingly, she shared what was happening with a letter to her grandparents in Arizona:

Dear Grandpa and Grandma

How are you? It rained here on Christmas My boyfriend had given me a necklace and was going to take me on a trip over Christmas vacation, but he went insane (really, he did!) Now he is in the state hospital. That's the main reason my Christmas was so horrible. I haven't really found anything to get my mind off of that. I bet you think I pick weird boyfriends, but I have no regrets. Now that I've had the experience of seeing a person with mental illness I understand it's not something to laugh about. I spent the day with Mark when he first started acting up and believe me, it was hell. I wouldn't want to go through it again. It helped me grow up a lot.

Well, that is all I can think of, so...take life in stride

Love, Barb

"Imagine all the people living in peace—John Lennon"

I visited Mark in the hospital, not to discuss his relationship with Barbara, which wasn't realistic to do so, but to find out more about his condition. He was a drug user, with more than only marijuana and his condition according to the medical diagnosis at that time was schizophrenia. I visited his mother and expressed my sympathy for her for what had been going on with her son. I appreciated the fact, and told her so, that she was willing to listen to me as to why he could not continue to see our daughter. The facts were obvious. Also, she admitted to me that at one point he had also tried to stab her with a scissors!

In January 1974 Barbara turned sixteen and obtained her driving permit. She was allowed to drive our second car, the Rambler, but not our Ford van as she wanted. She also decided she wanted to graduate from high school a year ahead—June, 1975. Her school counselor said she could do it if she took a summer course in U.S. History, which would then provide enough credits to do so. I had hesitations about her finishing earlier, but both John and her counselor gave her permission anyway.

After Mark was released from the hospital, Barbara became interested in him again. It was an on again, off again struggle with us. The prohibition from us usually didn't work, and one night when Mark came to the house to see her, John told him he couldn't, and asked him to leave. It was though John hadn't said a word, for Mark just stayed there and started to push John away. John wouldn't let him, so they scuffled and wrestled in our front yard! Patti came out, jumped on Mark's back, and pulled his hair! I called the sheriff, and finally Mark left when the sheriff arrived minutes later.

I had been taking her to a professional family counselor at the Catholic Charities office, hoping that would help her come to her senses, because she wouldn't take our advice. It was during that time span that I received a call from her high school's office one day asking if Barbara was ill, because she was marked absent, but there wasn't a written excuse from home for it. I was totally caught off guard because I thought she was at school, and that had never happened before. She had never been a discipline problem at school. I had no idea where she was, and said so on the phone, promising to call back. During this panic, I went to my previously scheduled appointment with the counselor to get advice. Barbara and Mark were both scheduled to be there with me. While I was there, the phone rang in the counselor's office, and it was Barbara! She was calling from Bolivar, a small town about fifteen miles south of Canton. She called to let us know that Mark had taken her out of town to marry her, but she was able to convince him that she wouldn't go through with it, and she wanted to call me. She said they would come back for the scheduled appointment, and she did. He did not. He just dropped her off. She stayed until the appointment was finished. We complimented her for having made the right decision and Glenwood High was called. I was so relieved and thankful.

Near the time of the last episode, Barbara and I were in her room heatedly disagreeing about something which I don't recall because of the incident which took over my attention. She foul-mouthed me, and because John heard her, he stormed into the room and angrily yelled at her. Then rage swelled; he grabbed her and started beating her head against the wall as his exploding passion took over! Suddenly, he cried out, "Oh my God—what am I doing?" He stopped immediately, realizing if he continued he would probably injure her seriously. The shocked, tearfully repentant daughter and stressed out, repentant dad understood better at that moment the power of rage. She never repeated what she had done to me, and John said, "I can't allow myself to get that enraged again. Until now I didn't even realize I had such a potential for violence. Now I know I'll have to work on preventing it the rest of my life." He did.

* * * *

Another day in the continuing Tate Saga, I received a call from Security at one of the large department stores at Belden Village Mall, near our home, because Patti and Carolyn were being held until we picked them up. They had been caught shoplifting a few cosmetics. What??! We were furious! Not only did we pick them up; the four of us also were given a report and an appointment with the counselor at juvenile court the next day. That night was the second part of humiliation for the girls after the first embarrassing one of being caught, lectured and detained at the store. As John and I railed at them for disgracing and dishonoring not only themselves, but also our family for the stealing, there were plenty of agonizing tears and apologies. They told us of the beginning "fun" of it and then how rotten they felt from their "episode". When John and I asked what motivated them to do it, they said a couple of neighborhood friends had been doing it, thought it was fun and encouraged them to do it. When I found out it was the children of the sweet, Catholic couple with ten children, I thought, "How can they keep track of all of their children's activities, when it was such a challenge for us with four?"

After interviewing us at court, the counselor said it was obvious the girls were not serious delinquents and came from a good family. And, since it was their first offense, they would be fined a modest amount, prohibited from shopping any more at that store, and released. We all went home relieved. The aftermath of that was that the girls had to pay the fine from their own meager monies and go to confession. Their final understanding from us was that John and I said we still loved them, and gave them hugs. We also said it was good they were caught, so hopefully, there would be no further thefts. As far as we knew, there were none.

52. BENEFICIAL INTERRUPTIONS

WHEN CHRISTINA WAS THREE years old, I felt the need to get her and me out of the house more often. Also, I wanted a good preschool program for her and I found what we needed at St. Mark's Episcopal Preschool Center at the church. When the woman director learned about my arts background and how I would teach music with singing and lots of movement, she asked further for ideas involving the children three through five years old. When she asked if I would do it for her school, I was delighted, and it would be the beginning of my new career path! I consented and stayed a school year. I enjoyed it immensely and that included the relationship with the woman director, who was so cooperative and considerate about Christina and my times for classes.

Even though I thought it was a good situation for me, the more I found out about Maria Montessori and the Montessori Method, the more I thought Christina might gain some additional benefits. A problem, then, was that it cost a lot more. She was accepted for fall '74, and in order to pay for it, I had to work more hours and get better pay. I was hired to work thirty hours a week at General Nutrition Center (GNC), located within Belden Village. It was for afternoons and evenings, so John had to help in the evenings at home with the children. It was with deep disappointment that I turned in my resignation at St. Mark's at the beginning of summer, even though it had been a start in the right direction for my teaching.

That summer I started back to college, also, thanks to John. One of the benefits he received from supervising one of his Akron University student teachers for 1972 was a course worth three credits and no tuition, which he or someone in his family could use before the deadline of 1975. When he offered it to me, I jumped at the chance! I qualified for an art course requirement for an elementary education degree. I chose *Design* and didn't mind the forty mile round trip commute. I received an A, which encouraged me to do more art work in the future.

53. LAMENTATIONS

BY CHRISTMAS DINNER AT our house, Dad was not feeling well, so it was good we treated him, Mom and Mary Jean's family for a change. Soon Dad developed pneumonia. By the time my John and the girls went back to school in January, I was able to enjoy the silence in our home, and it was marvelous! Then I developed laryngitis and the kids thought the silence was great, because I couldn't yell at them.

The rest of the year through August Dad Tate was weak. He had a bout with kidney stones and the polycythemia, which he had been struggling with for some time, continued to weaken him. The disease usually surfaces between the ages of 60 and 65, and is a rare disorder of the bone marrow which produces too many iron rich red blood cells which often collect in the spleen and cause it to swell. Another effect could be hemorrhaging. Regular phlebotomies were necessary then, a process which was similar to donating blood. According to his Jewish primary doctor whom we all respected, it was more commonly found in Eastern European Jewish men. We were not aware of any Jews in the family ancestry, but maybe someday we will find out if there were.

By the middle of September, Dad was in very poor condition. The doctors had told the family it was inhumane to keep him alive. We thought Dad should make the decision regarding his own life, but Mom was afraid it would break him up emotionally. Nevertheless, when he was given the chance, he said he'd rather be allowed to die than to go on like that, but then the medical team put him back in the hospital for more treatment and sent him home again soon afterward. We had to have constant contact with Mom and Dad.

On October 21, John went to Dad's Timken Mercy Hospital room late in the afternoon to visit him. Just as he entered there, it was total chaos! Mom and Mary Jean were wailing, because just moments before, Dad had hemorrhaged terribly all over his body in front of them, and had died instantly. His too thin body was still draining into the pool of blood when his son came in. The frantic medical personnel were starting to minister to Dad while some were getting ready to remove his mother and sister, so no one was blocking the doorway yet. Suddenly they had to remove three in-shock people. Soon there were no more rivers of blood, only rivers of tears.

Saracusta (prayer service in Romanian) was held two nights later at the Jacobs-Waltner Funeral Home, the place where many of the local Romanian-American families went for assistance during times of death. Mary

Jean and her husband John, together with John and me and our immediate families were sitting there with Mom.

It was the same the following morning at 10:00 A.M. at the sung Requiem Greek-Romanian Divine Liturgy led by Msgr. Carlo Capros. This Eastern Liturgy which predates the western Latin one was held within the small immigrant St. George Romanian Catholic Church on Seventh Street NE. Like Dad, Msgr. Capros was a recent immigrant who left Romania during the Communist regime that had been making life difficult for Catholics there.

The sacrament of marriage had ended for Mary and John, after forty-four years. The service of mercy and peace began with the tolling bell, calling people to pay last respects for John—a good man—who had suffered much. His friends and relatives as pall bearers slowly brought the heavy casket in, down the main aisle of the small church to rest in front of the iconostasis, and candles underneath the small, crystal chandelier below the blue sky and fluffy white clouds which were part of the artistry on the ceiling above.

Bilingual Dad had come to America from a village in the province of Transylvania Romania, speaking both Hungarian and Romanian because Hungary had control there at that time. Once here, he quickly became trilingual, but didn't gain more formal education beyond what he had up to his then current age of fourteen.

As an adult he became a citizen and asked for no more than the chance to work to provide for the family he loved so much. He worked hard in the steel mills and the Ford Motor Company, often in jobs where he sweat mightily in front of huge furnace fires to create steel, often to the point of physical exhaustion. He had usually worked the night shift, so he could garden and help his ailing wife by day. He had succeeded in these endeavors for his family, but they also had given him a lot of stress. Being a caregiver also prevented him from ever making a visit back to Romania, as his sister Vickie wanted him to do when she went to see their sister. He said he couldn't leave Mom long enough for that, even though there were other family members, including us, who could have taken care of her. Because my mother in-law was never really well all the time I knew her, the rest of the family assumed she would probably precede her husband in death. When that didn't happen, the stress factor loomed large as at least a partial cause for his illness. In his relationships with others, people liked him for his friendliness and sense of humor. My John had been very close to his father, and Mary Jean, his sister said that he was much like his dad. John senior lived to be only 65.

In the language of liturgy the service ended: "O merciful Savior, send your angels to conduct your departed servant to a place of refreshment, light and peace."

54. HAPPIER TIMES

FEBRUARY OF '75 WAS birthday time again for Christina, and since it was her fifth, we decided to give her a party. The main activity was taking the children to a youth symphony performance.

After John and I had attended a couple of jazz concerts with Christina at Peninsula, Ohio, near Cleveland, I decided I wanted to make the time to perform in one. Fortunately, for me, Canton was planning one to be held in March in the grand courtyard of the Cultural Center for the Arts and it was being organized by Walter "Moe" Klippert, the Peninsula organizer.

As I sat alone in the audience area before the concert began and noticed how many people were coming in, I started to feel insecure. I thought to myself, "Do I really want to go through with this? What if I get too nervous and forget my lyrics or music? What about my key for each?" But after the music started, "Yes, I do want to do it—I don't want to miss this opportunity—it's worth the risk!"

It was like a big sit-in, with musicians not only from Canton, but also, Akron, Cleveland, Peninsula, Pittsburgh, and Washington, D.C. There were no rehearsals ahead of time, and most of the ensembles that played were put together spontaneously during the concert by Moe, the reed man. This was the way it was in Peninsula, so I knew what to expect. I chose standard "oldies" New Orleans style songs to sing, hoping there wouldn't be any problems in accompanying me, because the musicians would know them. When I was called up, I gave the multi-city musician group the key for each of the three pieces and performed them. It was great! I didn't forget anything. The musicians were fun to perform with because they accompanied me perfectly. It had been worth the risk.

After the concert, I was invited to sing in Peninsula by Moe, and one of the musicians asked me to sing "St. James Infirmary" there. Another asked me to learn "Shiny Stockings" (a Frank Foster composition, and one of Ella Fitzgerald's performance pieces), which I eventually did. In the *Canton Repository* newspaper, writer Ralph Spencer wrote that over 1000 people attended, and that I sang "with pleasing effects", which encouraged me to keep singing. My tension after the concert was over and as it released, the burning stomach began. I went home and had to nurse it with a hot water bag the rest of the evening! I sang in Peninsula in April, and there was no hot water bag therapy needed.

John was doing very well in his Romanian language class with Professor George Leuca at Akron University. It was fun hearing him sound like a native Romanian. It helped that he had heard his parents speaking it when he was young.

Patti was happy to have received a little more than half of a scholarship from the Audubon Society for forestry camp and was looking forward to going in June.

After she came back home, she told us and wrote to her grandparents in Arizona that she had the best time with her outdoor classes for such things as tree identification and forest ecology while also having time to swim and go horseback riding. She was painting pictures again and created a beautiful sunburst with flying birds silhouetted in front of it.

Barbara *did* graduate early in June with flowers on her white graduation cap. She was accepted into the July—August Venture Blossom II art program at KSU, main campus, based on her art and recommendation from her high school art teacher. It ran for five weeks, was open to students who had completed their junior or senior years, and gave her college credits: She created art works and attended demonstrations and lectures by renowned artists from around the country. All the students had field trips plus free access to the concerts and Porthouse Theater plays at Blossom Music Center. Since there were also simultaneous music and theater programs for students at Blossom-Kent, it was possible for students in any of the three arts to meet and mingle. It was paid for by a combination of her own small earnings of kitty-care work and graduation gifts from Mom Tate and us.

Dear Grandpa and Grandma,

Sorry I haven't written you sooner, but I've been so busy down here at Kent. I really love it. I'm learning a lot. I am taking print making and design (where I use the wood shop). I am now working on an etching in metal. I had my picture taken for the paper doing my etching. I have seen the Cleveland Orchestra because I got a free pass from this course. I went with my roommate Cindy to her home in Cleveland, and we went to the Cleveland Museum of Art. It was so big and beautiful. Yesterday our two teachers took us down to a lake to make a water sculpture out of tire inner-tubes. We had so much fun. I wish I could go to school here this fall but I don't think I can afford it. Hope to see you soon.

Love, Barbara

Korb Guest House

KSU Kent, Ohio 44242

She didn't go to the main campus in the fall, but she worked full-time at the Scandinavian Health Spa during the day and attended the Stark branch near our place at nights. She thrived that school year because, as she said, "I love it here—they treat me like an adult!"

Carolyn was busy rehearsing "Peter Pan" in July after having taken the three day trip in June to Washington, D.C. with one of the student tours led by her dad. The plane flights were to and from Cleveland, and this is how she described the events:

Dear Grandma and Grandpa,

Sorry I haven't written in so long, but I have been very busy...

This year at the Players Guild we are doing the play 'Peter Pan'. I have the part as Wendy and it's great fun for Peter Pan and I really fly with harnesses and cables! The show opens this Wednesday and goes thru Sunday. We have so many people coming that we might have to make an extra performance. I've hardly been home for I've been going to rehearsals every day then building the set every night. I sure wish you could be here to see it...

This fall I'll be going into the 8th Grade at Taft and I can hardly believe it for this year went by so fast.

I went to Washington D.C. last month with a bunch of kids from school and Dad (the tour organizer). I was very excited for I had never been in a jet plane before and it's the greatest thing to do. It's a very beautiful city and so many things to do. I met a lot of really nice people from the other school who went with us. The girls in our hotel room had a blast at night playing tricks on the guys in the room beside us. It was only 3 days but I'd do it again for they were the 3 funnest days in my life! I took an awful lot of pictures in Washington D.C. and can't wait until they are developed.

I'm afraid I have to close now for I have to be at rehearsal in 30 minutes I miss and love you very much.

Love, Carolyn

The whole family went on opening night. It was awesome while I held my breath on and off when she was flying through the air. The whole cast production was done like professionals, and we were very proud, as indicated by our enthusiastic applause.

Carolyn was so busy, but still able to maintain her position as one of the top students at Taft.

John and I drove to Toronto and Hamilton, Ontario in October to participate in an ecumenical Catholic-Anglican/Episcopalian celebration. Our Episcopalian friend Al Gill, and his friends in Canada planned the event. Al, who was originally from England, had lived in Hamilton before he had come to live in the United States. In England and Canada he was considered Anglican; in the U.S. he was Episcopalian.

They were beautiful, sunny fall days going and coming back as we passed by colorful grapevines, loaded with grapes that hadn't been harvested yet in Pennsylvania. We paused a short while at Niagara Falls in New York, and were still able to make Hamilton that first night.

Highlights of the trip included the Eucharistic Celebration at Christ's Church Cathedral in Hamilton on Saturday, October 11. The welcome stated that "Ours is a house of prayer and praise for all people. Our principal service, Eucharist, or Holy Communion, is an act of Community." This pilgrimage to the cathedral was by fellow Christians in Ohio and parishioners at St. Alben's Parish in Hamilton.

The service was short and a meaningful celebration for John and me who believed that Catholics and Protestants serving together in unity was important. The reader was Al, and John and I were the presenters of the Bread and Wine. Musicians offered their talents, and the one who impressed John the most was Peter the piper, who with his bagpipes concluded the service by playing the hauntingly beautiful *Amazing Grace*, the iconic hymn for both Canadians and Americans.

We both enjoyed Toronto, and I thought it was a splendid example of the blending of both the old and new architecture downtown. First, we had a magnificent overall view of the city from an indoor observation deck atop the new, modern CN (Canadian National, originally the rail company that built it) Tower. Back on the street, I was admiring the beautiful, modern city hall when I was told it had been designed by a Finnish architect, Viljo Revell. "How understandable, I thought, as contemporary Finns are known for unencumbered, sleek designs for living—in architecture and otherwise. I was feeling fine as a Finn! The old, Romanesque city hall across the street from the new one looked good there.

We toured the historical wing of the huge Royal Ontario Museum and as we were walking away, we noticed a street performance of a costumed group dancing traditional Morris folk dances. I had heard of this Renaissance English country dancing, but had never seen any. For accompaniment there was a fiddle, a flute, and a drum. There were six men in white shirts and dark pants, with cascading ribbon streamers at their shins, upon which were tied multiple small bells, integral for the rhythms and vitality of the dances. In true peasant male fashion, the steps were vigorously sturdy, with stomping, kicking, and jumping. Their arms were generally linked backward and forward, then stretching up and down with the jumps and also twirling handkerchiefs in circles above their heads. I was delighted with their stellar act, rounding out my impressions of respecting both traditional and modern cultures in contemporary Toronto.

Al had another idea which reflected his British/Canadian roots, and one that was fun for all involved, two months later. He belonged to the Gyro Club, a fraternal friendship organization, with clubs in Canada and the United States. His local club celebrated Christmas that year at the Congress Lake Inn in Hartville, near Canton. The lovely, decorated program for the night stated on the cover: "Ye Ancient and Honorable Order of Gyro and Their Faire Ladyes Celebrate Ye Merrie Christmas at Ye Congress Lake Inn Friday, December 12 in the Year of Our Lord 1975. Inside, at the top, there was "A Description of ye Evening's Festivities": Beginning with a most hearty and gracious welcome and some faire imbibing of ye liquid refreshment; Then all be served a festive banquet of greate delight."

After eating was the entertainment. With a young and handsome priest with a great voice from my parish at my side, I performed Christmas songs and carols as part of the program: "Guitar and voice will then combine to charm Ye Gyros and Ye Guests. So lend an ear to Ye Singing Priest, Father James Johnston and Dolores Tate, a Maiden Faire."

55. LETDOWNS, BUT ALSO MUCH LOVE

NOT EVERYTHING THAT HAPPENED in 1975 was happiness or joy.

During summer, the everyday life of six people taking showers in a tub with only a shower curtain in our one little bathroom had taken its toll. To our dismay and unknown to us earlier, there was leakage that had caused the floor to sag and a gaping hole beneath it in the garage ceiling. Norm, our cousin, came over and helped John tear out the old floor and put in the new. John then tackled the walls around the tub, replaced them and did a professional looking job of putting in the new ceramic tile which looked better than the original, there only since the sixties when the house was built.

A year earlier, Dad received a call from his union that there was a job opening at the test site. He had been on out of work since February because the union had been on strike. He returned because he and Mom needed the income desperately. He passed the pre-physical well enough to get a higher security rating than he had before. The next day he was given a stiffer physical, passed it and was hired to work in the Air Force section. He opted to live in the dorm on base during the week and come home for weekends again, as he had before.

Then in 1975 after a medical examination Dad was sent the following letter:

This is to state that Mr. Hill has been examined by our Occupational Physicians in the Las Vegas Medical Facility and we find him to be totally disabled due to chronic pulmonary disease. His breathing capacity is approximately 30 percent of normal, which makes him totally and permanently unable to carry on his usual work of painter.

We recommend that he receive any and all medical disability benefits available to him.

Very truly yours,

L. K., M.D.

Medical Director

Because of that "bomb", all of a sudden they were panicked because they were without income. It seems Mom wasn't working, either. He couldn't get unemployment payments because of the disability, and the Social Security disability funds would take 5 or 6 months and were not retroactive. Small contributions and a lump sum from his union *would* be retroactive, but not available for about 3 months. His modest union dues of $56.00 were due and had to be paid, or he wouldn't be able to receive assistance from the union.

Their dog Laddie, who was like a member of the family, became ill and was too sick to save any longer, so had to be put to sleep. They had to leave a bill for future payment. Fortunately, they didn't have credit card bills to pay because they never thought it was wise for their income to have the cards. That was a bright spot in an otherwise depressing situation.

In the beginning, Warren, Byrle and we sent what we could. That took care of the mortgage and some other bills for the first month. Dad did a little painting for some of their neighbors, and that helped pay for some groceries and other daily necessities. Mom said in one of her letters, "Dad must either get a haircut or buy a violin, so guess the haircut is cheaper! I told him he was right in style, but he's uncomfortable with long hair." (Humor was helpful.)

Unfortunately, Christina could no longer attend Montessori School because of the cost, but we were fortunate in that public school kindergarten had finally been added. For her, William R. Day School was only a half block from our house and next door to Taft. She loved it.

In August Blanche Feiman, our original Jewish panelist on the Panel, passed away from the same illness that took Esther Brown. She was only 60—too young— and was a loss not only to me, other panelists, and her family, but also her reform synagogue, Temple Israel, and the Canton community. Also like Esther Brown, she was a native of Kansas City, Missouri. She and her surgeon husband sent their four children to the Canton Public Schools, in the advanced classes. She was an educator, having received both her bachelor and master degrees at the University of Chicago and an honorary degree for her work in Jewish education. For 25 years she volunteered her services as principal of Temple Israel Religious School, and became an expert on Jewish history, religion, literature, the Bible and Israel.

Even while helping Mom and Dad, and with college expenses looming in our near future for Barbara and me, I was able to travel by plane to Mom and Dad's for Thanksgiving week. Byrle and Warren were there also. It was so good being with all of them and having no emergency health traumas. John sent me wonderful cards:

I miss you and love you so much. Have a real good time and greet everyone.

He finished in Romanian:

La revedere, (Good-bye,)

Cu mult drag, (With much longing,)

John

11-25-75

Dearest Dolores,

I'm writing this from my cold, lonely bed tonight. How I do miss you 😊 You are constantly on my mind. I'm so happy for you that you got to make this trip 😊, but I'm sure looking forward to being with you again ♡ Sweat all again for me. I love you — I love you — I love you — I love you — I love you

John x x x

And this card.

56. FULFILLMENTS IN THE ARTS

WHEN BLOSSOM AND PAUL Perkins fully retired they moved to the country, to the little town of Carrollton, less than an hour away from Canton. They bought a small farmstead, complete with house and barn. We had picnics there and took the girls with us. Those of us who had been going to the Canton Jewish Community Center to do international folk dancing led by Blossom and Virginia were now going barn dancing as well. It was great fun as the recorded music played, Blossom, the teacher, would call the square dances and Paul, the lawyer, would play his fiddle.

It was at one of these outings in fall of 1976 when Blossom said,

"Dolores, I want to give you my books and have you take my place for teaching the children at the Canton Art Institute!"

I was stunned! "Me? Are you sure?"

She replied "Yes!"

Blossom was so good at what she did with the children and an icon in the Canton arts community, that it was an honor to have been chosen by her. It was also an awesome responsibility to try to follow in her footsteps (and her runs, hops, and jumps). I felt blessed and said "Thank you! I would love to!"

She was no longer with the music and movement program at Canton Art Institute (CAI) after she moved to the country and her replacement was faltering. I was still working at GNC, and had been accepted into a winter course toward an elementary education degree: *Physical Education Activities for the Elementary Child* taught by Assistant Professor Kathi Walz at KSU Stark Campus. It was the best university class for my future teaching. Ms. Walz, who was from Germany, knew I could do my student teaching with first graders at St. Michael's School, even though I was only a sophomore. A bonus in doing my student teaching at St. Michael's was that Christina was in the first grade there and benefited from it.

Near the end of my course, while I was still working at GNC, I went to see Mr. Joseph Hertzi, Director of the CAI, whom I didn't know, but was husband of the girls' former art teacher, and he hired me. By the spring session I was teaching, the beginning of eight years of happiness doing what I loved in an environment that was absolutely beautiful—the art museum within the Canton Cultural Center for the Arts. I was teaching in the arts again and would continue to do so!

* * * *

I had discovered the fun of folk dance in one of my high school gym classes. It was only for a short time but the wedding of movement with music was enough to help me appreciate it the rest of my life and was incorporated into my teaching. John's experience had been different than mine. As a kid he had seen ethnic dancing at Romanian weddings. His mother would do some, but his father would do none. We never found out if dad didn't have the confidence for it, or if he just didn't like it. After I started at the Jewish Center, John would usually go with me. He tried dancing, but he became frustrated because as he said, "Just as I'm learning a dance or more, they're replaced by others the next month."

At one point I said, "Do you realize what a rich and beautiful heritage you have in Romanian music and folk dance?"

"Well, yes, since I've seen *Ciocirlia* and the Duquesne Tamburitzans perform some of it, it is exciting, but I don't know how I'm going to learn any."

Then it happened. Not Romanian, but Greek! After he saw Anthony Quinn joyfully do a Greek dance in the movie *Zorba the Greek*, he was inspired. Not long afterward he noticed there was a Balkan Folk Dance night course offered evenings at Akron University and taught by Richard Vydra. John did well enough that when he had finished the course, Richard invited him to the Croatian-American Hall in Akron where he could continue learning dances from Eastern Europe informally for fun on Friday nights. John went and took five year old Christina, who learned some of the dances with him while I was working at GNC. Most of the dances were Croatian, with occasional Greek, Serbian, Israeli, Hungarian and Romanian. Eventually I was able to join him there and when Richard formed a performance group for the Nation of Nations Festival in Akron, John and I were a part of it.

In 1975 we learned of a small Romanian dance ensemble being taught by Director Valerie Musat at St. George Romanian Orthodox Church. We were acquainted with Father Tofan, the priest there, and he thought it would be good for us to dance in it, and introduced us to Mrs. Musat. She graciously invited us, and what followed were some happy times of performing.

Musat, an excellent teacher who had taken a youth group from Canton to perform at the 1964 New York World's Fair had John and me performing in 1976 with the adult group for the ecumenical Canadian-American Exchange when the Canadians were here after our trip to Canada. We also performed for the North Canton Teachers' Association and the Gyro Club.

The name of our performance group was *Transylvanian Folkloric Ensemble (TFE)*, and that included the exceptional Romanian-American musicians. The majority of Romanian immigrants, including both sides of John's family, came to that area of Ohio from Transylvania, a western province near the Carpathian Mountains. By fall we were fortunate enough to perform in the inaugural International Festival of Stark County, which also included Bicentennial in its name for that year. The festival, which became annual, was established to celebrate the different Canton area ethnic groups, which John and I thought was a splendid idea to learn about and enjoy our neighbors. There was a parade from Canton's downtown Central Plaza to its newly renovated Memorial Auditorium. Besides performances, there were booths with artifacts and delicious ethnic foods. John Serban Jr., a descendant Transylvanian and member of St. George's, was chairman of the festival and continued so for a few years. In stating the festival's goal, he stated: "It is an attempt to bring together many people from many different cultural backgrounds into a common bond of sharing, friendship, and good will. We are all proud to be Americans and equally proud of each cultural heritage that has contributed to the Stark County experience."

The crowning, highly emotional achievement for my John "the non-dancer" happened in June when he and our *TFE* (minus me) performed in Washington, D.C. for the Smithsonian Bicentennial Festival of American Folk Life in front of the Lincoln Memorial! Some of the male dances even required high stepping fast twists, turns and slapping of the thighs and calves while bells below the knees jingled for further excitement, and he was up to it all.

For the five days of performances John experienced a deep sense of connection between his own life and the history of Romanian folk culture, which was intensified by a professional folk ensemble from Romania, performing next to our group at different times. Our American ensemble of male and female dancers had no singer and fewer musicians than the Romanian ensemble, but our musicians were led by professional music professor John Lazar, formerly of Romania The beautifully attired Romanian group had a female singer and traditional instruments such as the *taragot* (similar to the clarinet and the oboe, but simpler), shepherd's flute, pan pipes, *cimbalom* (dulcimer), and violin. There were female as well as male dancers. Adding to the excitement of the circle (hora) and open circle (line) dancing and music are the *strigaturi* (poetic, often spontaneous, humorous shouts) among the male dancers. All the performances from both groups were excellent.

While the Canton group was leading the *Paranita*, a Romanian hugging and kissing audience participation dance, there was an interruption from a "breaking news" public announcement from the Washington Romanian Embassy. Barbara, one of the dancers, received the great news that the Romanian government had granted permission for her to marry George, a young Romanian professional folk dancer! Spontaneously, there was singing by visitors and performers of "Here Comes the Bride" before everyone settled down and the dance resumed.

Another emotional high began that first day on the Mall when Lazar discovered in the other group a friend and former classmate of his from the Romanian music conservatory. It was an unexpected surprise, so when they, in stunned awareness saw each other, there were passionate shouts, hugs and great tears of joy. Then, not only did they perform every day, but as my John remarked with a smile, "those crazy musicians played music every night at the dorm until 5 A.M.!" (It was a Georgetown University dorm where the two groups stayed during the nights.)

All these Romanian performances were part of the "Old Ways in the New World" category. Twenty-four foreign countries participated with their cultural cousins in America, creating an international family reunion on the Mall. In other categories and places, there were also Native Americans.

During one break from performing he visited the Hirshhorn Museum and Sculpture Garden and wrote me a humorous post card:

Dear Dolores: I made arrangements to put all your art work in this building. Get busy and produce! I miss you and wish you could be here to share these experiences.

I love you. John

* * * *

Back home, our Barbara had been air brushing beautiful nature scenes on a van and a motorcycle to earn money and was able to transfer in the fall to the main KSU campus to major in Graphic Design. She found furnished housing with Margaret, a graduate art student, in a small house in the community of Ravenna, near Kent. It was decorated with art works and lots of potted plants. Even though they did their own cleaning, cooking, and laundry, Barbara was happy, thriving, enjoying her independence, and had mellowed out some. She also had gone to counseling on campus and as a result of that decided to completely sever ties with Mark. She was finally able to see that it was not good for her to continue being with him. It was a *huge* relief to us as well.

* * * *

In 1978, John's cousin Gene Hedrick published a cookbook which he dedicated to his Romanian-American mother Victoria and entitled it *FROM ROUMANIA WITH LOVE* (using an older spelling of the country's name), subtitled *An Old World Kitchen*. Collaborating with artist J. Comstock, it was a beautiful paperback book written in appreciation of his Romanian roots, not only with recipes, but also with commentaries of the living history that he experienced growing up in Canton: *With words, as well as foods, it is in the sharing that the pleasure comes.*

Though his grandparents on both sides of his family and his mother who came over at 11 years old were living in America,

...the Romanian culture stayed alive. Each Saturday at church, language lessons were held and I remember hearing more Romanian than English while I was growing up. And I remember, too, that cooking, cooking, cooking for the next gathering of the clan was a constant activity.

In the afternoons, under the large grape arbor that produced wine each September, the relatives gathered at the tables and benches to argue politics, scream about the Bolsheviks and Nazis and buzz about the current union unrest. However humble, there was always plenty to eat in a Transylvanian kitchen...And, underneath, there was the joy of preparing it in a place where we were free. The memories of the war years in Europe—-of the food shortages and the armies moving back and forth through the villages—stayed alive in my mother's kitchen. It always seemed to me that there was a special beauty that here we were, day in and day out, doing what was common, but so thankfully received.

57. MORE ROMANIAN DELIGHTS AND CHALLENGES

IN EARLY MARCH OF 1966, my parents had attended a perfor-
mance by *Ciocirlia, The Romanian Folklore Ensemble,* and were so excited. Dad
had to write his impressions:

Mother and I attended The Romanian Folklore Ensemble at the new music cen-
ter in L.A. last Sunday. The entire troupe from Romania was indeed the rarest of
treats to the eyes and ears. They have a very distinct type of music my ears have never
before had the pleasure of hearing. They were new sounds that were very delightful!
Their instruments are different also, especially the pan-pipe. I've never heard such
clarity of tone from such a small instrument.

The group is currently on their first tour of 38 cities in the United States and
Canada. I certainly hope it will come to your area and you will have a chance to at-
tend. It will be one of your most thrilling afternoons in a long time.

Here's hoping you are all well and happy. Much love to you all,

Dad and Grand-pop

Yes, it was thrilling—we had seen them in Cleveland at that time.

Not long after the Smithsonian Washington trip in 1976, George (Gigi),
the professional folk dancer arrived in Canton. He and Barbara were married in the beautiful ceremony at St. George's Romanian Orthodox Church.
Very soon afterwards he chose and trained two folk dance groups—one
with young children, and the other with young adults. Each was larger than
our performance group. They were drawn from both St. George Orthodox
and St. George Byzantine Catholic churches, plus others who didn't attend
either. Gigi said John and I were too old to dance (in our forties and experienced), but Christina, who already had a little dance experience at the Croatian Hall was chosen, and was the youngest in the troupe at the age of seven.

I then became a seamstress, along with women at St. George's Orthodox Church, sewing authentically patterned costumes for the children. By
the time of the second annual International Festival of Stark County in
September 1977, both groups, which included Christina, rode on a special
Romanian float in the parade, which was on a longer route than the year
before. Then they performed once for both days as *Doina Romanian Folklore*
Ensemble. They danced like pros and we were proud!

I don't even remember how we met some fine Romanian-Americans
from Akron and how they learned I could sing. Maybe it was through John's

meeting Dr. George Leuca at Akron University for his Romanian language course, and Leuca's friendship with Professor Julius Burigan. The latter was born in Romania and was a former principal and teacher in a music school there. I was so fortunate, because once I was given the chance to sing folk and Doina songs in the Romanian language, they were my coaches.

Joining us was tenor Josef Bujorian. Symphony violinist Leuca and accordionist Burigan accompanied our solos and Burigan also played accordion pieces and accompanied his own vocals at our first gig. *Musica Romaneasca* was performed on February 27, 1977 at the KSU Student Center in Kent. It was sponsored by the Cultural Studies Group there to foster the appreciation and enjoyment of Romanian culture and it was open to the public. The organization was guided by Dr. Glee Wilson, Director of the Romanian Studies Program through the Department of History. Mary Lynn, student from Canton and St. George's, was president of the American-Romanian Cultural Studies and helped with the planning of the concert. It was fitting for us to be at Kent State, for it was a repository of Romanian literature and art. Dr. Anderson, resident ethnomusicologist, was also one of the persons in the appreciative audience. We had a good turnout, which included John, and many favorable comments. One of Leuca's female family friends wrote a nice note on March 5:

Dear George:

Just a note to tell you how very much we enjoyed the program last Sunday...I heard many, many good comments from the people we were with as well as others we talked with during intermission.

Two of the best signs that you reached your audience were Frank's obvious enjoyment even though he understood not one word and the fact that my mother was moved to tears by a couple of the pieces...

Please pass along my appreciation to the other members of your troupe. They were all wonderful and seemed to have a genuine feeling for the music, which was obvious in their performances. Thank you, and keep up the fine work.

Love, G.

Our second gig on August 14 was in Cleveland and we were written up in *America*, the leading Romanian-English newspaper for Canada and the United States. After Gigi had experienced my singing he asked me to do the same for the *Doina* group, at the September '77 folk festival, which I did.

At the November 1977 Conference of Romanian History and Culture at KSU, *Doina* was not involved. It was entitled *Patriotism and Independence*, celebrating the centennial of Romanian independence. It was two full days with films. Scholars from Kent State and other American universities, the Romanian Library of New York City, and Romania made presentations. Organizing it all was history professor Dr. Wilson.

At the Saturday evening banquet, Professor Leuca gave the opening remarks and performed with his violin. Professor Burigan performed on his accordion and also accompanied some of his own singing. Bujorian, and I sang solos in Romanian accompanied by Burigan on the accordion. For one of my pieces, I sang a vindictive Roma (gypsy) song with violin.

There were also performers under the tutelage of Ms. Botoman of Ohio State University. Overall, the conference was very successful and made the newspapers in Romania. There were Romanian centennial concerts at St. George's in Canton for *Doina* with Christina and my participations and St. Mary's Orthodox Church in Cleveland with the Kent State concerts group. After I sang *Cobzar Batran* in Canton, there were tears in the eyes of many in attendance, for it was a long standing favorite, especially of older immigrants, about the cobza (forerunner of the lute) musician.

At St. Mary's, there was great fun when Julius sang jokes in Romanian as he accompanied himself on the accordion. He almost had them rolling in the aisles! After the concert and my participation also, I walked away from the hall by myself and experienced a rush of overwhelming joy—a holistically happy, healthy feeling which was never exceeded. It didn't have to get better because I didn't think it possible to feel any better than that!

* * * *

Unfortunately, since Dad Tate died, my Romanian mother-in-law had not been thriving. In addition to still lamenting her loss, she fell and broke her hip. She was operated on, but that didn't work out too well, so then we realized she couldn't live alone anymore. There was no way we could have her at our then present house where we were bursting at the seams with that three bedroom house accommodating six people. So we and she decided to sell our houses to buy a larger one. It worked out very well. She divided half of the proceeds from her house with us, and half with her daughter and son-in-law. She would live with us and Mary Jean would be in charge of all her medical care, taking her to all her doctor and hospital visits. We moved May, 1977, and celebrated Patti's graduation in June at the age of sixteen.

The new house on Elberta Avenue was beautiful, much larger and about a mile from John's school. It was a brick ranch with shutters, gorgeous landscaping with large trees, flowering bushes, a vegetable garden plot and a small patio with gas grill, on two and a half acres. We gave Mom the master bedroom that had its own bathroom. She was able to walk with a cane. Our TV was in the large family room off the kitchen, where Mom could sit and watch TV, since that was practically all she wanted to do because she never felt well. There was a bit of conflict about it at first, because she wanted us to put a TV in the living room, which was what she was used to, since she had never had a family room. However, we were firm in telling her, "Sorry, but this living room, which is open to the formal dining area, is for music, meals and good conversation, not TV. Besides, the family room is lovely too, with bookcases, a hanging plant, new comfortable furniture and a beautiful dogwood tree visible out the window with a cushioned window seat!" Also, there was a half bathroom, and French doors that led to the patio and back yard. She never did consent to be in there, but grumbled and resigned herself to her new family room environment. She was on a lot of prescribed medications that contributed to her sullenness, caused side effects, and unfortunately didn't seem to help her enough.

John fixed the large downstairs room for Carolyn and Patti to share, and the house and yard were large enough so that all the girls would spread themselves around so they wouldn't have to interfere much with Grandma. Playing with Pepe, her little Chihuahua was fun, though.

58. DAD'S DEMISE

BESIDES MOM TATE AND her health problems, there was Dad Hill. By 1975 it was too late for preventive medicine for him. The only hopes for possible cures were based on crises and emergency treatments in Arizona and Nevada. By the end of March, 1977 he was in Mohave General Hospital in Kingman, Arizona for 17 days with pneumonia He seemed to gain extra strength though after his near death experience when he saw the beautiful, bright light. At that point he said, "I can't die. I can't leave Peggy alone." He then came home and had some measure of calm and recuperation at their quiet country home until the next episode.

One of the issues which should have been stressed by the doctors at that time was the connection of smoking to cardiovascular and lung diseases, including cancer. To his credit, Dad's primary care physician in Kingman told Dad that smoking was the most harmful habit he had.

John and I decided that I should be with my Mom and Dad, so by the last week of July I flew to Las Vegas, the closest commercial airport to their place, which was two hours away. Mom picked me up. Shortly before I arrived, though, Dad had gone first to the emergency room at Mohave, and after a couple of days it was determined that he should go to Phoenix for further care. Mom and I took him to St. Luke's Hospital, approximately four hours from Kingman, for graft surgery on his left leg to remove an artery blockage. It was done on August 2, and he was there 12 days, so I had to leave for Canton before he was out, leaving only Mother to take him home.

They were both strong survivors so far, even though his recuperation went more slowly than expected. By December Dad had improved and Mom wrote this gratifying letter on December 4, a time of respite:

Dear Ones—

We had such a wonderful time when Byrle, Warren, and the girls were here for Thanksgiving. The weather was lovely. On another day Dad and Warren prepared and painted the south end of the house. This is the hardest and highest to do so Dad was so happy to have Warren do the high work. They enjoyed working together and a robin kept them company.

What a beautiful day we have here today. Dad could hardly wait to have breakfast over so he could go out and paint the front of the house. He feels good and is having a ball!

By January 1978, the respite was over. Dad was rushed to the emergency room again at Mohave on the 5th and was in the intensive care unit for 24 hours. He was treated with oxygen for his lungs, electrocardiograms for his heart, and had draws for blood analysis. He was released on the 11th by Dr. R. with orders to go again soon to Phoenix for further observation and testing at the premier medical institute, believed to be the supreme place for heart surgeries in Arizona. A health history and physical exam were done January 23 by cardiologist Dr. K., who ordered further tests. He and Mom went back home only to return on February 1st at St. Joseph's Hospital on the 2nd, and then he was kept there through the 4th. The procedures showed blockages in three of his arteries, so Dr. K. scheduled cardiac surgery for March 3rd with "Dr. Arrogance", top surgeon at the institute. "Dr. Arrogance" was considered the best to be had, so Dad was confident he would be in good hands, would survive the surgery and go back to a normal life as had acquaintances of his who had experienced bypass surgeries and had done just that.

On the 3rd Dad's surgery was performed and considered successful. However, the surgeon never came to see my father after that time nor anytime in the future, which appalled the whole family and overly stressed Dad. He was in intensive care for six days, after which he went to a semiprivate room until his release on the 16th. While there, Dr. S., from the Center for Chest Diseases performed a thoracentesis to remove fluid from his lung area and put him in the ICU for 3 days. Dr. K., the cardiologist, made 12 visits to see him.

After just a short while at home he entered Mohave General in Kingman again on April 10, and spent 18 days there with 7 of those in the intensive care unit. He had his first heart attack and then heart failure! By the 28th Dr. R. determined Dad needed to go back to Phoenix on an emergency basis, for he had by then a blood clot from the heart surgery in the tube from his kidney to the bladder, cutting off oxygen to the kidney. He was flown by air ambulance to Phoenix, then rushed to St. Joseph Hospital where he was met by Dr. S., the urologist. Dad almost died that night! He was given a blood thinner and a cystoscopy was done on the 29th. His life was spared, but he lost one kidney. I flew to Las Vegas on the 29th. Warren and Byrle arrived at Mom and Dad's by car from California and on the 30th they, Mom and I drove to Phoenix and we were with Dad for three days. He was in the hospital until May 12.

From July 17 through the 29 he was back at Mohave General where he had multiple treatments for his chronic conditions.

In the meantime, during these agonizing experiences with my family, Patti had bought a car. She was able to take a vacation from her job, and Barbara was on break from KSU, so they made plans for driving out to the West Coast with a stop in Kingman to see their grandparents. Patti always enjoyed the desert; Barbara, not so much. Fortunately, though, they were happy to see Dad and Mom in August when Dad was not in a hospital! It was a gratifying visit for all. They also enjoyed seeing San Francisco, Lake Tahoe and Southern California, where they saw Warren, Byrle and their cousins. Overall they had a great trip and had no car problems!

Dad started getting oxygen therapy at home that same August of '78, but then was back again anyway in Mohave General in September for 15 days, 4 of which were in intensive care for the same chronic conditions. The hospital personnel knew he wasn't ready for home yet, but they did move him to a regular room for the rest of his time there, making him happy.

I flew out again in December for Christmas, but Dad was back in Mohave General Hospital on the 23rd. Eight-year-old Christina had written a note for me to take with me addressed to Mrs. *Arnalad* Hill:

Dear Grandma, I hope you are praying for Grandpa because I am too. So pleace pray for him. He's my last Grandpa and I don't want him to die or you either because I love both of you so pleace for me and Patti, Carolyn, Barb, and my Dad. Love, Chris

Warren and Byrle drove in again from California. The family was elated because he was given permission to spend Christmas day with us at home. He spent most of his time with us in his bed. Seeing his handsome profile of his face and full head of not very much gray hair has lingered in my memory ever since.

The problem was—-he didn't know any of us! He was on so many medications he was like a zombie! By the time Warren and Byrle took him back to the hospital and went to their hotel room, I was devastated. I went on his bed and the sobbing began. I couldn't stop, so eventually Mom came in and lay down beside me. She started by self-identifying with me. "I've cried so much, I don't have any tears left." Then, this ever patient and compassionate woman I was blessed to have as my mother lay with me, spoke softly at times, and stroked my head while I continued to sob for a couple of hours. It was the last time I saw my father alive, though I felt like he was gone already. That Christmas Day for me was joyless.

With the New Year, 1979, there was renewed hope. On January 14 Mom wrote that after taking him for his daily wheelchair ride at the hospital, he was able to take short walks by holding onto the wheelchair and pushing it.

He spent 4 more days in Mohave General, and then on the 18th bringing him home was another drama. Mom's neighbor Jack had gone with Mom and just as they were leaving, there was a rare, sudden snow storm! Coyote Pass, the road they needed to get back home from Kingman was suddenly closed and they were not allowed to go through. The medications they had with them for Dad were only the two they had just filled, and he would need the others at home soon. Then, as Mom shared in her letter to us, "I was upset, but Jack saved the day!" He tried the road that led toward Oatman and then took Prescription (Yes!?) Road across Golden Valley to Highway 68. It was a slow go, but they arrived at their destination safely, and Dad received the rest of his prescriptions.

In the early part of February Dad was having extreme pain in his left leg, so Dr. R., his primary care physician, consulted with Dr. K., a cardiologist who would fly in once a week on Thursdays to Kingman. After communicating on the phone with Mom and Dad, he and Dr. R. decided Dad should enter Southern Nevada Memorial Hospital for tests, cautioning that Dad's heart would not be able to tolerate any great surgery. On February 11 he entered that hospital in Las Vegas, two hours away. They learned that the same leg that had the surgical graft in 1977 had developed complications and gangrene had set in! So it would not spread, his leg had the necessary amputation on February 20. Warren, Byrle, and Mother were there, but I was unable to be with them.

Dad and Mom went home the evening of March 1st, only to return by midnight because he had suffered cardiac arrest again. Back at Southern Nevada, he was given heart resuscitation and was in and out of ICU until the 18th when he was moved to a regular room. One of his doctors said Dad didn't need so many medications, and took him off some. How great that was, because then his hallucinations ceased and he knew his surroundings better again. The doctor also said another reason he sometimes talked "way out there" is because his heart couldn't pump enough oxygen to his brain, so he continued to get oxygen often from a machine. He was there until March 30th when he could only be released to a convalescent health center in Kingman. He finished March there and stayed the whole month of April. Then it was back to Mohave General in May until the same convalescent center took over. While he was at Mohave, a Methodist minister, Rev. Bussey, visited him, putting him back in touch with a Methodist minister he could respect again, like Rev. Doran in Pittsburg. He liked the young minister a lot, and with him, received the peace of God for his suffering soul.

Everybody who worked at Mohave probably knew Arnie—he had been there so many times and had voiced his appreciation for their constant help. He often didn't mind being in hospital environments because they reminded him of the happy times he had working as an orderly at Minneapolis General Hospital assisting Sister Elizabeth Kenny from Australia in the early '40's, helping her with exercises for polio patients.

Even with those enduring memories, though, Dad's constant "visits" to hospitals had eventually become exhausting to both him and Mom, and he didn't like being in the convalescent center at all. Every time he was there, Mom would visit daily. By the time he was back in May, Mom listened to his complaints, scrutinized his care and saw that it was negligent and awful! Once she discovered that, she said, "That's it! I'm taking him home!" The personnel said she couldn't do that because she wouldn't be able to handle it. But, they didn't know Peggy! She said, "I'll find a way!" And, she did! She was able to get a hospital bed with a pulley on loan from the American Cancer Society, had it delivered to the adjoining room off the living room, on the other side of the wall from the kitchen, and took over his care. Dad was so happy to be home and appreciative to Mom and the Cancer Society. The next month my beloved father went to his final peace after his lungs and heart needed a rest from the struggles they had valiantly fought for so long.

Shortly after Mom walked into their kitchen after tending to Dad's needs the morning of June 18, Dad left her quietly. At that moment, a jarring, electric-like shock rushed through her body, then left quickly. She sensed what had happened and rushed to his side and lay down beside him to weep, to thank God that his suffering was over, and that she had him through 44 years of a good marriage, which ended too soon.

Arnie couldn't have had a better wife than Peggy. Her plants and paintings brought beauty and joy into both their lives. Her optimism, depth of love, wisdom and patience with him helped them both through the tough times. She handled the finances and was a good cook. She had the more difficult role in their relationship.

Dad was only 65—too young, we all said. Genetically, he had come from sturdy stock. Both his Finnish parents, born in the late 1800's, were hearty, and lived longer. His dad, with two wives, had fathered 14 children and lived to 79. When Maria, his first wife, died after having had 5 children, Grandpa married my grandmother Sophia, who was Maria's sister. Then, Grandma gave birth, not only to Dad, but also to eight others, including two who didn't survive. She lived to be 88. Though Dad's paternal family history is still lost to us in Finland, his maternal grandparents survived the trip to America from the Tornio River Area of Finland and Sweden near the Arctic Circle. After working on farms in Minnesota, they established a farm of their own in North Dakota with their four sons through the Homestead Act. They farmed that land, raised cattle and horses and built a two story home. They also raised five daughters, assisted raising a few grandchildren, and lived into their 70's.

June 19 was John's and my 25th Wedding Anniversary. To honor it, we planted a pin oak in our front yard, as much for our tree-loving dad as for ourselves.

59. ADDENDUM

THE JUNE 22 FUNERAL attendance was small, with only 30 of us in the Tucker Funeral Home Chapel in Kingman. Warren and Byrle were there with Dawn and Lisa, but only I represented our family. Unfortunately, we couldn't afford plane flights for five more people, so John stayed home with the girls and his mother. There were friends from the valley, where Mom and Dad lived, and Rev. Bussey, the minister from St. John's Methodist Church in Kingman, who gave a comforting eulogy and service. I gave the other eulogy and sang the passionate piece *Finlandia* successfully after breaking down and crying during two rehearsals with the organist before the service. Mother held up pretty well, considering all that had happened to Dad, and her loss. She shared with us, "I lost my darling and best art critic, but I have had so many wonderful experiences with him, for which to be thankful."

There were beautiful flower arrangements surrounding the open casket. Seeing him in that wasn't the way Warren and I wanted to remember our father, but Mother insisted on having him in the casket, even though he was cremated shortly afterwards.

The classical *Finlandia*, composed by patriotic Finnish Composer Jean Sibelius, was Dad's favorite piece and is loved by many. It has been used often as a hymn, with various words written for it. The passages I sang were brief and from the composer Lloyd Stone. They were published in United Methodist hymnals and were the best description of how my father felt:

This is my song, oh God of all the nations,

A song of peace for lands afar and mine;

For other hearts in other lands are beating

With hopes and dreams, and dreams the same as mine.

Oh hear my song, oh God of all the nations,

A song of peace for their land and for mine.

Concluding the service was recorded symphony music of German composer Johannes Brahms. It was the last movement, Allegretto Grazioso of Brahms' Concerto #2, Opus 83, which was another favorite of my dad's, and uplifting to all of us there.

As my mother had said, "Your dad was a musician, not a warrior!" During the latter part of WWII, Dad's draft board had plans for him to enter the military and he had passed his physical in San Francisco. He had no desire to kill other humans as a combatant so indicated his desire to serve in the

Merchant Marines instead, which was the commercial fleet of the U.S. It was non-combatant and non-military, but delivered troops and supplies to the military during times of war. It had a high risk factor, and during WWII suffered the highest casualty rate of any of the branches of the military.

Then, by government grace and possibly the Grace of God as well, they didn't take him, because the war was winding down, he had turned 30 years old, and he had a wife and two young children.

He was passionate about social justice and sometimes got into trouble for it because he also had a temper which would flair up at times in discussions that led to it with others. After he was a supervisor for workers at Disneyland he was fired after standing up for Negroes in a fiery vocal exchange at his superior's home in Southern California. He and Mom had been invited to dinner there and when the discussion afterward had become heated, Dad lost his "cool", and the host thought the rhetoric was threatening. What he didn't know about Dad was that he had never been—and never was—violent to others. Any violence he manifested had been self-destructive, smoking and drinking too much. He never drank at his jobs, or while driving. It was always at home, and usually on weekends. And he had a spouse who willingly joined him.

One of Dad's friends who had worked with him in construction, not a painter, came to my parents' house after the funeral that day. He said, "Every painter I have known became an alcoholic." This was before lead was removed from paint, as it was eventually in 1978, too late for Dad and many others. Knowing what damage breathing those fumes in paint, shellac and varnish causes, one can understand better why many would use alcohol to soothe their pain.

So, Dad and his health problems were complicated in a number of ways. But he taught me much just by living and occasionally sharing what he believed about love of life, the arts and culture, his family, his Creator and nature. He was opposed to thought control, hatred, greed and other causes of poverty. He believed in democracy for all, respected the U.N., had been disillusioned at times with some of their decisions, but still believed it was necessary for international cooperation in working on problems and positive progress for humankind. By some, he had been considered too much of an idealist, but sometimes he could also be reasonable about compromise. I still miss him a lot, and didn't realize how much I was like him until years after I left home at 18 to attend college.

Relatives and friends in California, Ohio and Minnesota sent letters and cards of condolences and gifts of money. From Ohio John had given me the following note in his sympathy card to take with me to Arizona:

Dear Mom:

I grieve with you over the loss of Arnie. The world was a better place because he lived his ideals and dreams, which his children continue to live. Arnie will be missed by us all. I'm sorry that his retirement years couldn't have been longer and in good health so that both of you could have enjoyed them. I grieve over his life cut short and over his suffering of these past years. I know it has been difficult for you. Peace be with you.

Love, John

60. IN BETWEEN THE AGONIES

THE ARTS ARE VERY therapeutic. They helped provide a balance from the stressful frustrations of our relatives' and friends' health problems and deaths. Our children benefited as well. It helped me cope and recuperate.

Little did I know that when I took the position for teaching the music and movement for young children that I would have opportunities for singing performances as well at the Cultural Center. Teaching and performing those last 4 years of the '70's had been not only work, but much enjoyment. I had been fortunate to have been doing what I loved!

One of the great bonuses from my having worked at the CAI was having met M. J., Associate Director there during those times. Not only was he pleasant of personality, but he was excellent in all he accomplished. Not only did he assist with art exhibits, but he also gave stimulating lectures on history and the arts and had published in the Cleveland Plain Dealer newspaper. As a music critic, he wrote reviews of Akron and Canton Symphony concerts for those area newspapers. He took many excellent black and white photos of my classes, and was so supportive of my teaching!

He also introduced me to James K., master guitarist. He was versatile, playing classical, folk, and especially Spanish classical and flamenco pieces. He had studied with Andres Segovia, and could also play the Renaissance lute. M. J. had thought that James and I would make a good duo for children's concerts, so I organized one and performed vocally with him for our first concert at Cable Recital Hall at the Canton Cultural Center to celebrate the United Nations' International Year of the Child. Joining us with the performances were percussionist Bobby and children from the Canton Suzuki Violin School, which included Christina.

My happy participation in jazz concerts with Moe and other musicians continued. My first one in picturesque Peninsula, in the Cuyahoga Valley, was in the spring, as was the second in the Cultural Center. In summertime and fall we performers at Peninsula were outside, enjoying the audience, weather and beautiful trees.

For songs, the pianists were foundational as accompanists for me, with the other musicians enhancing the pieces to make a whole, beautiful experience. One of those great pianists was Tom, a sociology professor at KSU who was expert at ballads, blues, rags, and stride piano style.

Bobby, a black percussionist, introduced me to another Al, a white reed musician who had worked out of New York with the Tommy Dorsey Band under the direction of Warren Covington and had toured extensively around the country with it. By the time I met him, he had returned to Canton, and had his own band. His group accompanied my singing of Billie Holiday's *Good Morning, Heartache* for a jazz memorial for a recently deceased black Cleveland musician who had been playing in New York. It had been his favorite song, and I was fortunate to have been asked to sing it. We performed it at the Bank Night Club in Akron, and it was a moving, enriching experience to have been a part of that and meeting the other people who came.

After I flew out to Arizona in July, 1977 there was a day before we had to leave for Dad's artificial vein surgery on his leg in Phoenix when they didn't need me. So I and their middle-aged neighbor Jack drove out to the Hualapai Reservation, in the Peach Springs, Arizona area, for I had a music quest. Jack and I both loved adventures, and he had more than one vehicle that was good for rugged traveling in desert terrains which he loved, but since we were going on roads, he took his van. He was familiar with Peach Springs, and it wasn't far from Kingman, just going north on U.S. Historic Route 66, southeast, and just hours from, Mercury and Las Vegas, Nevada. Because it was a spontaneous trip, I was hoping that someone on the reservation who could sing would share some Native American songs and allow me to record them on my tape recorder for my students. Ordinarily, it would seem like a rather dead end idea, since we had no contact with anyone there ahead of time. Well—it was amazing how it all turned out!

Just by asking a couple of people in among the cement block houses, we found our singer! He was a middle-aged man with grown children and two grandchildren—a darling chubby-cheeked little boy who was less than two years old and a lovely girl in upper grade school. One of his sons drove tourists on Colorado River raft rides at the bottom of the Grand Canyon, which bordered their land.

After inviting us into his home and introducing his grandchildren to us, he said he had to leave and get a native drum to accompany himself. Then, incredulously, he asked if we, total strangers that he didn't know at all, would watch the children! Before we had a chance to think much about the riskiness of it, we said "yes"! He left and the little girl offered us pine nuts to eat, which we enjoyed. He was taking quite a while, so we went over to the nearby Grand Canyon Caverns with them and took the short tour. The children were as trusting as the grandfather, so neither of them hesitated to go with us. After we arrived back at the house, this kind man came back with his drum and sang his songs about the Grand Canyon area. He sang in his native tongue about the beautiful nature surrounding them, which included birds, canyons, the Colorado River, and the rushing waters of springs and waterfalls, translating into English after each song. Then more of his family arrived, so we took snapshots, thanked him for the treasure he had given us, for which he wanted no money, and left. What a beautiful experience!

After Carolyn was at Glen Oak high school, she continued with drama and added singing. While she was in choir in 1978, she had the leading role of Queen Aggravain in the musical, *Once upon a Mattress (The Princess and the Pea)*, at the West Campus' Little Theater, and did well. I was also happy to attend the choir's beautiful concert of Leonard Bernstein's *Chichester Psalms* at the Canton Cultural Center for the Arts and couldn't resist buying a recording of it afterwards with Bernstein conducting the New York Philharmonic Orchestra and Abraham Kaplan conducting The Camerata Singers. She also had decided to stay in school for her senior year instead of graduating early like her older sisters. John and I were pleased about that.

61. REACHING FOR THEIR STARS

BARBARA TOOK A TRIP to New York City with her art class during KSU's 1977 spring break.

She discovered she was fascinated with big city life and wrote to her grandparents in Arizona:

Dear Grandpa and Grandma:

I hope you are feeling better, Grandpa. Mother wrote to me of your illness (pneumonia). I'm sorry I don't write often. When you're in college you seem to eat, sleep, and breathe school. I went to New York City with the art department. I used my income tax return so I could go.

We went to all kinds of art shows and museums and various art related businesses. We were told that if we were graphic design majors we would inevitably have to work in NYC—which I won't mind! I learned so much on my trip—I received one school credit—I should have received six for what I learned!

Love, Barbara

After another Kent art class trip to New York City, Barbara was absolutely convinced she should move there! So after three years at KSU, she left to work as an assistant to Canton artist/businessman Paul Anthony in order to earn money for it. One of her tasks was to paint music entertainers on the walls of an Akron music store, and she also helped build window displays for a store in Manhattan.

On January 7, 1979, a fairly apprehensive dad drove his daughter to New York to follow her dream, even though she knew only one other person there. Fortunately, this generous gay friend Bob, a Cleveland student whom she had met at KSU, offered her a place to stay in his apartment until she could find a job and her own apartment. For her 21st birthday on the 13th, Bob took her to Studio 54 and she enjoyed herself immensely. One of the persons she met was artist Andy Warhol, and she talked with him for 20 minutes.

Life for her in New York was built upon challenges, but also more joys. In her early February letter to us, she shared:

Looking for a job has to be the most straining thing I've ever done. It's a full-time job! Graphic Design is the second toughest occupation to get a job—so much competition. If you're from out of town, it's 10 times harder—everybody seems to want NYC experience!"

She had been accepted into the School of Visual Design, was enjoying her classes and reading from the vast variety of reading sources, especially the New York Times.

February 20, 1979

Dear Grandma and Grandpa—

I hope Grandpa is doing O.K. I'm concerned about him. I found a job last week after weeks of hunting! It's an advertising firm on Park Avenue, pretty close to my school, so I walk there after work (on the East side). BGA, where I work, has movie accounts. They design the advertising and posters for most of the major motion pictures. It's in a beautiful, modern office with most of the originals for the posters hanging on the walls. Of course, I don't get to illustrate...yet. I'm in a starting position, doing anything anyone needs help with. I love it. I'm so excited just to be in that environment.

My classes are going well. My illustration class is being taught by James, a famous illustrator (who is working me very hard, because I'm the youngest and least experienced in the class).

I found an apartment on the Upper West Side (103 W. 70ᵗʰ Apt. 3B), a walk-up with one very small bedroom. This is the cheapest place I could find in a safe neighborhood, (which is the most important factor). I'm just subletting it for 3 months from an actor who went to L.A. to be on soap operas. This will give me time to find a permanent place. My neighborhood is great! There are a lot of young people and people in the arts (a lot of actors). Everything I need is within a couple of blocks' radius. The grocery store is right across the street. The subway on Broadway is 2 blocks away. I just love it here!

Love you too! Barbara

We didn't have to worry about her too much anymore. Our vegetarian daughter seemed to be able to take good care of herself. She had found bliss in the Big Apple, so was willing to work hard to be able to stay there. She had always been such an energetic good worker, and reminded me of the times she accomplished so much earning her many Girl Scout badges in grade school. By October she was the assistant art director for East-West Network Inc., working under the hard taskmaster Jerold, the art director for two magazines simultaneously, *United Airlines Mainliner* and *All in Style*, a high end fashion magazine

* * * *

Because Patti loved the outdoors and nature so much, she had decided to become a park ranger. In searching within Ohio we found that the best programs of Wildlife Management, Recreation and Natural Resources were at Hocking Technical College in the rural southeastern part of the state, in the little town of Nelsonville, away from any major highways. She was accepted in 1978 and was looking forward to fall and quitting her job at the pizza parlor, which she realized, wasn't fulfilling.

As I was driving her to the orientation with a counselor we drove on the country roads within the peaceful Wayne National Forest, we noticed beautiful, lushly green, rolling hills. The outdoor environment was pleasant enough for her until we started noticing junk in people's yards, like parts of old, rusted vehicles and dilapidated refrigerators on porches of run down little houses. Well, the campus wasn't like that, so we thought that maybe she could still be happy working in the living science lab of the outlying areas. And, besides, it was the only two year college in the state that had dorms, so she could live on campus.

When we met with the counselor he complimented her on her grades and told her that she was also fortunate to have had a rich cultural background. In contrast, he said the students at Hocking came mostly from its general tri-county area, which was primarily rural, agricultural, and low income, so they didn't have what Patti had. But attending Hocking could help those students rise out of poverty and help them find fulfilling work (a good thing). "You, Patti, will develop your abilities better at a four year college, and I hope you will find what you want. You will probably thrive better there." In other words, he was telling her not to come to Hocking. We were both stunned, thanked him, took her applications and left. We didn't say a lot going home. Frustrated, she complained, "So, what am I supposed to do now?" She was in limbo again! I hoped she would find her star.

She switched jobs to work in a pharmacy. Then, she decided to do something really exciting for her: she applied to take a wilderness course with Outward Bound and was accepted! Fortunately, she had saved enough money so that she could take it, and her boss was nice enough to let her go and still keep her job. We were excited for her—especially John. He had wanted to do that himself for years.

Outward Bound was known for giving their participants challenging physical and character building experiences wherever it took them, and this was no exception. Because she loved the American West, our 18 year old chose to go to Colorado and climb Mount Massive, the 14,000 foot, second highest mountain in the Rocky Mountain Range! She flew to Denver and boarded a bus to Leadville, the base camp. After arriving there she met the leader and the 11 other young women and men. While waiting for the adventure to begin, Patti learned the leader had requested snow shoes. Because it was near the end of May, he was told they wouldn't need them. But he insisted, and later they found themselves quite fortunate to have had them.

Amazingly, she had been able to take time out to write to her grandparents in Arizona about it:

June 4, 1979

Dear Grandma and Grandpa, I am in Colorado now in the mountains. It is very beautiful. There is snow all around yet and we have to wear snowshoes to get through some of it. We will be here until June 14.

A few days ago we hiked to the top of Mount Massive, which sure lives up to its name! It's the third largest peak in the U.S. You can see everywhere from the top! I am taking a lot of pictures. All the people in my patrol are very nice and so is my instructor. He is very careful that none of us gets hurt. So far I haven't, and hope I don't!

We are doing a lot of exciting things, but they make me very sore and tired. I suppose that's to be expected, because we walk many miles a day with heavy packs. I'll sure be strong when I get home!

Thank you for the book on camping. I love it! I know that it will come into a lot of use for a long time.

I hope that you are doing better, Grandpa. I wish I could come and visit since I'm so close to Arizona now, but it's not possible at this time. I miss you.

Love, Patti

Before they completed their trek, each person in the patrol also had to survive in the wilderness by him or herself for three days, with only a few crackers given to them and the advice that they had to forage for wild food wherever they could find it, in or out of the snow. Fortunately, everyone survived (and no one had cell phones!) After arriving home, she said she loved Colorado, describing it as so pretty and clean. She had found some bliss there and hoped to return again someday.

62. MORE UNWANTED DRAMAS

BY THE END OF September '79, I was in a car accident. Immediately after I had stopped on Dressler Road to let a car turn left into parking at Roadhouse 77 Restaurant, I felt a horrible impact on the rear of my little compact that tossed my head and body like a rag doll! In the split second when I first realized what happened, I thought that was it until I was hit two more times as the offending car couldn't stop. The lady whose vehicle hit me had come down the sloped drive from KSU onto Dressler, had glanced briefly to the right and then slammed into mine full force because she hadn't seen my stopped vehicle in front of her. By the time the police and ambulance came, they had to cut and pry my door to get me out; the back frame and doors had been pushed forward onto my front doors. At the hospital I received a neck brace, nothing for my emotional trauma, and sent home after the x-rays showed no broken bones. I was fortunate. I had muscle and tissue damage to my lower back, so I went to my chiropractor, Dr. P., who helped me heal. Our car was beyond repair and declared totaled, so we had to buy another one.

* * * *

For several days in early November I went to New York City to see Barbara. She was seeking housing again and was living temporarily at Suzanne's apartment. Suzanne, a professional writer and mother of college students, generously let me stay also while she was on a writing assignment on Long Island.

When I was riding in the car with John on the way home from the airport he said, "You need to know that Carolyn is in the hospital."

"What? Why—what's wrong with her?"

"She broke her neck!"

"What?" I screamed, and then I broke down, flooding my face with anguished tears, thinking the worst. "Is she paralyzed?"

"No, fortunately not! Her neck has a fracture, and she has injuries on one of her hands and the lower part of one of her legs, near her foot."

"Why didn't you tell me?"

"Because it was almost time for you to come home, and I thought you could handle it better at home." He was right.

"How did it happen?"

"Drunk driver." By the time we arrived at the hospital, I was so weak in the legs I had to hold onto him.

It was quite an unexpected scene for me when we walked into her room. There she was, dressed and sitting serenely on the bed with her blond hair cascading around a neck brace and bandages on her lower leg and hand. My fears began to subside a bit. Then she stunned me when she made this incredulous comment: "I asked the doctor if I could go on that ski trip, and he said no!"

She didn't seem to realize the enormity of the accident, nor could she remember it—probably a good thing. It was in the afternoon and she had been in the back seat of a car without a seat belt, when the driver, who had just been drinking and she hadn't known it, fell asleep at the wheel and crashed into a tree in North Canton, not far from where we lived. The impact was so powerful it propelled her into the windshield, and cracked her neck! (The following year at the county fair, John and I saw a car put on display by the sheriff's department because it was so badly crushed, and then we learned it was *that* car! It even had some of Carolyn's hair still caught on the front door! It was such a mangled, dismal scene we had a hard time looking at it, especially knowing it involved her, so we didn't tell her about it.)

The wound on her leg was a hole about the size of a dime, and all the knuckles on her hand were crushed. Her situation wasn't good, but she could have been paralyzed for life, or killed! We were so thankful she was as good as she was. My mind raced back to that other family alcohol-related accident when my mother's brother, who was near Carolyn's age at the time, didn't make it when his drunk cousin driver crashed into a tree. That driver survived. In Carolyn's tree crash case, the two other young men, also in the front seat, survived with minor injuries. Because of the driver's teen age, he received no legal penalties.

How did it happen that Carolyn was in the car in the first place? Carolyn knew Craig, who had been dating Patti, and who was not the driver, offered her a ride home when she was done from her part-time waitress job at a restaurant at Belden Village. She had called her dad, who was planning to pick her up because there were no sidewalks. She told him she didn't need the ride home because Craig and his friend offered to take her home instead.

So, Carolyn didn't finish her senior year the usual way on campus, but completed the graduation requirements and graduated with her class in June of 1980. By the end of that summer she was getting ready to move to southern Ohio to attend Ohio University and major in journalism.

* * * *

Mother Mary (Tate) was not doing well. For years, she didn't appear to have much joy in life, which we noticed more after she moved in with us in '77. Even though it was a loving environment for her, she didn't change.

Later, in November of that year, all her family hoped that by including her in the gaiety of her oldest grandson's wedding, she might gain a limited measure of happiness, at least for a short while. She even danced with him briefly without her cane, but even then she never smiled in any of the photos of her and didn't enjoy the occasion.

In 1978 we learned that she was having trouble with the first hip replacement, and needed a second surgery. She survived it and the recovery. Then, during the greatest snowfall of the year, she had given up. John and I had driven the short way to Belden Village while Barbara, home for the weekend from Kent, found herself outside her Grandma's locked bedroom door, hearing her screaming that she had deliberately taken suicidal amounts of medications! Barbara coaxed, pleaded, begged and finally ordered her to open the door! By the time she did, the medics and ambulance were there to take her and Barbara to the hospital, where the doctors pumped her stomach, kept her long enough to get her stable, and sent them home.

She couldn't be left alone anymore. By fall of 1979 she had so many things wrong with her, even her doctors didn't seem to know how to diagnose or treat her. In the middle of an angiogram, she had a heart attack, so it was discontinued. They thought she had symptoms of cancer. The poor thing looked much older than her age. She was down to skin and bones. In December she went back to the hospital and died on the 12th. She was too young, at only 68. Her slender, older sister and an aunt each lived to be 100. What had gone wrong for Mary? Her immigrant mother was too large from cooking and baking excessively and died of colon cancer in her fifties. Her younger sister had a life style much like her mother and passed away too young from cancer and too much radiation not long after Mom. Their immigrant father—and John's Grandpa—Nick, lived a bit longer.

Another health tragedy in the family, it was a loss of an originally vivacious and friendly young woman who, even together with the medical experts, couldn't maintain her love of life. Mary had suffered through 17 surgeries, starting with back surgery, and several heart attacks, including one shortly after moving in with us. She had taken massive amounts of prescribed medications with too many side effects to her, physically and psychologically. She had ¾ of her stomach removed, many adhesions from the surgeries and not enough sunshine on her bones living in an overcast, cloudy climate. No wonder she had felt lousy!

After Dad died and my sister-in-law took over some of the caregiving, she responded magnificently, constantly taking Mom to her multiple medical procedures and treatments, which helped me tremendously.

In hindsight, I wonder if I had been too busy with my work, performances, and rest of the family to give her enough personal attention for her spirit. Also, the stress factor must have been enormous when her husband died in the explosion of the blood bath in front of her.

The death certificate stated acute peritonitis, etiology (causes and origins) undetermined. Peritonitis, a painful inflammation in the abdomen is usually from bacteria which can spread into the blood and organs, causing multiple organ failures and death. She had suffered terribly for too long. It was amazing, to some extent, that she had lived as long as she had. It seems to me that somehow some of that suffering could have been prevented by getting more to causes and some better treatments for her problems.

For the daughter of immigrant parents who thought it was enough for her to have only an eighth grade education—like they were used to in their agrarian village in the old country—she had her accomplishments. After finishing school she had worked in a pottery factory. After marriage and two children, she had worked during WWII at Republic Steel until she injured her back. She was bilingual, had learned to read, write, and spell pretty well and took care of the family finances. Through careful budgeting she had always maintained a savings account, which helped them buy their homes, starting in the 1930's. She always bought good quality clothes, furniture, and food without spending a fortune (on a working class income) and had a knack for decorating the house. The baby clothes she crocheted were beautiful. Also beautiful were the jars of dill pickles she canned with carrots, celery and yellow, long, hot peppers. The peppers gave just enough "bite" to everything in the jars, making the finished products the best pickles ever! She had been a great cook in other ways too and passed on those creative skills in the kitchen to her daughter. Mean spiritedness was not her style. She had loved her family and we had loved her.

John requested the Requiem Mass at the newly built and beautiful St. George's Romanian Byzantine Catholic Church, and conducted by Msgr. Capros, who had led her husband's funeral. It was the last loving act he could do for his beloved mother. All our family was there except Barbara. In her hand made card with a rosebud gracing the cover, she wrote: *"With all my heart—deepest sympathy for the loss of Grandma. I loved her very much. Love you, Barbara."* Afterward, the beginning of recovery from loss started with the traditional Romanian style meal in the social hall, consisting of chicken, stuffed cabbages with sauerkraut, rice pilaf, vegetables, wine, desserts and coffee.

She was buried near her husband and in-laws from Romania, George and Anna, in Forest Hills Cemetery in Plain Township during the last month of 1979—too much of a heart-wrenching year for us Tates.

63. SUPPORTING THE ARTS AND COLLEGE STUDENTS

FUND RAISING FOR ARTS organizations is a constant every year. Besides the umbrella "United Arts Fund" for all the organizations at the Canton Cultural Center for the Arts, the staff at the CAI started one also for its sake with the Museum Guild in the late 70's by having a Casino Royale party. Besides the gaming tables, there was a cocktail party, dinner and other entertainment. The Canton Repository editor Flo Lynn entitled the article, "Casino Royale was a royal treat." She declared that the gourmet dinner staggered the imagination. There were hilarious comedy acts performed by Al, Steve, and Dick, humorous displays from the former Meyers Lake Amusement Park, and a magic act with Tom. I performed turn of the century songs for the Gay Nineties Review wearing a period costume with Dave accompanying me so well on the piano. As Lynn concluded, "It was a happy night...the conversation was light, but animated. The crowd (more than 180) was most compatible...as far as a successful party went, everyone was a winner!"

The Canton Civic Ballet raised funds through performances and the 1980 Spring Season Gala featured stellar dance performances accompanied by top-flight musicians. Highlighted in the press were virtuoso classical pianist Ms. Baxtresser and guitarist James, who were joined by three other string musicians. John and I were especially pleased to experience the tribute to our friend, Blossom—my mentor and—founder of the dance movement in Canton. It was a top-flight and delightfully touching performance of "The Preacher Said We Could Dance", an artful original created by Co-directors of the ballet, Mr. and Mrs. Wilkins, based on a true story.

From the time Blossom was a young girl, she had loved to dance. But at home and church there was a problem. Her father was a minister in a Protestant church where dancing was considered an evil, so members were discouraged from participating in it. Her father then changed from that denomination to Methodist, hence giving cause for the ballet performance. Imagine Blossom's joy when that originally took place! Her exuberance, her sense of freedom—as portrayed by the dancing—burst out of her, causing her to leap, skip, twist and twirl through the fields of wildflowers near her home in the Middle West.

Blossom was so thankful to God and her father. She remained an appreciative Methodist the rest of her life, involving herself in the many aspects of its avenues of service and education, eventually becoming a physical education teacher at Mt. Union, a Methodist College in Alliance, Ohio.

* * * *

Carolyn was more than fortunate—she was especially blessed too, that she could eventually walk, run, ski, swim, or any other athletic type movements after that '79 auto accident. By fall, as a student at Ohio University in Southern Ohio, rooming with three other girls in a dorm, she was keeping up with her classes, had a part-time job and a loan, and was still asking me to bring items down occasionally and money from home often. She was enjoying her independence, as indicated by her signature on her September 9 letter: "I love you all a lot and miss you (but having a ball being so grown up.) Carolyn."

She came home for spring break in '81 and planned to work at Ocean Beach, Maryland upon the suggestion of one of her roommates who had done the same. Once there, she had some time at the beach, but not a lot since she had jobs as a waitress and sales clerk, amounting to 6 days a week. She was learning what it was to work in the real world and pay rent, food and other essentials on minimum wage salaries. "I tell you, the cost of living sure becomes noticeable when you're out on your own!" By the end of summer she didn't have much for college. What she had accumulated were some fun times with girl roommates whom she liked a lot. She thought the location of the apartment was ideal "with the Laundromat, the bank, and grocery right down the street and the beach a block away!"

She went back to university in the fall, and continued through winter quarter. "Hello Parental Beings, I just don't like the party 'till you puke' attitude around here. It's really demeaning to one's intelligence and I find it really silly. My, don't I sound mature! Really, I think I'm changing my ways. I don't smoke pot anymore or drink to the point of being drunk, or enjoy going uptown anymore. It's a meat market and I'm not doing that anymore either. I went uptown last night and I was in bed by 10:30. I've been surprising my mod-mates around here because I've been so studious and sober. Oh no, it sounds like I'm becoming an introverted bore! I've even made plans to go to church tomorrow. My goodness, what's happening to me? I must be growing up—ee gads! Next weekend I am going to see the theater-dance show. I'm really looking forward to that. I'm going to start taking advantage of the good things they do have to offer at O.U."

She came home over spring break '82 and then returned immediately afterward to Ocean City so she could have better chances at summer jobs. That summer she met Walt from Delaware and her studies were, unfortunately, interrupted quite a long while. The family met him on a trip to Canton when all the girls were home during summer of 1983 and Barbara introduced us to Charles from Connecticut, whom she had met also in '82.

Patti had new resolve, and had become discontent with her life at the drug store pharmacy. She decided she needed to further her education. She wondered if it could be related to art, and explored possibilities at Stark Technical College near KSU in North Canton. First she enrolled at the technical school where she could learn to design machinery. She lasted less than a week. She came home in tears and said, "I hate it there—I don't want to do that kind of work!" So she enrolled at the KSU branch, lived at home, and found contentment. In 1982, then, one of her first courses was in pottery, and I still have some of the beautiful pieces she did on display here at home. Another of her favorites (not surprising for a rock hound) was geology. Soon she was on the dean's list for her high achievements.

It wasn't long before Patti stunned us with another decision: she didn't want us to help her with college expenses except the living at home part while she was at the North Canton campus! She knew she would probably be going to the main campus in Kent eventually where she would need more food and lodging expenses in addition to her university expenses. But she was adamant about our not helping, telling us we had too many other expenses. We were touched by her unselfishness, generosity and love.

She obtained a waitress job in an elegant Chinese restaurant in Canton, which meant that she was traveling back and forth after she was rooming near the Kent campus, more than 30 miles away. She had an orange Volkswagen bug which she used in all kinds of weather, until it started to fall apart and she was done with her university studies.

Earlier, while she and I had been checking out Stark Technical, I was introduced to Mr. Pridgen by Norma Marcere who had turned the inner-city Saturday PAX (Project for Academic Excellence) directorship over to him, and his office was at Stark. That meeting turned out to be great for me as I shared with him my hopes for finishing college. He told me to check out Capital University in Ohio which, in addition to the traditional classes for college-aged students, had degree programs for working adults.

Thank you, Mr. Pridgen—for helping with this Godsend for me! It was perfect for finishing my Bachelor of Arts degree, which I could accomplish in a little more than a year, even though I was starting at the mid-sophomore level. My prior college work would also be included in the credits needed for my graduation. Through the University Without Walls (UWW) program for working adults, I was able to transform work and volunteer activities into college credits for my major by writing competencies in them, while also taking courses with Capital instructors, some at other colleges and two educators at the CAI. Though the main campus was in Bexley—a suburb of Columbus—about two hours from Canton, I only had to go there several times because I could work mainly out of its downtown Cleveland campus, about an hour away. That was a *great* benefit to me.

It was going to be an intense amount of work, and before I started I was told that some students' spouses had lost patience with being ignored too often and asked for divorces! So, what about John—how did he feel about it?

"What? I can put up with it. You have waited so long with so many interruptions to finish this goal, you helped so I could get my degree—go for it!"

After being accepted into UWW by Admissions at the Cleveland Center, I had my formal degree plan accepted for the baccalaureate program. To graduate, I had to satisfy the following requirements: the University Core; College of Arts and Sciences Core; UWW Core; selection and approval of my major; and completion of a minimum of 124 hours of course work, including at least 30 credit hours of UWW course work.

Before any of those could be started, however, I had to attend an Orientation Workshop in Columbus in fall of '80 for learning about everything I had to do, which included four Prior Learning Portfolio workshops. I also learned that the costs, less than $6,000, equaled what I received in the balance of settlement from my car accident, so I didn't have to go into any debt! I met others in my class of '82, which included our then Ohio governor Richard Celeste's wife Dagmar—First Lady of the state of Ohio—majoring in Women's Studies. I would start formally fulfilling my Bachelor of Arts degree, spring of 1981. I had a few courses in classrooms with other students, but most courses were independent studies. I would have a first meeting with the professors to learn what was required of me, and then I would fulfill the studies on my own.

In June of '81 it was so helpful to me to have sent eleven year old Christina to her grandmother's by plane for a few weeks, after one week at Mount Hermon in California with Alyson, Glen and Eleanor's counselor daughter. Christina did well—flying by herself—with airline personnel helping her all the way to her eventual destination in Las Vegas, where her grandmother could pick her up.

One of my pleasures was meeting with my Core faculty advisor Pamela in the Capital UWW Cleveland Center office in the beautifully restored Cleveland Arcade. In 1890 it was America's largest indoor shopping center, with five tiers of shops. It was the first building on Ohio's list of historic landmarks. Fast forward to my time there, it not only had shops, but also offices and restaurants. It was light, bright and gorgeous with its gleaming brass railings with cascading plants, a huge glass roof and live trees. It was a people-friendly place!

I was fortunate in having such cooperative university personnel to assess my prior learning works. Critical to my music/movement teaching of children in the early childhood span was a music professor knowledgeable of the purposes and techniques of the Orff-Schulwerk Approach, which was based on child development and originally from Germany. That person was Ruth Hamm, Orff Music Education Specialist at Cleveland State University. She was also one of the founding members, in 1968, of the American Orff-Schulwerk Association (AOSA) in the United States (Cleveland) after studying it in Canada, the first country in North America to establish it. The Orff Approach was created after much research by educator Gunild Keetman and composer Carl Orff and utilizes singing, chants, poetry, clapping, movement, melody and non-pitched instruments. It is designed for all children in classrooms. I was so fortunate that she assessed my teaching for the CAI, Canton City Schools and also the concerts and other programs for the community. She gave me advanced ratings on six competencies, and intermediate on the one which also included influences on my teaching from Kodaly and Suzuki approaches. I was very grateful to her for all her assistance.

I attended my session with her in Cleveland, at her house. It so happened that after I spent hours with her until dark, the winter temperature had plummeted to below zero, one of the lowest of the year. John had driven me there, so after some snacks and voiced appreciations, we both bundled up and went to the car. It got us nowhere, however, because it was so cold, the battery was dead! So Ruth's husband jump-cabled our car with his and got the motor going. By then, they invited us to spend the night, which I definitely wanted to do!

But did we? No—my stubborn husband said, "Thanks so much, but I think we can make it home now."

"What? Are you crazy? What if we don't make it—we have only our coats and each other to keep us warm—we could freeze to death in the car!"

I was too weak, so I gave in and we two lunatics left after thanking the Hamms for everything. Even before we reached the highway we had to drive below our usual speed, and because it was so quiet, we could hear our tires crunching on the snow. Once we arrived at the highway, the wind broke the silence and created snowdrifts across and behind us. Fortunately, (or maybe unfortunately), there were no other cars to get in our way, not even the Highway Patrol. Our car was the only one on the totally snow-covered Highway 271 because everyone else was sensible enough to stay away. I was beyond apprehensive all the way home, which took us *twice* as long to get there, but at least, thankfully, we did. Like I humorously declared on our honeymoon as John and I plowed through the Wyoming thunder storm alone, "If we die, I'll never speak to you again!" I guess he liked somewhat risky challenges such as these—puzzling phenomena for an otherwise reasonable guy. His only other kind of "living on the edge" behavior was teaching adolescent students—another challenge he thoroughly enjoyed!

John was 50 years old when I started at Capital University.

I finished my studies during the spring-summer session 1982 and graduated in August at forty-seven years old, with a major of Arts Performance, Education and Child Development. I was so happy and grateful! That same August I spent six days and my birthday at the national conference of the Dalcroze Society of America at the Oberlin Conservatory of Music in Oberlin, which was closer to our home than Cleveland. It was to further enhance my teaching of eurhythmics for music education, and I used it later for dance, too. I was almost as elated there as I was with my graduation as I participated with the outstanding faculty. They were from three universities and three colleges in the United States, Canada, Holland, and Switzerland. Professor Porte from Switzerland was the Director of the Emile Dalcroze Institute there, as well as a composer and teacher. (Emile Dalcroze, one of the pioneers of music education in the 20th Century, used rhythmic movement, ear-training, and improvisation to increase musical awareness.) One of the teachers from Duquesne University also taught later at the International Music Festival at Andrews University when I taught there.

The children's concerts didn't end with the one in '79 at Cable Hall. James and I gave three more for the Canton City Schools, and then M.J. at the CAI asked if we would do one in the museum for "The Children of this World" photographic exhibit organized by UNICEF and the German magazine, *Stern*. How could we refuse?

The reception and concert were held in the Fry Gallery on Sunday, September 7, 1980. The international folk song repertoire fit in so well with the international exhibit. The Best and Worst of the world of children, from the happiest to the most unfortunate had been photographed by 238 photographers in 94 countries! The children at the exhibit-concert were fortunate in that while they were there they could experience an awareness of the great varieties of people their ages and the places where they lived different than their own, and then participate in the joys of music and movement. These are the kinds of activities I'd like young people everywhere to have.

James and I appreciated being there and enjoyed it immensely. M.J. kindly reported:

"The talent of both Mrs. Tate and Mr. K. made the program a real pleasure for both children and adults alike. As a team, these two performers possess a magnetism and sense of cooperation which resulted in a flawless performance that moved to a finale without a dull moment." — M. J., A Music Critic: *The Canton Repository* and *Akron Beacon Journal*

James and I had no more performance opportunities after that, but we did see each other briefly twice one evening. After he had left Akron on his way to one of his performances, he realized he had forgotten his guitar! Fortunately for him, he stopped at our place and asked if he could borrow my seldom used folk guitar. I hope the concert went well, considering he was used to his Pena Fernandez guitar from Spain. He returned the guitar afterward, but I didn't get that information, so I'll always wonder how well it performed in the hands of such a master...

How can one not enjoy working in the arts, especially when your co-workers are of such high caliber? From the other teachers, artists, Director Joseph and Associate Director M. J. at the CAI to others in the various arts organizations (ballet, opera, theater, and symphony), we had a thriving arts education and performance center at the Canton Cultural Center for the Arts (CCCA). It also meant extending its personnel into the broader community. An adapted production of Russian composer Prokofiev's *Peter and the Wolf* especially for preschoolers was held May 5, 1981 in the restored and beautiful Palace Theater on Market Avenue, sponsored by The Canton Jaycee Women and The Mayor's Downtown Commission. The cost was to be fifty cents a ticket, so no child would be left out.

Wilkins of the ballet, Wilson, Associate Conductor of the Canton Symphony and Conductor of the Canton Youth Symphony, Ms. Winter, head children's librarian at the Stark County District Library and I, representing the CAI, worked cooperatively to present the classical music production on the young children's level.

I led a pre-concert session on the stage with some of the children from the audience. Joining me were Peter (the conductor), and John with the young dancers from the ballet who represented the characters in the story. We explored elements of the story by drawing upon the children's natural senses of wonder, curiosities and humor. Not only did they hear the instruments (by youth symphony and Canton Symphony musicians) with their representations of the human and animal creatures; they eventually saw the instruments and also had the delightful visual effects of the dancers, whom, in some cases, they were invited to imitate. After this brief encounter, they were then able to understand the usual kind of presentation better, complete with narration, which was spoken by Ms. Winter.

We repeated the production the next year with Ms. Crowley, new director of the ballet, Ms. Biehl of the library who planned sign language for the audience, and Albert the actor, who gave the narration.

64. FAITHFULNESS

DURING THE 60'S AND 70's John and I noticed some curious activities regarding marriages and divorces near us, in addition to the unrealized divorce of Rick and Nora. One of my Catholic friends married to an Episcopalian left her husband and six young children to nurture a lesbian relationship. Two Panel of American Women panelists were stunned when their husbands suddenly asked them for divorces. One of our neighbors was granted a divorce after his wife had a hysterectomy, which freed her of the fear of more pregnancies, and so was having sex with other men, even though she and her husband had two young sons. Two priests at our new parish were laicized and got married quickly afterward. One who was a favorite of ours had given Christina her First Communion and married a former nun. The other married a lady who was a layperson and was hired by our mayor to work in his administration. Both left our church and we missed them.

* * * *

Not only does music bring people together—on occasion, there is also dancing, such as the Romanian Paranita (Little Pillow) dance at performances and other celebrations such as weddings. This friendly "choose a partner from the circle" dance involves a male or female in the center who, after choosing by standing in front of someone, takes that person by the hand to the center where they kneel on the pillow, hug and sometimes kiss. The newer one then becomes leader as the first person leaves the center and joins hands in the circle again. It had always been an enjoyable, casual entertainment for John and me, with usually a hug, and sometimes a light peck on the mouth. But one time where we attended a wedding, it became more. I was chosen by a young man unknown to me and he French kissed me! I thought, "What? Is this the way we do the Paranita now?" Dumbfounded and *really* dumb, I chose one of our family friends from the circle and did the same.

This mutual family friend and I would occasionally go to lunch at the European style restaurant near our house because his work schedule was more flexible than John's. Our behavior and conversations had always been platonic—as between good friends. We always had much to share in our conversations. He liked the fact that he thought I had a lot of interests similar to Europeans. However, soon after that wedding, he shared more than I ever wanted to hear. "It's vital that you know that your French kiss resurrected in me passion I haven't felt for decades! Ever since our son was born (he was in his twenties) my wife hasn't wanted any sex. She has a Madonna Complex. You made me feel alive again! I know this could affect the relationship that you and John have, but if you ever felt for me what I am feeling for you, I would be willing to leave Aurelia."

I was speechless. I felt awful that I would have been so stupid as to have done it. He waited about a minute until I could find words to respond. "Nick, from the time I met you, I have enjoyed your friendship. Your kindness, advanced education, your interest in the arts and other good qualities have meant a lot to me, but I'm sorry, I cannot be what you want me to be. John is the only lover that I desire. I love him very much. I want to be just your friend, and if we can go back to only that kind of love relationship, I can do that. If it's too difficult for you to go back to that which we had prior to Paranita, we will have to stop seeing each other like this. Again, I'm so sorry I have caused you this misery and hope you can forgive me. I so much wish and pray for your complete happiness with someone beside me. With help, maybe Aurelia can change and you might be able to resurrect your marriage? Please let me know your decision," and I left.

I hate unrequited love, and here I was, responsible for initiating this situation. On my brief ride home I remembered an eight year old girl who was taken by her parents in 1943 to her first operetta experience in San Francisco. It was "Blossom Time", based on the music of Franz Schubert, and the story of unrequited love from the lady he loved. The young girl thought the music was beautiful, but that the story was so sad in that he was refused. I cried all the way home that night to Concord, about an hour away.

* * * *

Ed had been a priest at one of the churches where John and I had been members, and then we kept in touch with him occasionally even after we and he had moved to other churches. One beautiful warm afternoon John and I had visited him in his small college town parish house while on a pleasant country drive. Always friendly, he wanted us to call him by his first name, without the "Father" title with it. Always hospitable, he shared glasses of wine, food, and interesting conversations. We had a tour of the church and parish house, which many years before had been the home of a famous author. When we left, he said to come again, and we could also stay overnight some time and go to church or a concert at the nearby college. Eventually an opportunity for attending a concert there opened up. It was all percussion and I was vitally interested in it.

Due to other obligations, John could not go that night to the percussion concert, and neither could Ed. So, after wondering what to do, I called Ed and he said to come anyway. John and I both felt satisfied that because he was a celibate priest friend to both of us, we thought it was okay for me to spend the night there. So, I came again on a beautiful, sunny afternoon, and before dinner, Ed and I took a brief walk down a country road near the parish house, talking about the usual subjects, including jazz which we both loved. The dinner he made was good, I helped with cleanup, and drove the short way to the campus in time for the concert. I was in awe afterward over what had been accomplished with no melody instruments, so I was glad I had been there to experience it all!

Even though I was elated over that, I had a gnawing discontent in what had happened with Nick. Since Eddie was a priest, I wanted to go to confession, get his counsel, and put the experience behind me. I was looking forward to forgiveness and feeling free of my burden. We sat across from each other on chairs in subdued light while I confessed what I believed to be my sin regarding my Romanian friend. I mentioned what I had done and the result, that he was interested in both of us leaving our spouses. I felt so low, but Father didn't show any emotion. After I got it all out of me, he said,

"I don't think that kiss was as serious as you think it was," and gave me absolution. Then, he stunned me again when he said, "I care a lot for you, too, and I'd like you to be my "Bunny" (as in Playboy). Will you?"

"This is a joke, right?"

"No, it isn't!" He wanted me to be intimate with him that night.

"No I won't! I value you as a friend, but love only John. And you're supposed to be *his* friend!"

I went to my bedroom and locked the door, anxious and my head reeling about what had happened. I didn't think he would bother me anymore, but cried myself to sleep after thinking about how much I was missing John, and wondering if Ed had any girlfriends or if he had fathered any children while he was a priest. He was a leader of Marriage Encounters for couples but was basically lonely himself, craving a companion with whom he could share the ups, downs, and beautiful things in life. I thought how good it could be for him to find a soul mate he could marry, love deeply in every way, experience joy in doing for that person and have those experiences of love returned by that other person, like John and me. Ed was a good person, and deserved a good mate.

In the Roman Catholic Church, where the leadership seems dysfunctional on the subject of sex, it seems it's not easy to gain an understanding of loving intimacy for priests—something for which he seemed to have had the potential. For someone such as he who enjoyed his vocation as a priest it would not have been easy for him to have left the priesthood, so maybe, with changes in the church's rules, he could have had both a religious vocation and marriage, like many Protestant, Orthodox and Eastern Catholics. I realize some people fall in love after being friends, but I hoped and prayed it would not take very long for his interest in me to pass away.

The next morning he apologized as I left the bedroom dressed and was ready to leave for home without breakfast. I accepted it, told him I wasn't upset anymore and we parted by just saying good-by. For both of us, it had been an awkward situation, and I shared the last part of the experience with John because his friendship had been affected too, not only mine. If I had done what Ed wanted, it would have obviously affected John's and my relationships with each other. We decided to see him in group situations, if at all. I did not want to share the experience with anyone else, and how many Catholics would have believed my story at that time anyway?

Ed wrote a note: "After your visit I had a painful reflection. I felt myself so vulnerable in that experience. That will never happen again. I want to be friends." That I could accept.

After I told John about this experience, I decided not to tell him all the details of the other. What he knew was that I had gone to confession and what had followed afterwards. I was putting the wedding experience behind me and I didn't want to put the Paranita in a negative light. I would go back to the usual "hugs only." I did not tell anyone else about it either, feeling it would do more harm than good.

As for Nick, he couldn't turn off the spigot of creativity, or the desire to have contact with me. He created beautiful poetry which he mailed to me anyway. I wished that he could have found someone who was lovingly inspired by it. He was a good person, and deserved happiness, but I was not the person for that longing. I just enjoyed his friendship. As far as I knew, he never found another for what he wanted and was unable to improve his marriage before he passed away a few years later. It was a lamentable situation for both me and my good friend.

* * * *

After I encountered problems from the very beginning on my trip alone to Fairfax, Virginia, I might have guessed that this trip for the Harnes Voice Class was going to be different than any other. The weather was cooperative — beautiful and sunny — as John dropped me off at the Akron-Canton airport where I rented a car and drove away. By the time I was on the other side of Akron, though, the steering wheel started shaking. It became progressively worse, then uncontrollable, so I returned to the airport and exchanged cars. I started again and was still looking forward to taking the voice course, since it was a graduation gift for finishing my degree at Capital that summer of 1982. I was 46 years old and so happy I had attained it, after so many delays. My serene state of mind was interrupted then, as I encountered so many trucks that I decided Sunday would not be the day for me to drive the interstate anymore!

By the time I cruised onto the Washington Beltway it was too late, very dark, and I missed my exit. I was lost and ended up in a seedy part of a Maryland town and stopped at a gas station for directions. I was fortunate—the man there gave me good directions—so I finally arrived at my destination, George Mason University. But it was so late everything was locked, including my assigned dorm. No one answered my knocks and doorbell rings. I resigned myself to sleeping in the car, but felt safe because I was in a lot near my destination, and could see no one around. Just as I was getting back into the car, a male voice asked, "May I help you?"

As I saw him coming my way, I quickly locked the door and rolled down the window just enough to speak to him. I thanked him for asking, explained why I was where I was and told him, "No thank you, I will be fine in the car until morning."

"But it's not right for you to do that. I'm living in that dorm over there, and you can stay in my room."

"Thank you for your generosity, but I can't do that."

"Don't be afraid, I won't hurt you. You can come with me to see it and then decide."

He was about John's height and build, with a foreign accent unfamiliar to me. He was dark haired, nice looking and appeared to me like he was a little older than typical college-aged students. I assumed he was younger than I. Racing in my brain was, "He seems nice, but can I trust him enough to follow him? Can he really be just kind and helpful? What should I do?"

He waited the couple minutes patiently until I decided,

"Well okay, I'll look at your room, but then where will you stay?"

"It's big enough for both of us."

"What? I don't think I can stay in your room!"

Then I surprised myself— I got out and walked the short distance with him because at that point I felt safe enough to do so. As we entered, I saw that the place was two rooms—a small entrance sitting room with a love seat-sized couch and then a long room with a twin bed at both ends. I was so exhausted I hoped I could stretch out *somewhere* to sleep. However, I didn't think the couch was an option, because it wasn't any larger than the back seat of my car. So, I opted for the bed at the farther end from the doorway of the larger room, as it looked more than welcome to me. As he brought in my suitcase and shoulder bag I hoped I wouldn't regret my decision. I used the bathroom, put a few curlers in my hair to look unattractive and lay down in my clothes, which were my Romanian ivory, long sleeved blouse with the hand embroidered brown flowers and ivory colored skirt. He came out of the bathroom in a long black nightshirt down to his ankles with a beautifully white embroidered collarless neck opening. I told him I liked his nightshirt, and he told me it was Moroccan. He lay down on his bed and we said good night with lights on. There we were, two tired strangers sharing shelter and a common interest in artistry, as indicated by our clothes from cultures other than our own! I couldn't fall asleep until he was sleeping, which, fortunately, did not take long. The last thing I noticed before I fell asleep was that he looked so sweet and peaceful...

He was dressed in jeans and a long sleeved blue striped shirt when I woke up feeling refreshed. I used his bathroom off his room to shower, and then changed into a white eyelet peasant-styled blouse with three quartered length sleeves and black pants. When I came out, he told me I looked beautiful. I thanked him, and told him that I appreciated his great hospitality and kindness to me—a stranger—very much and then thanked him again. Just before I went out the door in a rush for my assigned dorm room and singing course, we introduced ourselves. He said his name was Saied. Then he grabbed a piece of paper, wrote on it, and said, "I want you to have this."

After looking at it I said, "Thank you! It looks beautiful, but I can't read Arabic—will you translate it for me?"

"It means, 'By the name of God.'"

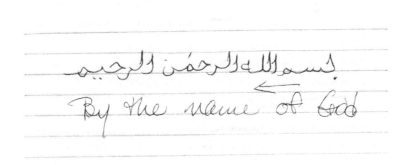

I wrote it down. I mentioned briefly my keen interest in international cultures and we decided to meet another day so I could learn more about his—I thought I was fortunate that he was interested in sharing.

I saw my new friend only four times. Except for the first night they were very brief. After my class on Tuesday at the university, we took a short walk on campus. He took me to see his car as we chatted about him, his family and how he thought he wanted to go back and help them. Wow! After viewing it, I understood better why he had a suite of rooms instead of one dorm room. It was a gorgeous blue expensive sport car! Our visit was less than an hour and during that time he shared that he was Palestinian and soon after Israel was recognized as a country, his family had fled to Kuwait where his parents had started a landscaping business which had become very successful.

Before I left him I shared that Pete Seeger the folk musician/singer would be performing Friday night on the Washington Mall and I was hoping to go with my new classmate friend Nancy. We discussed a little more who Pete was and I asked him if he would like to go if I could I get more information for him. He said "Yes." By Thursday I only had time to drop off a flyer advertising the concert, and told him I hoped he could go and if he liked, he could invite someone else to join us.

After my classes were finished Friday afternoon at GMU, I stopped by Saied's dorm room to finalize plans for attending the evening concert. I asked: "Hi—did you get anyone to go to the concert?"

"No."

Still standing, he paused to light up a joint. Then he said, "I won't be going to the concert, but now, I want to make love to you!"

Stunned, I wasn't sure I understood him correctly, or if maybe it was a joke! "Did you say, 'Make love to me'—as on your bed—do you really mean that?"

"Yes!"

(Oh my God, he had broadened his hospitality!)

After a few seconds, the words poured out of me passionately. "I'm sorry, but I won't do that with you because I love my husband John so much. He is the father of my four beautiful daughters, and we have shared so many great and also difficult experiences together. He is a teacher, and because teachers are not paid well in our country, he works hard even at other jobs part-time so he can provide a decent life for his family, whom he loves. He's intelligent, kind, strong, handsome, and loves me deeply. Doing what you want would hurt our relationship with each other. I wish you future happiness of the same kind that John and I have, with someone else!"

He was quiet several seconds, looked disappointed, but then said, "Say hello to John!"

I was stunned at his answer, and not knowing exactly what to say, I responded with "Thank you for all your kindnesses," and left.

I was not away more than 5 minutes on my walk back to my dorm room when it started. There was a rush—encompassing my entire mind-body complex. There was eroticism—sheer and simple—an intensity which I had never experienced with anyone but John! It was like a prelude building up to the huge orchestration of Finlandia, (but then minus the percussion!) I couldn't figure it out. I went into my dorm room to sit down and do just that, while I assumed I would be left alone quickly.

Wrong! It didn't want to leave—the surge was unrelenting—just kept hangin' 'round the whole time while I wrestled with 'why?' Was Saied physically attractive? Yes, but I had been around other attractive men, and this hadn't happened. We hadn't even flirted, so it didn't make sense.

I left early to get my classmate Nancy so we could get a bite to eat, catch the Metro train and arrive in time for the concert. I could not help but share with her what had happened. She, a divorcee (I was not told why) said, "It happens."

"But, again, it doesn't make sense. It's crazy how it affected me when we hadn't even touched each other the whole four times we saw each other!"

"It happens anyway!"

It did not help to eat, and I kept thinking about it at the concert and on the way home in the taxi because it had toned down some, but not entirely. Back at the dorm, Nancy and I said our good-byes and parted because we were leaving for our homes the next day.

I didn't feel like packing, so I laid in the dark, agonizing and analyzing what had happened to me. Why did I refuse, when it might have been a thrill?-Besides, who would have known about it since it was far from home? But I knew myself, in that what might seem good in the short term, would not, in the long term, be so. It would be damaging to my marriage. I would carry the memory home with me and the feelings for that would probably affect my feelings for my husband. I made a commitment to faithfulness the day I married him. I loved him so much and was interested in keeping the love which I had from him.

That which I felt in Virginia, for me, was not love; it would have been only a facsimile of my love for John, so therefore unfulfilling. I hardly knew the person, and over time it might have been able to evolve into a loving relationship, but only if there were totally different circumstances. I have no idea how he reacted soon afterward. He might have been able to pass it off as no big deal. He was younger, and probably had or eventually loved one or more his own age, gaining great happiness with someone. I hoped so.

What made me so hot and bothered was not so bewildering after I continued to relive the experience in my mind. It was holistic — the combination of being desired by him, his attractiveness, the way he handled his rejection .He was strong in his acceptance of it and in his consideration of John, with respect, graciousness and hospitality, even without knowing John personally. That was all so seductively sexy!

I thought about him a lot driving home, but then it was so great being with John again. I told him about the singing course, Nancy, and my other new friend—everything but the last event except the "Say hello to John" part. He said, "I'd enjoy meeting him some day."

Knowing John, I knew he would.

65. NEW AND DIFFERENT DIRECTIONS

AFTER 18 YEARS, JOHN decided in 1983 to retire from supervising student teachers for Kent State and Akron Universities. At the end of the school year, Dan and Cheryl, parents of a young student of John's at Taft expressed their appreciation in a thank you note:

Mr. Tate,

Dan and I want to thank you for the support you have given Ken this year. You have helped him to gain the self-confidence and self-esteem that wasn't there.

We've always tried to develop these qualities, but when they are encouraged from those other than parents, they mean so much more. Your notes of praise and encouragement were greatly appreciated. The Eaglegram was a special added touch!

You practice so much of what is important to a child's development.

Thank you again for the important role you have played in Ken's education.

Gratefully, Dan and Cheryl

In '84 John received an Outstanding Teacher Award from all of Taft's parents.

Meanwhile, Barbara had accomplished much in her career. In the early eighties when East-West decided to discontinue *All in Style*, she had the option to continue at its other publication but chose not to, because she thought the work wouldn't be as creative and interesting as it had been for *Style*. She resigned and took work with a couple of advertising agencies, and then went as a freelance art director with many clients, some as varied as Polo Ralph Lauren, Harper's Bazaar, I. Magnin, and Avon.

When it came to marriage, she said she would only marry someone wealthy, if at all. Then, after dating Charles, she realized she had fallen in love with him. He was middle class, but not wealthy. When they decided to get married, she said to us, "Mom and Dad, I think you will be proud of me, because I'm marrying for love!"

We were, and we had a sigh of relief, remembering her earlier encounters. We liked him a lot. He loved to ski, so he helped Barbara become a better skier on the icy slopes of Vermont! Of good character, he had been raised a Catholic, and was a graduate of Drexel University. He had been a marketing director at Langley Products in Beacon Falls, Connecticut, and after moving to New York had become an independent marketing consultant. We happily consented to the engagement party she requested for them at our place during the Christmas season, 1984. We felt they were mature enough for marriage since they both were in their late 20's and she had the expertise and desire to plan the wedding she wanted.

There was a casual, friendly wedding rehearsal dinner at one of Barbara's photographer friend's Manhattan studio apartment so we could meet Charles's family. They were married the next evening in the beautifully ornate Convent of the Sacred Heart ballroom on Fifth Avenue in Manhattan, May 25, 1985 with many New York friends attending. Patti was her maid of honor and John, Charles's brother was best man. Carolyn and Christina were the bridesmaids.

The highest point of the ceremony was the Mozart music and sacred vows. The reception, which included dancing, was so exciting I forgot to eat! As Mother-of-the-Bride hostess, I had been walking with a glass of wine in my hand and talking endlessly to the many guests, hoping at least to greet all. John, whom I never knew to be drunk, was a little high – but unfortunately looked drunk in the photos! Concluding our trip was our visit to the top of the World Trade Center for the spectacular view of the city.

* * * *

Even though I had years of happiness working at the CAI, by the time of my graduation from Capital University in '82, I wanted to expand the music/movement part of the integrated arts classes for preschoolers. I wanted the CAI to hire Eleanor, a gifted pianist who could help me give more varied experiences to the children than I could do alone and give me more access on the floor with the children. She was already working within the CCCA at the Canton Ballet, and could add these to her schedule there. She wanted to do it. We got along well with each other, and she had accompanied my singing once at a local performance for a national charity. When I made the proposal to the CAI Director and board, I was informed she could work there if I paid her salary. I didn't think it was fair, and I resigned.

Eugenia, Program Director for the Cultural Center, offered me the chance to teach outreach dance education programs in the area public and private elementary schools. Before I left the institute in 1984 I had started the "Joy of Movement" program in '83, in cooperation with the Canton Ballet, for the Massillon, Ohio City Schools. By the time I finished, all the kindergartners and first graders in that school system had participated. My own joy there had been twofold: interacting with the students and knowing that the staff of a public school system understood the importance of it for their students and were able to get funding for it.

For three years I led the dance program for first through third grades, with a core group of third graders at St. Peter's Catholic Elementary School in Canton. Sister M. Lucille, SND, the third grade teacher, could not have been more supportive. She even sat in the classes while I worked—never interfering—and I loved having her there. Her presence meant that she learned along with the students that the beauty of creative movement and music could be as one entity and how the children's self-esteem and brain power increased as they strengthened self- discipline and spatial awareness with joy. She understood. One of the girls who had been struggling with her classes improved in her academic learning after the dancing.

One day while I was teaching third graders at St. Joseph's Catholic School in Canton, we had an unannounced short visit by our bishop, James Malone. I did not even notice him at first as he stood and observed briefly. When I offered him a seat after my greeting so he might stay a while, he declined politely. "This is all so good. Thank you for providing this for our students." This was beautiful—sharing the joy together—different than what we were doing in 1968 as my concern with him then was over racism and fair housing. This time all of us with our racial differences were living harmoniously as the children romped before our Pastor of Peace!

66. QUESTS

AFTER I LEARNED THAT Leonard Bernstein, one of John's and my heroes in the music world would be performing as Laureate Conductor of the New York Philharmonic Orchestra at Blossom Music Center, I decided not only to attend it, but also to meet him in person. Because Barbara was acquainted with his personal assistant, she was able to obtain a pass for the Green Room, enabling me to succeed!

The August 14, 1986 concert was part of a six U.S. cities tour which ended with Cleveland. The program consisted of Bernstein's *Candide Overture* and *Serenade* (based on Plato's "Symposium") plus Tchaikovsky's *Sixth Symphony*. Not surprisingly, all were outstanding. What *were* surprising to me were his occasional flamboyant high jumps, with legs tucked under, while he was conducting. It startled me. It was amusing, but also puzzling.

When I met this magnanimous man, his white summer performance jacket complimented his white hair and tanned face, as he sat, with jacket open, seemingly relaxed with a cigarette in his hand. His broad smile, resonant voice, and gracious friendliness were impressive. He also seemed kind. In general, I told him how much I appreciated what he had done positively for music and music education, which included the Young People's Concerts. Then, I mentioned his concerts in Japan for the Hiroshima and Nagasaki Memorial that I had seen on TV and thanked him for being there. At that point in our conversation, he eyes became intense as he exuberantly shared with passion his view of its importance. "You know, there were practically no Americans there! We need to have more attending and participating!" I agreed and told him of my interest to be there. He signed his autograph, which I received with enthusiastic gratitude and left.

* * * *

Even though we had a lawyer for Carolyn, the check for her injuries in the car accident amounted to practically nothing because she did not appear to be injured. The crushed bones in her hand and fractured neck had healed somewhat, as well as the hole in her leg. The drunk driver did not get prosecuted because he was still only a teenager. The amount, which we hoped she would put toward her university studies, was enough instead to buy a used Volvo, so she and Walt could travel more. There was nothing we could do about it because she was an adult. They had been living in Florida while Walt worked, and then went back briefly to New England where Carolyn met his parents. After Barbara's wedding, they came to Canton, where they lived with us for a few months, and went with us for an enjoyable night at Blossom Music Center before leaving for Southern California.

Walt was cute and photogenic, with blond hair and a stunning, wide smile. He worked well with his hands in some of the building trades, could repair boats, cook, and was a high school graduate, but didn't seem to be a good match for Carolyn intellectually, culturally, or spiritually. I was crying and losing sleep over it, while John took it in stride—which upset me, too. His thinking was "that it probably wasn't going to last long anyway." When they left I was crying for the loss of Carolyn far away in California and worried about what their partnered life would be out there. They decided to stay in San Diego, and it was not long before they both had jobs.

✳ ✳ ✳

Before Patti finished at Kent State in Graphic Design, she had her work exhibited in the spring senior art exhibit. Patti didn't want a graduation party, but she was interested in a tentative trip with her dad, which he was planning for California. He had not had a break for years from working at his teaching and part-time job at Sears, and really needed one. So, summer of '86 John and Patti went to San Diego and a few places in Baja, Mexico. I couldn't go because I had my first opportunity to teach at the Suzuki International Music Festival at Andrews University in Michigan.

Carolyn and Walt were thriving and accompanied Patti and John during much of their time in San Diego. They all liked everything they experienced there, which included the many beautiful sights that draw so many tourists. Whether it was Balboa Park, the ocean for tide pools or swimming, Wild Animal Park or Old Town Mexican cuisine, John and Patti would have enjoyed visiting them longer. Two of his sister Mary Jean's sons had moved to California for job opportunities and adventures, were living in the L.A. area, and came south for a one day reunion. When he came home and shared the photos and his enthusiasm for having taken the trip, he suggested that in retirement he would like to live in San Diego.

I had my opportunity to fly there in late November. I had a reunion with Nancy and Paul Preddy and Doc Vriend, who were still living in San Diego. The visits with people I loved, the beauty of the city and its natural surroundings, plus so many cultural attractions there convinced me that this city was where I also wanted to live if we returned to California. Just before I left, though, I told Carolyn again that I didn't think Walt was good for her. He also had a drinking problem. She listened to me and that was it for a while.

Patti had a great time in the city by the sea, and then after she was back in Canton busied herself at the Chinese restaurant and her new job as a freelance artist for the Timken Roller Bearing Company.

67. CANTON FOOTBALL AND THE HALL OF FAME

ONE OF THE PLEASURES I had when I moved to Canton as a bride in 1954 was being surrounded in the football frenzy of Stark County. I discovered that the fervor and games started early. A legend in that area is that infant boys are given miniature footballs while still in their cradles! There is flag football in early grade school years and then tackle football starting at age nine.

John's public high school, McKinley, whose team was named after the first professional team, the Canton Bulldogs, was a football powerhouse when he was there in the late 1940's. He enjoyed the sport as a spectator, having preferred swimming instead and swam for a while on the McKinley swim team.

It was different with his (now deceased) cousins, Gene and Mike Hedrick. Both started football at St. Benedict's Catholic Elementary School and played for Central Catholic High School. Gene went on to play for Notre Dame University and coached youth briefly in Montana.

Ten years younger than Gene, Mike enjoyed playing at Central Catholic, which included playing with Alan Page, who was a year ahead of him and who he respected highly for his athleticism and intelligence. Mike became a football coach in addition to being a speech pathologist in Canton City Schools soon after graduation from KSU in 1968, even though he didn't play for KSU. He loved coaching, so he continued with it much longer than his brother.

After leading junior high students, he assumed posts with McKinley High as freshman coach and assistant varsity by 1973. In 1975 he assumed the varsity football coaching position and in 1981 led his team to the State Championship of Division 1 (largest) schools in Ohio. He resigned after football season in 1989 and returned to coaching junior high football so he would have the time to attend the university games where his son Mike, Jr. played football.

In 1993 Mike, Sr. became assistant football coach at Timken High School, and led as Head Football Coach from 1998 until retirement in 2003. While head coach he maintained a weekly TV show on the Canton City Schools' station and Warner Cable. *Coach's Corner* was a great way to get exposure for their football program and get recognition for their student athletes as Mike would go over the previous week's game, show highlight film, discuss future opponents and have player interviews.

While his dad was coaching, young Michael Jr. was immersed into football culture when he accompanied his father to practices by the age of five.

He loved playing with the other coaches' sons and getting teased by the coaches themselves. By the time he was at Crenshaw Junior High, not only did he get the Student of the Year award, he also received Male Athlete of the Year, excelling in football, basketball, track, and had won the city championships in the hurdles and long jump.

While at McKinley High School he was district champion in the hurdles and lettered in football and track every year. His senior year was a time of multiple accolades: *Mr. McKinley* for Outstanding Senior Male Student and Male Athlete of the Year; named Most Valuable Player in football by the McKinley Booster Club, WHBC Radio and Stark County Coaches. The Akron Beacon Journal newspaper named him Stark County Male Athlete of the Year and he received a full football scholarship from KSU where he played each year until graduation. He coached football four years at McKinley and five years at Canton South High School. In 2014 he was requested to coach football again at McKinley and he accepted.

After Mike Sr.'s retirement from actively coaching students, he was president in 2001 of the Stark County Coaches Association and helped host international high school level American football games for the World Championship at Fawcett Stadium in Canton.

Not surprising, Mike Sr. was a trustee of the Pro Football Hall of Fame Club which hosts athletic speakers from all areas of sports from September through May. In the summer, he helped with the NFL Hall of Fame activities for the inductees and included his wife Carol and their daughter Kristen's attendance at the celebratory dinner.

* * * *

In 1987 John Henry Johnson, legendary football superstar at my Pittsburg (California) High School (PHS), was inducted into the Pro Football Hall of Fame, along with six other Enshrinees on August 8 as the class of 1987. We did not know each other in Pittsburg because he graduated five years before I did, and neither did we know each other at his induction. I knew of him because of his fame at PHS and John knew better than I of his professional football career. After college he had played for the San Francisco 49ers, Detroit Lions, Pittsburgh Steelers and Houston Oilers. When I learned of his induction (we didn't have the opportunity to attend), I was excited and called my Pittsburg friend, Anna Marie, who lived about an hour away, to ask if she would join me in sending flowers to his hotel room as "fellow" PHS alumni. She did.

When I thought of calling him to invite him and his wife to a performance of Wynton Marsalis in Akron that week, Anna Marie and Oscar said they were unable to join us, but Mr. and Mrs. Johnson were able and willing!

John and I treated them to dinner and the concert in Akron. Dinner was at Quaker Square, and the concert was in the beautiful University of Akron E. J. Thomas Performing Arts Hall.

It was the first time any of us had seen a live Marsalis performance, and almost unbelievable on such short notice that we were only a few rows from the stage on the main floor section! It was a trio—Wynton Marsalis on trumpet, Marcus Roberts on piano, and Mel Torme, surprisingly, on *drums*. He didn't sing a note the entire time. We thought the concert was great, and we had such a friendly visit; it was as though we had known one another much longer than what we could pack into that one legendary night!

They said they enjoyed living in Pittsburgh, P.A. at that time not only because he had played pro football there, but also because of its close proximity to Canton, where every year he attended festivities with pro football buddies where he said he "had a ball!" He remembered Pittsburg, California, with fondness, not only for his alma mater, Pittsburg High School, but also for the ongoing friendships of alumni and others in the community whom he visited often. One of my classmates, Bob Rouner, was one of the organizers of those get-togethers, including a memorial for Johnson when he passed away in 2011.

* * * *

Since the Pro Football Hall of Fame opening in 1963 and in conjunction with the annual induction of players, there is also a professional football exhibition game, parties and a parade in August. When Patti started working at the Timken Company, she submitted a design for the company float which was accepted and won the top prize for floats in the 1987 parade! However, she wasn't there to bask in the glory of her achievement.

We received a very nice note from Mary, who worked for the Timken Company:

Mrs. Tate:

Enclosed is a picture of our float. I'll send copies to your talented Colorado daughter.

Everyone at the Timken Co. was pleased with the design of the float, and many comments were made 'that this was the best we've ever had!' I agree.

Thanks to your daughter for a grand prize winner! Enjoy your photo!

* * * *

Almost a year before that time, in Canton, she had met Eric, who lived nearby in Massillon. He soon had become the love of her life. But before the Hall of Fame festivities he and Patti moved to—yes—-Colorado! The city they chose in '86 was Boulder and they are still there. Cat lovers, like John and I, they took the beautiful white with ginger spotted offspring of our family cat, Kitty. They were Nicholas and Holly, born on Christmas Day, 1985.

Nicholas and Holly, Boulder, Colorado 1995

68. CALIFORNIA, HERE WE COME—AGAIN!

IN THE SUMMER OF '87 John and I traveled together to California, where we saw Carolyn, Walt, Eleanor and Glen. In Arizona and Nevada we were with Mother, and Colorado where we hiked with Patti and Eric. Everything we did confirmed our desire to move back to the west! Coming back to Canton with us were three awesome books: David Muench's *Santa Barbara* from Eleanor and Glen, Greg Lawson's *San Diego County*, and Ansel Adams's *Yosemite Valley*. Later, in August, Christina took her own trip to California, with "I love California! It's so cool!" on one of her post cards to us.

Since we would be retiring from our Ohio employments in 1988 and were hoping for more of the same in California, we requested letters of recommendations from necessary resources. We were moved with emotion when we received them, because they exceeded our modest expectations. They were written in 1987 and 1988 starting with L.M., Superintendent of Plain Local School District, who started by saying that it was an honor to recommend John...that he was an outstanding professional educator, who was one of the top ten teachers in the district of 450 teachers...In describing more, he said John's personal commitment meant that he would be successful in any task he would accept.

Mr. G. R. B., Assistant Superintendent of Public Instruction for the State of Ohio's Department of Education in Columbus said he would be most pleased to have John list him as a reference. In another from his principal, D. M., he stated that John had been a loyal and highly professional staff member through the years...an integral part of the middle school concept that they had been using for Taft (originally it was a junior high school)... and child-centered teacher who had done an excellent job with middle school students...a very cooperative and dedicated person. Mine were from university professors; a headmaster, a classroom teacher; CAI, CCCA Outreach Education, and Canton Symphony personnel.

Life was good. At this time, Christina graduated from high school, the only daughter who did four years! She entered the University of Cincinnati in the fall. Barbara the artist, with her "eye" for photography, opened with a beautiful exhibit of "Details" in nature and architecture at the CAI in November of our eventful '87. She had taken the photos in Europe and the United States after having studied photography at the International Center for Photography in New York. It was awesome to view our own daughter's works.

All was going well until an agonizing call came from Warren: "Dolores, I've just returned from taking Mom to a throat doctor surgeon friend of mine in Southern California, because she has cancer of the larynx! He said she needed a laryngectomy, which would remove her voice box! She said, 'no way', so I'm going to have to send her to you and see if you can get the help she needs."

"What a shock! Oh, man, what else can I do? Her care is primary, so send her and I'll see what I can do. It's a rough time for it since we're right in the middle of planning our move and employment in California—and that seems so selfish to even mention it when her life is threatened!"

Well, she came—and she and I went— to the Cleveland Clinic. After the throat oncologist examined her he asked, "Mrs. Hill, are you, or have you ever been a smoker? "

"Yes, I am a smoker, and I've been one for many years!"

"Did you ever drink alcohol when you smoked?"

"Yes."

"As far as your throat is concerned, that's a double whammy! I'm so sorry you have this cancer, but there may be some help for combatting it. If you're willing to have consistent radiation treatments five days a week on your throat for about 3 months, you can have improvement. *It'll only work, however, if you quit your smoking—and then, if you do, you have a 50 %.chance of beating it!* What do you think? Are you willing to have the treatments?"

"Yes, but I'm dependent on my daughter. Dolores, are you willing to take me?"

"Mom—of course! But do you realize what this means, driving an hour each way to Cleveland, plus dealing with a lot of congested traffic?"

Then the kind doctor said, "If you desire, there is a facility closer to you that does the same therapy and is in communication with us. It's in the small community of Hartville. Do you know where that is, Mrs. Tate?"

Did I? Absolutely. I had been through there many times. It was only about 20 miles from our house! I could have kissed him when he told us that!

"Yes, that would be great, and where I'd like to take Mom!"

We were fortunate in that I had retired from all my teaching in the summer, so had been able to take her.

"Mrs. Hill, what about your smoking? Are you willing to quit?"

"Absolutely."

After expressing our *huge* gratitude to the doctor, and doing the necessary preliminaries for the treatments, we went together five days a week from Thanksgiving time '88, until Valentine's Day '89. Fortunately, the rides were pleasant through Mennonite farm country.

She amazed me as she quit "cold turkey" the day of her Clinic appointment and never smoked again. Since I had never smoked, I could only guess it must have been difficult.

Her comment was, "Smoking was the dumbest thing I ever did in my entire life!"

Valentine's Day was a glorious "heart day" for both of us—full of gratitude to God and the doctors because they said the cancer was gone! Mom came out of the treatment room to greet me with her arms stretched up and outward, as high as she could reach, triumphantly, with a beaming smile "as wide as the lobby".

The only negative was that the radiation treatments destroyed her thyroid. She told me she could live with that because she could take thyroid medication. What a joy for our whole family that she hadn't had to lose her voice! In time, the quality of her vocal sounds actually improved, for she no longer had that gruff, scratchy smoker's sound. On the way to her home in Arizona that spring, she stopped in Minneapolis to visit relatives and share the great news.

* * * *

As far as our beautiful home was concerned, we prepared it for sale, and it sold in one day. We didn't have to change much because John had been improving it in many ways the last few years that we lived there, such as replacing a new furnace and roof. He had taken down the areas that had wallpaper, painted the interior, and had new carpeting installed.

Carolyn was a big help in finding us temporary rental housing in Tierrasanta, a planned community within San Diego before we arrived.

When it was time for our move in '89, we were sorry to leave our relatives and friends and hoped we could come back occasionally for visits. Christina moved out with us, as well as our two cats, Jasper and Kitty. He told me that as he was getting off the plane in San Diego he had "an emotional, overwhelming feeling of joy that I was coming home!"

He and I had left separately, since I had to teach at the Suzuki International Music Festival at Andrews University in Michigan for a week in June.

John teased me because I had two job interviews scheduled in San Diego before he did. By the end of summer I was hired by the principals of those schools. I was to teach music education at St. James Academy in Solana Beach K-8 and the same at St. Vincent de Paul's in San Diego K-6. In addition, I was to provide student Christmas concerts for both, and teach art for K-2 at St. Vincent's. I loved living in our new place by the sea and looked ahead to my new teaching adventures!

Warren Dunes State Park, Berrien County, Michigan.
Dolores Teaching the Romanian Paranita for the Music Festival.

69. BORDER "WELCOME"

JOHN HAD AN OFFER of a teaching position by Tony, principal at St. Columba Catholic School in San Diego. Tony was so appreciative of John's professional background that he was anxious to hire him. As a practicing Catholic, John thought he could be comfortable teaching there. The pay was lower, but because he was receiving his public State Teachers Retirement System from Ohio, he felt he could do it, and he would consider it to be a form of ministry, as well. Tony, also a Catholic, had a working wife and three children to support. After starting in the fall of '89, my spouse was delighted to learn how well his principal and he worked together. Like most of his classes in Ohio, he would be teaching sixth through eighth graders social sciences, but also additional ones—science—which he also loved, and some English. He received his California credential for public school teaching by passing the California Basic Educational Skills Test (CBEST) exam easily.

There were unintended bonuses for us when we attended the church there occasionally. It was a San Diego diocesan church, like the parish closer to our residence, with a priest John respected highly. Father seemed to be a conscientious leader of his parishioners and a great supporter of the school who would also attend parent-teacher association meetings. Then John soon found out he was also a lover of jazz, and knew I would appreciate that too. The priest promoted a jazz quartet composed of young men, some of whom were members of the parish. We enjoyed one of their concerts in the parish social hall and also the music played for folk masses led by music director Peter, a great guitarist with a great voice, and member of the jazz ensemble. Everyone could tell they enjoyed working together!

Life was again good, and I was happy with my two part-time jobs at St. James and St. Vincent's. The way I taught music required a lot of space, so I and the children were so fortunate that we were able to use the church social halls on the same campus as the schools. I bonded immediately with Sister Karen, a Sister of St. Joseph of Orange, California, and the principal at St. James Academy. She was very intelligent and compassionate. She expressed high academic standards and fair discipline for the students and faculty. She would come into my class unannounced once a year to observe and then give me a written report on how well I was teaching. One of the primary reasons she hired me was because of my inclusion of physical movement as part of my music curriculum, which we both knew helped develop not only musicality, but enhanced intelligence and balanced brains.

I was elated that all the students had excellent music textbooks. They had also included teachers' supplementary resources for Orff instrumentation; I could hardly believe my good fortune! However, while the school had a piano for me, but did not have any instruments for the students. The challenge, then, was to find out if providing them could become a reality.

Sister was slender, wore no religious habit, had nicely styled short hair, and was modern in her style of dress as well as mode of leading, which appealed to students as well as staff. Her overall appearance was modest and unassuming, which included no makeup or jewelry. The children were mostly from affluent or middle class families, but they also had projects helping their sister school in Tijuana, Mexico, the homeless of San Diego, and needy mothers and babies of Casa Maria, a place of refuge. Ecology, recycling, and even earthquake drills were important, as well. She lived and hoped that the students would also live abundantly well. This meant living by one of her favorite scripture verses from the Old Testament books, Micah: "to act justly, love tenderly, and walk humbly with our God".

Sister U, whose order was the Sisters of Mercy of Ireland, was the principal at St. Vincent's, and wore an abbreviated black or blue habit of a short veil and skirt below the knee with a white blouse. She kindly allowed me to borrow the few Orff style melody instruments that they owned for my use at St. James on my alternate teaching days. That consisted of a bass xylophone, an alto metallophone, a soprano glockenspiel and an alto one. I added my own alto xylophone and percussion instruments.

The teachers for the first and second graders were friendly and enthusiastic over the art projects I had for the children in their classrooms. One was young and the other was near retirement age, but both were energetic and fun.

The Christmas concerts of all the music students at both schools went well. I had hired a pianist, at my own expense, so I could direct the singing, dancing, and instrumentation. As I had in Ohio, I had spring programs for each class to share with parents what they had been learning. By the end of May, 1990, while making grades for over 300 report cards, I was rather exhausted and had been catching colds. The doctor said my immune system was breaking down. I was looking forward to having a break at summertime, but also my commitment to teach for the fifth time at the week-long Andrews University music festival in June. I was disappointed that I couldn't do it. Director R. was sorry, but had to hire a replacement—which was understandable— and I never went back.

After teaching at St. Vincent's on May 29 near four o'clock in the afternoon, I was lugging instruments, books and props up the long wall encased staircase leading from the sunken social hall to my car parked above on the street. Just as I was putting them into the trunk, I noticed a dark haired young man less than a block away on the sidewalk walking toward me. After shutting the lid and thinking nothing more of it, I went back down and up with another load, and by the time I was almost done filling the trunk that same person was near me, picked up the book bag I had on the sidewalk and handed it to me. I thanked him, tossed it into the trunk and slammed down the lid. He was short, had on a filthy white t-shirt showing through his open, short jacket and was unshaven. I didn't feel comfortable near him. By the time I arrived at the top of the stairs the third time, he was there and in a Spanish accent, asked if I could give him work.

"No, I'm sorry, I have no way to give you work. I'm just a teacher here at the school."

"I'm embarrassed."

"Why, what's the matter?"

"I don't know where I am."

He was disoriented; I wondered if he might be on drugs, and told him he was in the Mission Hills area of San Diego.

"I need to get home."

"Where do you live?"

"San Diego—in San Ysidro" (which was at the border with Mexico).

Just then a bus stopped about half a block from where we were. I gave him two dollars and said I didn't know if it was enough or not, but then added, "Quick—run to the bus and ask the driver how you can get to San Ysidro and how much it costs. If it costs more I'll give it to you."

But he just stood there. "Will you take me?"

"No."

I went back downstairs and hoped he had left for the bus. Finally, for my last trip up I stuck three more dollars in my pocket from my purse just in case he hadn't, took out my wooden alto xylophone from the storage cabinet and then put it down until I locked the cabinet. After that, my purse went onto my shoulder. I picked up the xylophone with both hands with my keys still in my right hand and turned around with my eyes looking down. Just as I stepped up onto the second stair I heard a downward rush of footsteps pounding on the several stairs just above me. I looked up. *It was that guy, still!"*

He grabbed me first with his one arm around my neck and his other hand poked a silver metal weapon which looked like a knife into my side. Then he left my neck and started to pound my head! The xylophone fell onto the stairs as I put my left hand on my head to protect it and my previously whip-lashed neck.

He shouted, "Give me your keys!"

I screamed instead, hoping someone on the street would hear me from the pit near the locked patio *but no one was around!*

"Don't scream!"

I was afraid to scream by then and he knocked my keys onto the stairs. He grabbed them and as he raced up the cement stairs my knees crashed down on them because my limbs were too weak to stand. I heard the engine of my car start up above and then take off.

I sat down on the stairs for a few minutes to try to recuperate. I reached for the railing and tried standing a couple times, and after that second time went up the stairs, slower than a snail, while peering cautiously as a spy as the parking spot came into view. Its emptiness was enormous relief, thinking he wouldn't be beating me up again! I walked the best I could, holding my purse until I arrived at the school office. Fortunately, it was still open. I was injured, but not badly.

Sister Ursula and her office assistant were stunned after they heard my story. It was not a high crime district. Sister seemed embarrassed. The police were called, and there was one in the area, so it did not take long to get help. I called John at St. Columba, and since we did not have "wheels", one of the teachers brought him. After the police report, we both went in the ambulance for a hospital checkup.

They gave a brief physical, some x-rays, but no emotional exam. Since the only visible sign of any injury was a huge dark clot on my hand which we were told would dissipate with time, we were sent home via an emotionally shaken Carolyn. I felt so emotionally drained and physically exhausted, I went to bed for a rest. I was surprised how upset Christina was too. Both girls stayed, sharing their concerns and appreciations with John and me. I was so thankful also that I hadn't been harmed more seriously. It was comforting to be home and to feel so loved.

I felt like everything was going to be okay. John and I had just bought a brand-new, lovely Mediterranean style, two bedroom, two bath condo in the Tierrasanta neighborhood of San Diego and would be moving into it in a couple of days. However, having moved from our spacious four bedroom house in Canton meant that in downsizing to a condo we didn't have much storage space, so John solved the problem. He created a large, sturdy loft of wood with steel supports and seven long wooden shelves along one whole wall of the garage. Near the washer and dryer he put up two shelves for laundry needs. Even with all the alterations there still was enough room for a moderately sized sedan, but we didn't need that space for a while!

San Diego, 1990, near our new condo.
Front row: Dolores and John.
Back row: Barbara, Patti, Carolyn and Christina

We had a considerable mortgage because our beautiful home in Canton sold for only about a third of the purchase price of the condo. But, John was elated that he no longer had to collect tons of leaves off our yard in the fall and shovel the snow off our long driveway! Another consolation was the two framed Ansel Adams photos we bought in a gallery to hang above our living room fireplace mantel. One was of El Capitan in Yosemite—so appropriate to have in a California home! The other is of trees in another location. Neither have his name on the front, which was the only way John would hang them on the wall. He didn't want them to look like posters, but like fine art.

When Sister Karen found out about the assault, she was appalled and sent a beautiful large bouquet of flowers from the school staff. School was almost out and some of my teaching resources were missing. She thought my teaching for the year should be over because it was important for me to rest and recuperate. She graciously invited me to the eighth grade graduation, which was being held in a country club near Solana Beach. I was pleased to be invited and went, even though I still felt somewhat tired and weak.

I still had my job for the next year at St. James. There were mutual agreements for my termination at St. Vincent's. The work load of the two schools' hundreds of students was more than my health would tolerate any longer.

By June I received a nice letter from the Victim's Assistance Office of the San Diego Police Department and by calling their number, I made an appointment with a Ms. G. to discuss my case. As a crime victim, she said I was eligible to receive psychological counseling for the trauma I had experienced. "Thank you, I appreciate it, but I'm pretty strong psychologically so I don't think I'll be needing it."

Soon after John and I had gone to bed in our new bedroom, I received a call between 11 and midnight the night of June 2.

"Hello?"

"Is this the residence of Mrs. Dolores Tate, and if it is, may I speak with her, please?"

"Yes, this is she."

"Mrs. Tate, this is Patrolman S. from the San Diego County Sheriff's Department and I'm calling from the Vista Patrol Station. I apologize for calling you so late, but I have found your stolen 1988 Nissan Sentra!"

"Great!"

"However, I'm sorry to say, you can't have it back."

"Why not?"

"It was totaled in an auto accident."

"Oh no—excuse me while I tell my husband! I hope no one was killed!"

"No one was killed, but there were injuries. I need to tell you from the beginning how all this happened."

"Please do."

"First of all, I pulled over a car of your Nissan's description in Vista because it had a stolen license plate on it. A young Hispanic was the driver, and another one was in the passenger's seat. I had the driver get out, and he didn't have a valid driver's license. He spit at me, jumped back into the car and sped away, with me chasing him. It was crazy dangerous! He started in the bike lane, went through one parking lot at 50 miles an hour, and another at 70! On one straight road he was going 80 miles an hour! He even went on the wrong side of some roads and went through a few stop signs. On the last one, he finally was caught because unfortunately, he ran into a 1989 Nissan Pulsar with all young passengers. Fortunately, they seemed to have survived so far without serious injuries, but they are going to get treated. So your car was totaled, and the passenger in it was found covered in blood from lacerations to the forehead. His left eye was shut because he had shattered glass in it. His left shoe was off and his ankle was so swollen he couldn't stand on it."

"What about the driver?"

"He was hardly injured! Anyway, I arrested him and during interrogation he waived his right to be silent, said he knew his driver's license had been suspended, and that he stole the license plate that was on your car from an apartment complex in Vista. He admitted stealing your car. We know about this guy because he's had a history with drugs and gangs. We recognized his passenger, too. We're pleased that the driver had a birthday recently. Now he's old enough to be prosecuted! His name is Francisco and his passenger's name is Mario. Are you willing, Mrs. Tate, to be a witness and identify him for the assault and robbery? If so it will be in the Vista Courthouse."

"Yes, I will."

"Also, you have to identify your vehicle and it's at F.'s Towing in Vista. Here's the phone number... Thank you, Mrs. Tate."

"Thank you, for doing such a great job of getting Francisco despite the risks, and giving us such a great report!"

I received a subpoena to appear on June 19, and John went with me. I worried some that I might not recognize him, but when he appeared I had no trouble at all, even though he was in bright orange prison garb. I thought about the tragic life Francisco had been living, his "fried" brain from drugs and hoped he could get the help he needed for permanent spiritual and health repair, away from crime.

John and I were required to visit the Vista lot to claim our destroyed, useless car. It was a depressing scene, with the body ripped and full of holes, shattered glass, and a frame that was twisted, dented, disjointed and collapsed. We were able to see the inside of the front seat and saw that there was a photo of a girl clipped on the sun visor, which we thought might be a girlfriend. There was an athletic shoe on the floor of the passenger side that probably belonged to Mario.

We were able to unlock the trunk and confirmed my dread that it would be devoid of any instruments and other music paraphernalia. My anger and frustration was also over the loss of lesson plans that I had created. The man there said they were gone when the car came to him. As far as I know, no one ever learned what Francisco did with them. He probably threw them all away or sold the instruments. Besides the car, there were economic losses of $1866.00 to St. Vincent's, St. James' and myself. Insurance policies paid some, and the balances were to be paid by Francisco's prison salary, which we never received. Maybe it required me to follow through on it more myself. I typed and submitted lists of the losses, but there were no receipts for the instruments because too much time had elapsed since purchase.

By September 1990 Francisco had been sentenced to prison for five years, with multiple crimes against him.

As fall and classes near the holidays were thriving for all at St. James, life was good again for me—until I started having some nightmares. They happen occasionally to most people, so I didn't pay attention to them at first. But then they became a little more frequent and by then I was also more sensitive emotionally than usual, which also created stomach distress for me while awake. There were times when I didn't have my normal confidence in driving. Once I woke up in a sweat after feeling terrorized by someone asking me to give a singing performance I didn't feel I could do! I decided, then, that I needed professional help and discussed it with my chiropractor. He recommended very highly Dr. G., a psychologist who was an emotional trauma specialist.

My initial session was February 11, 1991, and afterward I was already feeling better about my situation. We communicated well, and because of his knowledge and understanding, I felt there was hope for my healing.

Driving there the next day I was more relaxed and confident on the highway. In talking with Dr. G., I learned I had to take an active role in my healing by keeping a stress management journal daily, entering my subjective units of discomfort with my daily activities with a unit scale from 0 to

100. 0 represented very, very relaxed and 100 was very, very tense, angry, and frustrated. I was also told that I would go through stages of healing, starting with feels of guilt and blame, then anger, then calm. ("Yes!" I told Dr. G., "It was partly my fault because I didn't take the other door out of the social hall where the storage room was. How stupid I was!") This had been my initial reaction.

In gauging the stress levels, I never reached 100, but I did hit 90 once when I rescued a cat injured in a hit and run car accident on the road near our place. Immediately I had a splitting headache, but fortunately, I was able to drive the victim to a vet nearby where care was given as soon as I brought him in. When I left him the headache left me, knowing he had good care. I put signs in the neighborhood, and I was so elated the next day when I found the owner! From that Tuesday to Wednesday, my number went down to 20. The numbers went up and down from 80 down to 0, depending on my other activities.

The only times I had zeroes were after John's and my love making! Teaching reactions with the students were occasionally 80 and 70, but mostly in the lower numbers, because I enjoyed teaching. Our trip to Disneyland was sure different than usual. I had taken my journal to write in it that day. The highway was crowded, which stressed me out. At breakfast with our nephew, I felt sick to my stomach and couldn't eat much, but by the time we were out and about I improved greatly. The last thing we did before we left was to dance with live Big Band music, and my score went from 80 down to a mellow 10!

During Easter vacation we drove to Mother's in the Arizona desert with no problems and had a happy time helping her and pouring over old family photographs, which I loved.

I hadn't cried at the attack, and my psyche knew I had the need to do so. I would do so spontaneously a little bit, as when I would become too nervous, or worried about Carolyn and her problems. One of the triggers for it was (just) the high notes sung at Mass by congregation and choir. I had not joined the choir yet and was with the congregation when I had to stop singing at that point.

A weekend in April was especially healing. At the peak of our love making Saturday night I cried for the first time since the attack! I was a little awkward about it, but John was patient and understanding, believing it was probably needed and good for me. On Sunday I went to Mass alone and struggled against crying from the time I entered church for Mass. The homily was helpful, as though it had been designed for me personally, and the congregational song was "How Can I Keep from Singing?" Then—The Lord's Prayer—I was finally able to sing it without crying, and sang the alto part! Then—what? I started crying uncontrollably coming home! I parked the car at the end of the drive near our condo by the open field of wildflowers and wailed with enough water to soak the foliage! As I looked out the windshield the tall, pale yellow mustard flowers were swaying beautifully in the gentle breeze as gracefully as dancers. The longer I gazed, the shorter the sobs were. The graceful rhythm became a part of me as I swayed slightly in my seat until the tears stopped. Then there was peace. I felt healed and told John, who shared my joy.

The next day I felt good about myself. My remaining sessions with Dr. G. were very helpful, and on May 13, 1991 I was released from my therapy, almost a year (May 29) after the crime.

70. OUR CALIFORNIA AND
NEW YORK CELEBRATIONS

THE SAME MONTH IN '91 that I was considered healed John and I attended Carolyn's graduation for her Bachelor of Arts degree in Communications at San Diego State University. Her two student film creations had been accepted into film festivals in San Diego and Los Angeles. What joy the three of us had in all her university accomplishments! What a strong spirit she had to finish, despite the stresses of living with Walt. They had both been working (she was a photographer for J. C. Penney's photography studio); his leg had been injured on his job earlier, but had eventually healed as Carolyn had taken him to medical appointments and cared for him otherwise. He still drank too much, charged thousands of dollars on her credit card, and then left her shortly afterward before she was done with her studies. We ended up going to court to pay that debt because she didn't have the money, and she moved in with us as a temporary measure.

John and I took her to Coronado Island across the bay for a Polynesian lunch after the ceremony, and then had a small family celebration at our place within days with our nephew Randy and his family; Charles, Barbara, and Mom, who flew in for it.

* * * *

When Christina married John, a California native, in San Diego near the end of April, 1993, it was the first of three weddings that we Tates had in two and a half years at our new locale. We were satisfied that the choices all the girls had made for marriage seemed to be good ones, giving us a sense of relief for each. Besides the name, John was like her dad in that he was an Air Force veteran. When they had met, both were part-time college students while working full-time.

His father Tom and stepmother Helen provided a fine Italian wedding rehearsal dinner at a restaurant in Seaport Village along San Diego Bay. Christina wanted to take the major role in helping me plan everything else. She was the one who made most of the choices, from choosing the clergyman, ceremony and classical guitarist to her lovely traditional white gown. Particular about food, she chose a wonderful Italian cuisine buffet and the D.J. for the dance music.

Having it in beautiful Balboa Park, full of gorgeous landscaping and Spanish architecture provided a perfect environment for the sunny outdoor ceremony. John's good friend was his best man. Carolyn was Christina's bridesmaid and Laurie, her best buddy, flew in from Ohio to be her maid of honor. Other friends and relatives from California, Arizona, and

Oregon filled the guest area as two handsome ducks also observed from the small reflective pool there. A surprise at the conclusion of it was the sound of chimes played from the nearby organ pavilion — how perfect that was!

* * * *

When Patti and Eric finally decided to marry in 1994, their invitation stated "...will make it official after a seven year rehearsal...the eighth of October." They chose the Princess Resort in San Diego on the edge of Mission Bay. The lush, tropical setting looked like we could have been in Hawaii! Since they were both working a lot, they asked if we would make all the other arrangements, which we did. It started with a scrumptious sunset rehearsal dinner at the ocean in La Jolla, provided by Eric's parents Roni and Eric.

It was an outdoor, small and intimate October wedding ceremony with 25 people from our families, followed by a candlelight dinner and entertainment by another Eric, a classical guitarist. Barbara, the maid of honor, and Patti's only attendant, had flown in from New York with Charles. Eric's paternal grandmother had flown in from Illinois with her son Ty who was best man. His aunt and uncle came from Connecticut, and Mother was there from Arizona.

When busy talking at happy occasions, sometimes it's easy to miss how many glasses of champagne and wine are being filled by the waiter. When we all rose to leave and walk to our cars, mother could hardly do it, because she weaved and wobbled uncontrollably down the dark sidewalk, until John assisted her. It was the first time I had ever seen Mom drunk! Maybe I shouldn't have been so irritated with her since everyone else thought she was a humorous sight.

* * * *

After Walt, Carolyn was jaded. She didn't care if she dated anyone ever again, not trusting men much anymore. In fact, she wasn't in the mood when, after attending a party at a friend's home someone she had met there liked her laugh and showed a bit of interest in her. Surprisingly, she gave him her phone number, which was ours, so when he called I happened to answer. She didn't want to come to the phone, but I encouraged her to do so because he sounded so nice. They had been at a mutual friend's home, so she weighed that into the equation, thinking for a moment that it might be safe to try. She finally consented, and when he came to pick her up, I liked him right away since he had such good manners (must have been raised well, I thought).

Slowly she adapted to Mickey until there was a joyful relationship, doing much together. She even helped him with his orchid business and shows.

On March 28, 1993, though, there was a heartbreaking event for him and his family. One of his brothers and his wife were killed in a small plane that he was piloting in the Pacific Northwest. He was one of four brothers in a family that also included a sister. We were touched positively when Mickey unexpectedly asked not only Carolyn, but also us, to attend the April memorial service for emotional support. It was held at the First United Methodist Church in San Diego, and was presented with grace and beauty by Rev. Mark Trotter, Mickey, and another of his brothers. Mickey's photo of a beautiful sunset over the Pacific Ocean graced the front of the written memorial program. There was a reception line after the service which included the rest of the family, and we were impressed by how special all his family seemed to be. It was our first meeting.

Eventually he asked her to marry him while they were in Hawaii for 1994 Thanksgiving and she could not have been more ready, so she accepted enthusiastically! On July 14, 1995, the wedding rehearsal dinner was held, overlooking fantastic San Diego Bay.

Theirs was the largest and first summer wedding of our three and was held at First United Methodist Church on the next day with Rev. Trotter officiating. John and I had heard him preach occasionally and respected him highly. We were inspired each year as we attended each Advent concert there soon after we had moved to San Diego.

The Sanctuary is illuminated with natural light through the gold, red, and clear glass windows and a large window displaying outdoor trees, bushes and flowers behind the altar. The massive organ pipes for the organ that Mickey's family helped establish complete the magnificent sacred space. It's conducive to prayer, words of wisdom, inner peace, and joy, wedding vows and commitments. Christina was her Matron of Honor. Barbara and Patti were her bridesmaids, as well as Mickey's sister, sister-in-law and a friend. John was so proud of all his daughters and enjoyed being in all their weddings.

Even though our family had not lived in San Diego long enough to know a lot of people to invite, Mickey's family, well established in the city for generations, made up for it. There were hundreds in attendance.

The outdoor reception, which was at Mickey's parents' home, included dancing to a live tuxedoed band. Also special to both of them was the attendance of Carolyn's maternal Grandma, in her 80's, and Mickey's paternal Grandma, in her 90's, at the wedding ceremony and reception. What a joy for John and me that Carolyn was finally so happy!

* * * *

June 19, 1994 was our fortieth wedding anniversary. Months before, our girls told us they wanted to give us a party. As we were looking forward to it, I started to doubt the affair. "Hon, Mom is going to be 80 this year. She's been living out in the desert alone for 15 years now, which isn't easy, so I wonder how much longer she'll be alive. I wonder if we should forgo our party and do it for her instead."

"Well, it seems like a good idea. I wonder how the family will respond to it." We both decided that maybe they would be interested in giving us a celebration of our fiftieth instead.

We could not have had a better response! Everyone we invited came. John and I and Carolyn and Mickey were the only ones living in San Diego. Others came from Colorado, Minnesota, New York and various places in California.

Her birthday was not until October 29, so I planned to have it as a surprise near our June anniversary time. The soonest I could get the reservation was Saturday, July 2 at the Sheraton Hotel East, Harbor Island, overlooking San Diego Bay. We had a perfect size banquet room not only for guests but also for our other needs. The restaurant providing the buffet was Harbor's Edge, with breathtaking views of the waterfront marina and San Diego cityscape.

Fortunately, Mom arrived from Arizona, fully believing that she was going to *our* party! Mother-To-Be Christina greeted her Grandma Peggy with a mixed flower bouquet with plenty of roses. Mom was overjoyed, but puzzled as to why *she* was getting flowers while she continued walking further into the room, holding onto Warren's arm. As the music began, Warren guided her to the balloon decorated seat as she needed to sit anyway just to try to figure out what all the attention was about! She was seeing so many people she loved, photographs plus a poster of herself, and her clown painting on an easel.

While I was explaining and singing from the microphone, the musician was playing on the keyboard and Carolyn was filming everybody. After everyone had shared the food and great conversations, Mother stood at the mike and thanked everyone from the bottom of her heart. She was so overwhelmed, she couldn't say much else. But Dawn's daughter Lauren—about kindergarten age—thought it was great fun to talk on it! "Happy Birthday, Great Grandma Peggy!"

As for a fiftieth anniversary party for us, that unfortunately didn't happen, but there were never any regrets that we had chosen this substitute.

* * * *

When the Saratoga Limited traveled to Saratoga Springs Racetrack in August 1993, it was the second August for the rail excursions, planned by our entrepreneur son-in-law Charles. The first year they were so successful the New York Times ran a feature travel article before the second run helping to make the trip assured, with twice as many passengers as before. This time John and I were invited, as well as Charles' mother Helen, our welcome companion for the day. John was the Tour Supervisor for the 15th of August, overseeing all tour guides and on board programs, while Helen and I just relaxed and felt special to be guests on the private luxury train.

The engine pulled two restored vintage cars from the 20's and 40's, on Amtrak rails which began daily (except Tuesdays) at 8:15 A.M. out of the Pennsylvania Station in downtown Manhattan. From the time we boarded with the help of a tuxedoed porter, it was red carpet treatment all the way in classic French style service. Meticulously planned by Royal Northern president Charles, no elegant detail for customer comfort and satisfaction was left out.

Upon entering the refurbished cars in Victorian style, I was in awe over the fine mahogany interiors as well as decorating done by our daughter Barbara. In the dining car there were huge classic urns with dried flowers bouquets in various colors which coordinated with the drapery window treatments and Muirfield china. There were beautiful landscapes of the famed Hudson River Valley outside the windows as well as some in illuminated frames on the walls that passengers could view from their dining tables. The gourmet meals began with a European style champagne breakfast.

Sitting in the relaxed ambience of the observation lounge car lent itself to extended enjoyment on the three and a half hour rail ride to the first arrival in Albany. Helen had made beautiful pillows for some of the seats. There was an outdoor platform on the back of the lounge car where people could stand and feel the wind!

We were met in Albany by limousine drivers who whisked us away to the racetrack because the Amtrak rails did not run to Saratoga. We arrived by noontime, ready for the gourmet lunch and races at the Saratoga Racecourse Clubhouse. There were outdoor tables and seating, shaded by a huge tent covering with broad red and white stripes over tables and chair decorations, continuing with the red and white theme. Our priority seating, looking out at the lovely pastoral grounds, was located trackside, along the first rail, adjacent to the parade path, so we enjoyed seeing the thoroughbreds up close as they paraded and raced past us!

John and I spent a little on the betting and Helen did more. Some passengers had an interest in sightseeing, antiquing, or relaxing at the spa in the splendor of the Victorian village, but we didn't have time for them—

as attractive as they were—even though there was an executive shuttle provided.

After the exciting races we returned to the train. It was evening, and we were greeted with champagne and hors d' oeuvres to celebrate. John and I hadn't any winners, but Helen made out very well at the track, so she was in quite a celebratory mood. A professional personal trainer had won $4,000, so he was also feeling great!

A sumptuous five course dinner created by the James Beard award-winning chef was served by candlelight, along with cocktails, fine wines and Saratoga sparkling mineral water. From Poughkeepsie to Yonkers, New York we were serenaded by two young men who played classical music on their violins. There were a lot of us in mellow, relaxed moods, and actor Tony Randall, sitting with friends in the back, was more than just mellow, boisterously enjoying the night!

It wasn't long before staff from *The Today Show* took the trip. They had such a great time they decided to film it for their program. Because they felt the time allowed for the weekly show would not do it justice, they aired it on a Saturday, instead, to give it more time.

71. FAMILY HEART PHENOMENA

IN 1957 WHILE JOHN was an undergraduate at KSU, his father's cousin, Professor John Popa died suddenly of a heart attack at the age of 55. Deeply disappointed, the student couldn't understand why Popa left at such a young age. He clearly felt the loss and regretted that he would not be able to learn Romanian history from his Romanian expert relative.

One evening a year later, there was an episode at our home. John suddenly experienced breathing difficulties with tightness in his chest, erratic heart beats and pain shooting down his arms. He was sweating as he weakly said, "Call an ambulance!" I did and we went to Mercy Hospital. The doctors checked him thoroughly for a week with a tentative heart attack diagnosis. Fortunately at the end of the week the final conclusion was that he didn't have a heart attack. What he *did* have was his body's response to drinking *ten cups of coffee daily.*

In the late 60's, my mother-in-law Mary had her first heart attack while in the hospital with an acute case of asthma and a lung infection. Her husband's oldest sister (and John's aunt) Anna died of a heart attack in her sixties. Some years later her son had heart surgery twice but is still alive in 2016.

During the 70's and 80's John's Dad's younger sister Vickie had heart attacks until she had open heart surgery; she lived many years after that. Her oldest son also had open heart surgery at age 42 and is also still alive in 2016. It was different with her second son who died at 42 from a sudden heart attack. Her youngest son died at 66 from a heart attack in 2015.

Dad Tate himself avoided heart disease, perhaps because he took large amounts of aspirin for arthritis. Perhaps that aspirin came back to haunt him later.

After the wedding, white water rafting and train trip in the summer of 1993, John and I went back to teaching in September refreshed. Life was good until November.

Near the beginning of the month John developed a slight sore throat and stiff neck. At night when he could lay flat, he would have a moderate cough and some difficulty breathing, accompanied by discomfort in the chest and back, radiating into both shoulders. He would feel better in the daytime, so he just hoped the symptoms would eventually go away on their own. However, that did not happen, and on Saturday of Thanksgiving weekend, the 27th, those symptoms got much worse. This attack lasted for several hours and John was exhausted.

John was also frustrated. "What the heck—what's going on here? I'll have to call Dr. A. on Monday." He then grabbed the phone, and was able to get an appointment with our primary care physician for Tuesday. He had to take an extended Thanksgiving "vacation" the rest of the week from school.

He was able to drive himself to the XMed (Medical) Building, adjacent to Scripps Memorial Hospital in La Jolla. I taught that day, so he took me and picked me up from school when I was done. Feeling even worse than before, he told me what happened with the doctor: "When he listened to my heart on the stethoscope, his eyes got intense, and he looked like he was in a panic!"

John continued, "'My God', he said, 'I can hear a lot of blood swishing in there! I have to get Dr. G! Fortunately, he's in this same building!' He ran out of the exam room and continued to Dr. G.'s office. He's a cardiologist and Dr. A. was able to get me an appointment for tomorrow."

When that doctor gave him a physical exam for evaluation, he concluded that the regurgitation was severe, and seemed it was originating from the aortic valve, which could have been caused by congenital heart disease, a bicuspid aortic valve, or rheumatic heart disease. His cough could be related to congestive heart failure or upper respiratory tract infection.

He ordered two x-ray views of his chest for that same day which showed the heart was slightly enlarged. The other conclusion was that he did have mild congestive heart failure. As a result, he received medication for it and appointments for an echocardiogram, a thallium treadmill stress test, and lab tests for Friday.

He returned home and that evening and Thursday evening he developed chills with a fever reaching 102. Friday, December 3, with his fever down, I drove him to his tests and returned home with the understanding that I would be ready to pick him up whenever he was finished. The echocardiogram on Friday revealed a thickened aortic valve with severe (4+) aortic regurgitation and dilated left ventricle. There was no evidence of regurgitation of his other valves. The stress testing had to be interrupted due to his growing weakness, but there was enough to confirm severe aortic regurgitation and a worsening cardiac murmur. When the testing was finished, I received a call from the nurse. "Mrs. Tate, you can pick up your husband now."

Five minutes later, just as I was about to go out the door, I received another call. "I'm sorry, Mrs. Tate, there has been a change. When you arrive, please see the doctor in his office."

"Okay. Thank you for calling. I'll be there in about half an hour."

As I walked into Dr. G.'s office, John was sitting in the chair opposite the doctor at his desk and he looked ghastly! His complexion was ashy; he looked pained and exhausted—worse than he had looked at home. I got a lump in my throat and had to sit down. Even though I had just met the doctor for the first time, his compassionate look gave me some calm as I listened to him.

"Thank you, Mrs. Tate, for coming. I need to talk to you because John is in such a dangerous state with his heart he needs to be put in the hospital immediately."

"And if he doesn't go to the hospital at this time, what would be your prognosis?"

"He would die very soon of massive congestive heart failure—he already has congestive heart failure and it's progressively getting worse. So far it seems like he is going to have to have emergency surgery for his aortic valve. If you take him home it will be against my professional judgment, and I cannot give permission to do so!"

I looked at John, then Dr. G. and said, "Absolutely, he needs to go into the hospital!"

John said, "I'm so relieved! Because you usually say surgery should be the last resort, I was wondering if you were going to argue with the doctor over it, telling him you had to think about it first." With a determined look in his eyes, he said, "I need the surgery."

I agreed. "Honey, there is no choice in this matter!"

Doctor G. gave a sigh of relief too, as I nervously hoped and prayed the hospital personnel would be able to save John's life! As I was leaving Scripps Memorial Hospital my Rock noticed I was shaken, and exuded a serene confidence as he kissed me good-by and said, "Everything will be okay."

Well, evidently my body and psyche had not digested what he just said. I didn't have as much confidence as he had. I felt physically and emotionally drained, but my thoughts were racing. He was dying, and he looked like it! I was exhausted driving home to Tierrasanta in the dark. I got breathless walking up the 13 steps of our condo, and when I walked inside my jarred immune system reacted. I started getting a sore throat, cough and tightness in my chest. I crawled into bed and, in tears, called our girls in Manhattan, Boulder and locally, to tell them what had happened that afternoon and evening, and how bizarre it had seemed. I could hardly talk, but the emotional support that they gave helped relieve some of my anxious stress. I was so proud of them as each responded voluntarily and without hesitation, "I'll be there with you for the operation!"

I wish I could have seen my honey on the weekend, but I was trapped in the house with my own ailment. Monday I was able to get prescriptions for my cough and respiratory infection after Dr. A. saw me. I was just across the drive from the hospital, but obviously could not be with John. Every time I spoke on the phone and heard his voice, I was elated! He was still alive! Otherwise, he was being thoroughly checked for infections because of his recent elevated fevers. There was a concern that they could be related to dental work he had done in October. Urine and multiple other blood tests were being done as well. Lung and heart monitoring were constant.

He also had a cardiac catheterization procedure that day. Dr. G. wanted me to be there to review the angiogram, but since I couldn't, Carolyn was chosen. She consented, but her immediate feelings were, "At first, besides feeling very responsible, I was somewhat apprehensive—particularly if my conclusion was for the surgery and then later learn that he shouldn't have had it!" But after viewing it, her hesitation completely vanished. She was absolutely convinced that he should have the surgery! "I could see where the blood wasn't being pumped! The aortic valve wasn't functioning at all and the heart was larger than it was supposed to be because of the non-circulating blood rushing uncontrollably into it. And, there was actually some good news—there were no arterial blockages!" This last revelation from Carolyn's call was a great aid to my own recovery and thankfulness that he had not been a smoker and that he had eaten right!

Cardiologist Dr. G. chose surgeon Dr. M. and Carolyn and I went to see him together. Compassionately, he put his arm around me to help calm my worries and tears. He told us of the general surgical risks involved, but also the benefits of the superior Ross Procedure, which was a double valve surgery. He said John would probably do well with it, because like the other doctors, he had concluded that except for the current valve problem and related heart enlargement, John was generally healthy. Yes! My Rock was strong! If his arteries had been blocked, he would not have been a candidate for the Ross surgery. Other medical staff searched for infections all week and found none; this also would greatly improve the chances of using the Ross. When we were done, Carolyn and I could not have had more confidence in any other surgeon to fully restore John's health.

Thursday was the first time I was able to see John and we went over the medical facts together. John had tolerated the angiogram well, with no complications. It revealed that his aortic valve was bicuspid (two leaflets), instead of the normal tricuspid (three leaflets), and the conclusion, then, was that the abnormality was apparently congenital. Fortunately, his pulmonary valve was a normal tricuspid; this was necessary for the kind of surgical procedure we hoped to have.

John was blessed to have been in La Jolla. The proposed surgery was uncommon in the United States, and most common in the United Kingdom, where it had been developed in the 1960's by surgeon Donald Ross in London. It was also gaining use worldwide. Our cardiologist said Dr. M. was one of only six surgeons in the United States trained to use the Ross Transfer, the improved human valve replacement surgery, and Dr. M. had worked with Ross. It involved taking the patient's own tricuspid pulmonary, transferring it into the more critical place of the aortic, and replacing the patient's pulmonary with a human donor valve, which had been freeze-dried, and would be flown in from Georgia. We were told if either valve deteriorated it would happen more with the donor's pulmonary than with the patient's own. Prior to the Ross Transfer, single human donor aorta valve replacements had not been as successful, and the only other choices were porcine (pork) and of synthetic materials, such as stainless steel. The latter would make audible clicking sounds, and both would develop calcification in about ten years, necessitating surgery again. The Ross transplant, utilizing living, human tissue, had a longevity of twenty years or more, so was used for patients who would probably live that long. John was 62, but the doctors thought he was healthy enough to live that much longer. Beside the possibility of rejection by the patients' bodies of porcine or synthetic valves, there were other lifelong issues with them, as well. Clots could develop causing stroke, so anti-coagulants, with the possible risk of hemorrhaging, had to be taken by the patients, and those valves were more prone to post-surgical infections.

Since it had appeared to both of us that this complex and lengthy surgery technique was superior to the other options for John's situation, we had consented to the Ross Procedure surgery scheduled for the next day and spoke with the anesthesiologist. We parted with prayers, confidence, and knowledge that all of us Tate girls would be at the hospital.

Besides us five, there was Mickey, Carolyn's future husband, who took time away from his orchid business. Warren, who was at his job in the Sierras, and John's principal kept in touch on the phone. It was coffee time again when we gathered, because the surgery started at 7 A.M. Some of us prayed in the chapel. Nobody talked much. There was a lot of silent reading done when we could concentrate on it. Some of us were edgy, wanting the time to pass faster as each succeeding hour went by. The tension just kept building as we wondered how John was doing all that time, and if he would survive. It was the longest morning of my life.

Initially, it was a 4 hour wait, and when the nurse came down the hall to report to us, Barbara ran there to meet her. Right after the nurse gave her a message, Barbara burst into tears. I was on the phone with Warren, and when I saw Barbara through the window, I dropped the phone. Alarmed, I started crying. As the two came into the room, Barbara excitedly blurted, "Mom, don't worry—everything is fine! Dad's doing great! The surgery went well, with no complications! I was crying because I'm happy—it was a tension release!" I felt so much better as I thanked the nurse.

Dr. M. was beaming as he eventually walked toward all of us anxiously eager to greet him. He said John had no infection anywhere inside, so it had been possible to go ahead with the Ross Procedure, which he tolerated very well. "Amazingly, the aortic cusps were torn completely away from the aortic wall. Apparently, the cause of the bicuspid valve failure was that it wore out due to the work load that normally a tricuspid valve would do. Well, now that he has a tricuspid in that position, he should do well for many years!"

How could we show our appreciation to him for saving John's life? He had performed a demanding and long surgery. Words were inadequate for the profoundly joyful emotions swelling within our chests, but of course we bombarded him with many appreciative words. As he left, I picked up the phone to confirm with Warren what he may have heard already, and then called Margaret, John's principal. Barbara grinned as she shared, "I could have kissed his feet and more!" Eventually the family showed our appreciation with notes and an orchid for his office. For lunch that day we celebrated at nearby Pizza Nova.

When we girls returned to the hospital, John was slowly waking up in the intensive care unit. When I was in there the nurse was gently slapping his face to help bring him out of the morphine-induced sleep. She also said, "This man is no longer a sick man—you are to treat him as a well man."

"Okay," I said, "That's encouraging!"

Barbara did not last more than a few minutes after seeing him with the multiple tubes attached to his body. "I had to leave Dad—I couldn't stand to see him like that!"

After he was moved to a regular room, walking was one of his daily activities. During resting times, some people walking past his room wondered how he rated head and foot massages from three lovely young ladies, until they learned they were his daughters!

I received an unexpected bonus when I visited him one day and accidently found a little coffee shop in the hospital. Not only did they have coffee, but they had half chocolate and full chocolate biscotti, which I had never had before. Wow! I loved them, and discovered I felt especially good after eating them! Until John left the hospital on the 16th I got my daily choice of a little "medicine", which has continued to this day when I need an occasional little boost of comfort food for my blues.

At the time of John's release, he was eating a regular diet, still taking walks, and had an appointment to see the surgeon in two weeks for check-up. I was a bit apprehensive about caring for him.

For years, I had tried as much as possible to have whole foods, non-processed, organic foods to eat, and one of the habits John had when eating meat was to carve away any fat that was there, even though most of the meats were lean anyway. Except for occasional Romanian stuffed cabbages, he had cut out red meat in the 1980's and ate some fowl. After his surgery, he wrote the following letter to our girls and their husbands:

I am especially aware of the problems of heart disease after going through surgery last year to replace the valve. I consider myself very fortunate to have known about preventive care for many years. Probably the best thing I did was to have taken vitamins E (free radical fighter which helps prevent clots), C (infection fighter), and minerals, plus walk as much as I did. Because of this I did not have to have the bypass surgery. I credit my lifestyle for my recovery. I am sure that you probably know about some of this information, but I thought it would be useful for you to review it again for your reference.

I send it to you with love, Dad

When we considered the events of the past year, we thought he was also so fortunate that the valve didn't go out on him at Christina's wedding, the Saratoga trip, and *especially* while on the whitewater rafting. As we celebrated the birth of the very Special Child at Christmas, we rejoiced again with thanksgiving the gift of life that had been restored to John. So did John's class at St. Columba as they sent a colorful, huge humorous card designed by Louis, one of the students, and signed by everyone. "The Sixth Grade Class Wishes You A Happy Christmas!" On the front were a cool Santa and one of his reindeer flying through the air, both wearing "shades", above the greeting, "Have a Cool Christmas".

After six weeks when John was allowed to go back to his teaching seventh and eighth graders history, geography, literature, English and science and his normal other life of activities, John said, "It's time we go back to 'Makin' Whoopee', which we did, and it was glorious—our perfect gifts for each other!" And again, we looked forward to long lives together!

Carolyn sent a card:

Congratulations! You're alive! Isn't it wonderful when good things happen to nice people! You're healthier than ever! You're back to work! We love you Dad! Glad to have you back to normal and healthy!

Love, your Four Lovely Daughters (especially Daughter Number Three)!

San Diego 1994
John had survived his emergency heart surgery in December 1993 and had recently celebrated his 63rd birthday in October.

San Diego 1995
John the teacher at St. Columba School

72. GRANDCHILDREN AND OUR YOUNGEST CHILD

OUR YOUNGEST DAUGHTER AND second to get married was the first to have a child. Birth day for Cameron, our first grandchild— a boy in this family of girls—was exciting for all of us. He surprised us, having arrived a month early, but he was already 19 inches plus on the 19th of December, 1994 in Oceanside, California. She did not want us present for the birth—just in the adjoining room—while Carolyn was requested to be with her as well as her husband John and the doctor. How fortunate they were to have had her John to help with the delivery in her room—cultural wisdom had finally been established by then for the father's presence.

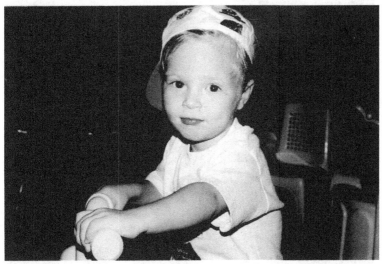

Fremont, California 1996. Our grandson Cameron at two years old.

Cortland, our second grandchild was conceived in San Diego during the happy week of Carolyn and Mickey's wedding. Cortland at 19 inches long also came a month early. I was puzzled by both premature arrivals, since my first three children came two weeks later than estimated birth date and the last one was a week "late". However, John's sister had premature births, so we decided it must have been genetic. On March 8, 1996 our sweetly fragrant plumeria plant from Hawaii bloomed to welcome our sweet New York City granddaughter!

New York City 1998. Our granddaughter Cortland at two years old.

* * * *

Raising our last Bundle of Joy had been almost like raising an only child. When Christina was nine, we finally were able to start her music lessons, though hers began differently and later than her sisters'. She started with Suzuki violin. It was great training for developing her musical "ear", memory and ensemble playing. It also exposed her to great classical and folk music literature. I was committed to attending all her lessons and supervising her practicing at home. A bonus during practice times was seeing Kitty, our adopted cat, choosing to lay in the violin case!

Attending Capital University for a Suzuki Music Institute was special for both of us, especially for her outstanding solo performance. Since we had a piano, she eventually gravitated to it on her own, playing music by ear that she had learned on the violin. She requested piano lessons, and for a year was taking both while learning how to read music, too. By the time she was at Taft, we allowed her to quit her violin so she could focus more on the piano, which she preferred. She began studying with piano teacher Betty W. and was awarded a superior rating for her solo work by the Ohio Music Association. I also took her and Laurie to two summer music institutes at KSU because Laurie was studying piano too. They both did fine at the recitals and John and I were pleased.

Laurie and Christina had met in grade school, lived in the same neighborhood, and immediately became best friends. In some ways, she was like our fifth child. She spent a lot of time at our home, and Christina was at Laurie's often. This friendship continued through middle school as they each decided to have their own paper routes and private music lessons, but performed together at various venues with Doina, the Romanian dance ensemble.

In high school, they both committed themselves to getting up at dawn to be on the swim team. Christina's art teacher encouraged her to continue with art in college. Unfortunately, the passion for active participation in music waned in both girls; they decided to be spectators only.

They both went to University of Cincinnati in 1988 and Laurie eventually graduated there. Even after Christina moved to San Diego with us in '89 and later to Portland, Oregon they have continued their faithful friendship.

After marriage, motherhood and employment,she discovered that cooking was her greatest passion. She eventually received her company's first place Top Chef Manager Award for the Pacific Northwest and flew to California to accept it.

73. SADHANA

JOHN'S WORK LOAD AT St. Columba in 1996-97 had been reduced in preparation for full retirement in 1997-98, making it easier to take time for other activities. As much as he respected the contemplative lifestyle of Thomas Merton, he had not developed it for himself. That is, until 1996, when he took a class at Ascension Parish with Louis, a layman, who led him into Centering Prayer. The book they read for guidance was *Sadhana, A Way to God*, (Sod-ah-na) written by the native Indian Jesuit priest, Anthony de Mello, for a Christian perspective on inner silent prayer. I had always felt that John's spirit would be open to this. And Anthony, the author, was a contemporary, the same age as John, whom he could respect, with a background of philosophy studies in Spain, psychology in Chicago at Loyola University, and spiritual theology in Rome at the Gregorian University.

One of the exercises in the book which is common to Orthodox Christians is simply the ceaseless repetition of the name of Jesus, which is considered a foundation of their prayer life and their spiritual life in general. "The Name as Presence" therefore becomes a mantra as a means to God's Presence, the name itself not being an end in itself. This, as a form of prayer, has been developed and used by Hindus over thousands of years. It is called the Remembrance of the Name. Mahatma Gandhi claimed that the repetitious name of God as *Ram* brought him wholeness of spirit, mind, and body, which he said was more powerful than the atom bomb! He lived those words which brought him non-violent strength, so that when he was assassinated in 1948 by a fellow Indian with three bullets, he not only gasped the words *"Ram, Ram!"* but also in a split second touched his palm to his forehead in an act of forgiveness, inspirational to all who are moved to non-violence. John had committed himself to non-violence years before in Christian imitation of Christ himself. Eventually he also became a Eucharistic minister, distributing Communion to parishioners at Ascension Parish's Sunday mid-morning masses.

74. "BY THE WAY…"

ONE OF JOHN'S FAVORITE spots in San Diego was the tide pools on the western rocky side of Point Loma, where sandy cliffs meet the ocean and barnacles and other small sea creatures survive amidst the churning tides and winds. We felt good exploring there in the sea air whether it was sunny or cloudy. Occasionally we would continue down the road to the Cabrillo National Monument, where the panoramic views of sea, cityscape and bay often dotted with sailboats leading out to the open ocean were breathtaking. In the distance are mountains. The huge statue is of Juan Rodriguez Cabrillo, the first European to explore the western U.S. coastline, sailing up from Mexico and into San Diego Bay in 1542 before proceeding up the coast.

San Diego 1995. John in Point Loma near the tide pools.

Whether going to Cabrillo or coming back there is only one road and it passes through the middle of Fort Rosecrans Military Cemetery. Sitting higher above the ocean than Cabrillo, it also has the views of city and bay on one side and on the other side all that is seen is the open ocean. On one of our trips to Cabrillo in '97, John said, "I love this area—it's so beautiful!" And as we drove past Rosecrans, he said, "By the way, because of my military service during the Korean War, I qualify to have my ashes interred here."

I didn't know how to answer, so I only made an entry for it in my memory bank.

75. DAMN ROCK!

JOHN HAD BEEN GETTING cardio checkups by both Dr. G. and the surgeon, Dr. M. since his heart surgery in 1993, and had been doing fine—still a healthy man, we were told. By January of '96, because he had chronic discomfort in his right side, he went to his urologist, Dr. I, and after testing it was found that he had a possible cyst in the right kidney; the left kidney was diagnosed "unremarkable." By September 19, Scripps Memorial Imaging confirmed a 1.4 cm nodule, possible cyst in the right kidney and a solitary 4 mm non-obstructing calcium-based stone in the left. This testing had been requested by his primary physician, Dr. R. and he received the results. No intervention was mentioned because at that stage, most stones pass on their own. He was advised to drink lots of water.

September, 21, 1997: Inside the Tate bathroom—extreme moaning, groaning and yelling, which then combined with a wretched vomiting from the depths of his being! "John—what's the matter?" (He couldn't talk, so I paused momentarily.) "John—what's going on? I'm coming in!" In between gasps and "yuk gunk" he yelled, "Pain in my back! It's the worst I've ever had! It's making me puke!" This went on for a little while, so I said, "I'm taking you to the hospital!"

The doctors at Scripps Memorial Hospital found that he had passed a kidney stone from the kidney, but it was lodged high in his ureter! While he was being examined, the receptionist in the emergency room said sometimes people who with genetic roots in Eastern Europe where sheep milk products have been the norm for centuries have more trouble digesting cow's milk than people from Western and Northern Europe. Sure enough, his dad had suffered with one, and had not lived long after that. (However, there are people who pass them and live longer.)

The doctors told him to go to his urologist immediately—which we did—but to complicate matters worse, he did not work through Scripps, but at Alvarado Hospital instead, located in San Diego, but not in La Jolla. So I raced him over there and the stone was found to be 4-5 mm and was blocking his urine flow which had started to leak out of the ureter! Dr. I. did surgery, but could not get the stone out, so for the time being he had to attach a pouch outside his body which would collect the urine. The situation with the bag stayed for a while and the doctor eventually attempted to surgically remove the rock again on November 12, with the same failure of acquisition or destruction. Poor John—he vomited big time after that afternoon surgery. Frustration was everywhere with anyone affected by the stone! Two days before Thanksgiving, there was a consultation with surgeon Dr. M., to find out if he might help. There was hope as he considered it.

John's painful situation notwithstanding, our whole family had a joyful Christmas together at Christina, John, and Cameron's house in Hillsboro, Oregon. The extra "baggage" accompanied John so he could go. He was a bit weak, but it didn't stop him from enjoying the visit.

January 1998 came and we were told Dr. I. was turning John's problem over to Dr. M., a surgeon at University of California San Diego (UCSD). The first week of February was tense, as we wondered if we dared to hope for success, even up to surgery time on the 5th. Then Dr. M. rescued the *stubborn stone* with no difficulty and no complications, making it seem to John and me like he had mined a *rock of gold, bright enough to have made the whole day golden for us!* What a skillful surgeon—we were so grateful!

A week later the catheter and the rest of the collection system was removed, freeing John, finally, to enjoy his first year of full retirement from teaching in California. Since this and my vein surgery on my left leg in January were behind us, we looked forward to a great 1998!

After those stresses, during a quieter time when we could think more calmly, I asked John, "Hon, remember when we were renting our apartment the first year ('89-'90) we were in California, and you were having trouble swimming in the pool because your shoulder hurt you so much?"

"Yes!"

"Do you remember going to the clinical nutritionist who prescribed magnesium citrate for it and how it helped dissolve the calcium deposits she said you had in your shoulder, and that eventually you were able to swim okay again without pain?

"Sure!"

"Are you still taking it?"

"No, after the problem seemed solved, I stopped taking it."

"Sorry, that wasn't a good idea."

76. SAVING PEGGY

THE CAR ROLLED TO a bumpy stop with the cloud of sandy dust behind it dissipating onto the unpaved, country "washboard" road. The driver parked it near the Palo Verde tree and row of short Prickly Pear cacti in front of the modest two bedroom desert house. There was a gray Dodge parked on the gravel driveway. There was no activity outside except the constant wind, but it was assumed by the couple in the car that there would be someone inside. Walking from the car, through the creaky yard gate and onto the dusty porch they noticed a weathered, ragged-at-the-edges, small note stuck on the door. By the time they were at the note, knocking at the door, a small brown spider was crawling up the door toward it also. The lone spider added to the eerie feeling of emptiness that Lisa and Marcus were getting as they started to read the note that looked to be scrawled in haste: "Your Grandma isn't home. She's in the hospital. Come to my house and I will give you the details. (Signed) Neighbor Dee Loris." Attached on the back were directions to her place, a couple of miles away.

When they arrived, Dee Loris greeted them and proceeded to take them around *her* desert place, which included the display of her gun. While they were walking around, getting her "chatty" tour, she then told them that only after Mom had talked with neighbors on the phone about how sick she felt was she willing to let one of them take her to Mojave General, twenty-five miles away in Kingman.

After thanking Dee Loris, Peggy's granddaughter and her boyfriend left for the hospital. Even though she had just been fighting a terrible lung infection, Mom became excited and smiled as she walked slowly to greet them in the hall near her room. She greeted them cheerfully with "You are my angels!" Well yes, the visit from the pair had worked out well, even though it had turned out so differently than they had planned—just a brief stopover on their way home to California from April camping trips in Bryce and Zion National Parks.

John and I didn't know what had happened until Mom was home and Lisa called us from there. We drove the seven hours from San Diego on Sunday, May 3 after we had notified my school, packed, and had a good night's sleep. Lisa was at the dinette table arranging her medicines as she was making a list of the schedule for taking them when we arrived. Mom was incapable of doing it herself. She looked old for her 83 years, frazzled and at times was confused. She had almost died!

Marcus and Lisa needed to get back home, so soon after we arrived we were put in charge as they left and we told them how much we appreciated all that they had done. Upon leaving the hospital, Lisa was given instructions to call Dr. K., Mom's medical doctor in Kingman. After we took her to the medical appointment, the doctor said she had over 90 percent blockage in a carotid artery and needed surgery otherwise she was ready for a stroke! Since it wasn't possible to do it in Kingman, he would have to schedule it in Las Vegas.

So it was that John and I stayed at the modest Continental Hotel Casino, complete with a dining room devoted to an interesting array of 50's Elvis Presley paraphernalia, and where we were generously given a discount because of Mom's necessary stay at Desert Spring Hospital. She survived the surgery well, and when we arrived in her room the day after, she was cheerfully eating spaghetti as heartily as any lumberjack, with a portion seemingly large enough to satisfy one! Her health was bouncing back, and then with a cleaner artery, her mind was becoming a little sharper. What a great experience for the three of us! Shortly before the time of her discharge, John took me to the airport so I could return to my teaching. When Mom was discharged, John drove her home. He contacted assistance for her medical and home care, stayed until that was secured and then left.

77. TEACHING THE ARTS IN CALIFORNIA

WHEN I WAS WORKING at one of my two happiest places, the CCCA, whether teaching at the CAI/Museum's music, movement and art classes for children or the Center's dance outreach in the schools, I wasn't concerned with job insecurity. I lost my work because of my resignation at both places and our move to California. Some public as well as private school administrators there were enlightened enough to know the arts are critical for balanced brains and education for all classroom students, especially before their educations become more specialized.

Working in elementary schools for the Roman Catholic Diocese of San Diego provided for me mostly happy experiences, whether teaching Orff music or providing art experiences with the kindergartners through second graders at St. Vincent's. The staffs at the schools were always cooperative and treated me well. The problems lay with funding, over which the individual school administration had some, but not full control.

Such was the case with St. James Academy, my other happiest place, where I taught from fall 1989 until summer 1992. I loved teaching there. Sister K. of the Sisters of St. Joseph couldn't, in my opinion, have been a better principal. She was tops, working well with her staff for quality student education. Even I, as a part-time arts educator, didn't miss her scrutiny as she would evaluate my classroom teaching each year, arriving in my class on a single day unannounced to see and hear what I was doing. Fortunately, I passed her scrutiny.

I couldn't believe how good the circumstances were when I arrived. Each child, from first grade through eighth had excellent, beautiful music textbooks. There were teaching resources for the kindergartners, as well as the other grades, music literature for Orff melody instruments and a decent in-tune piano. The only problem was that there were no Orff instruments so I used a combination of my instruments and some which we borrowed from St. Vincent's. But after my assault and car robbery in '90, there were no more from St. Vincent's or me. Soon Sister obtained a small amount of money to start a supply at St. James.

Activities were going well until there was a robbery of the Orff instruments. Then she purchased some again. Eventually there was an announcement from the diocesan office that soon there would be eliminations of both the pastor and all part-time employees, which would include me`. The reason given was that finances needed to be better handled. The problem with the pastor was *huge*, since he was respected and beloved by so many at the school and church. The replacement was going to be an American priest who had been stationed in Rome. Sister was upset over the losses, and the staff gave the departing priest a beautiful coffee table book about the ocean. When she learned of the music budget cut, she asked me if I would give a workshop to the classroom teachers on how to use the instrumentation so they could do some music in their classrooms, which I did. The staff gave me a lovely piece of pottery, which I still have. Sister became so upset over the whole situation that she resigned as principal and announced she would be taking a sabbatical at Notre Dame University, which I assume she did.

Fortunately, in the following fall I was able to get a reduced grades job at St. Columba. The principal decided that I would teach K thru second the first year and add grade three the following year, and more after that. The classes would be in a multi-purpose room with teacher aides from each class accompanying the children during the whole classroom time, which made possibilities of misbehavior nil and easy for me. There was a piano, but no Orff melody instruments except a few new ones that I had purchased. I had also restocked my own supply of percussion instruments. The social hall, where we would perform concerts for parents and teachers was ideal, with plenty of wooden floor space, and a stage with an excellent sound system, which included a cordless microphone. I was pleased.

I was asked to produce a concert by the end of September, which was only weeks away, when my concerts at the other schools had not been until Christmas, so I wrote a short play and created an instrumental piece which the students could learn quickly enough. I created pantomime with instrumentation to the poetry of Hans Christian Andersen's *Sandman*. I taught a second-grader with white-blond hair to move quietly and skillfully with the "magic" umbrella, which helped him to be the *perfect* sandman. Student concerts for parents continued to flourish until summer vacation in 1994, when the budget for Music Ed had been cut – which meant that I was laid off. The farewell card, with comments from the staff, was heartwarming, since my heart was aching.

It was a great family summer and rest of year, though, with John still doing well with his health. Mom's 80th birthday party, Patti and Eric's wedding and Christina's baby shower consumed plenty of my time. Then there were Christmas time activities and our greatest gift, which was our first grandchild, Cameron. It would have been hard for me to squeeze in teaching, too, and besides, I wasn't fired up about it like I had been—the passion had waned.

When I did apply to both the public and private schools in San Diego County, there was no opening and no funding. In some cases, a band teacher was needed, and I was not that. My pupils began music at earlier ages, and involved all students in the classrooms. Because I was primarily an Orff educator, I continued my membership in the organization and still attended some of the county wide Orff music workshops. At one of those in 1996, Karen—another member—revealed that she was giving up her music specialist job at a small private school in downtown San Diego so she could accept a fourth grade classroom teaching job. She asked if I might be interested in applying for it, and I said yes. She left the school at the end of 1996, and after the holidays I applied for an interview and received one.

I promised not to tell detailed stories of my classroom teaching to you, the reader, but this is one exception, a story that needs to be told because of the critical issues involved for educators, and what parents should know about the school environments involving the teachers and principals for their own children.

When I applied, Seaview School included three and four year old preschool, kindergarten, and combination classes of first/second and third/fourth. My prior teaching experiences included all of these, and so much more. The school had been established by T., the wife of K., son of one of the wealthiest families in the United States, who also had some interest in education. Their grade-school-age son was a cancer survivor but behind in his school work. I was told the school had been established primarily for him. A neophyte for this endeavor, she relied on others to help her. Since it was a private school, and Catholics have had a long history of running their private schools, she tapped people who had an association with Catholicism. I don't know if she or her husband was Catholic at that time.

After a successful interview, Mr. B. B., consultant to the school with a background in Catholic education, hired me. The principal there had been one at a Catholic school in north San Diego County.

I started February 3, 1997 and was given the assignment of having a concert soon on March 19 for all the parents and staff in the community room, a space too small, so we could hardly squeeze everyone in. As each group performed, I had to have them leave the room. One little three year old (whose name I don't remember), after romping with his class to Leopold Mozart's sleigh music, surprised us all as he stood in front of us, ready to bow, and nonchalantly wet his pants, which drained then onto the floor and caused a brief cleanup interruption! I was pleasantly surprised afterward when I received a note in April from grateful, gracious parents M. and G (I don't know if they were the parents of that little boy or not):

"Thank you for your extraordinary work with the children! We loved the March 19th concert—it's obvious you work very hard and enjoy what you do very much! Keep up the good work—we look forward to the next concert. If we can be of any assistance, please let us know." (A note like this is what helps teachers continue their work.)

Somehow we all survived the various less-than-perfect circumstances at Seaview until the end of the school year. The building wasn't large enough to have a music room, so my classes had to take place in the day care room which was used primarily for drop-off and pick-up before and after my classes. I always had to act as custodian, too, as I had at other schools, by re-arranging the room to accommodate paperwork, singing, instrumentation, eurhythmics and folk dance activities. There were no instruments for the students except what I was able to bring in each teaching day. No textbooks or teacher's lesson books were provided, and there was no storage room for any resources. When I started, there were no guidelines given to me for curriculum, but Orff teachers are accustomed to developing it and being creative in various ways. I had also built up student and teacher resources with my own pay after my losses in 1990.

By June 1997, we teachers had been given the Core Content Guidelines for all the grades and music classes. The Guidelines were sequential and published by the Core Knowledge Foundation of Charlottesville, Virginia. Some of that content I had already been teaching sequentially for years and had gone even further than those guidelines toward my goal for music literacy.

Since I incorporated a variety of music and music styles for all my stu-dents, I had also used classical occasionally. I wanted the students to learn about composers, so when I couldn't find writings about them that I liked well enough for the students, I wrote some myself, such as *Mr. Bach* for young children. While at Seaview I wrote two one-pagers on Wolfgang Mo-zart, one for the younger students—*Wolfgang the Wonder*, and one for the older—*Why Mr. Mozart?*.

In the fall, the older students studied European classical music from Baroque to Romantic, which included Mozart's period—the Classical—and were studies for the Core Knowledge Sequence required by the school for me by the end of the '97 school year.

Seaview was located near Copley Hall, home of the San Diego Symphony, a vital resource for the community. When I learned that the symphony was going to perform Wolfgang Mozart's *Magic Flute* with children from the San Diego Ballet dancing in it, I organized a field trip for the first/second grad-ers, with the help of parents who formed a car pool. Everyone who attended was spellbound! Our children didn't talk during the awesome performance, for the feasts for their eyes and ears mesmerized them into concentration and quietness. Also surprisingly, no one even asked to go to the restroom.

When we teachers returned at the end of summer, new grades had been added—fifth/sixth and seventh/eighth. Guidance was given to all the teachers with a workshop on Stephen Covey's *The Seven Habits of Highly Successful People*.

T. and K. invited the teachers and spouses to a wine and hors d'oeuvres reception at their Victorian style home near San Diego on September 5. Everything was lovely. Delightful music was being played on a piano inside by H., a versatile musician. The other activities were outside, and I was especially impressed with the beautiful, terraced organic garden. I was told that she allowed only organic foods for her son when he was sick. The host and hostess were gracious, and everyone was friendly, including a prominent Catholic priest in the San Diego community. We learned that he was on the Board of Directors for the school. He was the only board member I recall meeting. I didn't see K. after that. It seems that the school was his wife's project. Overall, I was looking forward to teaching in a pleasant, supportive environment.

I was used to concerts in the fall and spring, so I planned a fall one with all the grades, kindergarten through eighth. Holiday concerts were not requested, but I incorporated a Thanksgiving celebration of thankfulness for the harvest and Planet Earth through narratives, Native American songs, round dance, storytelling, poetry, a song from Peru, and the *Rhapsody of the Rain* percussive piece. They were all part of a sacred trust of living in harmony with our beautiful place in space.

The long table was decorated with "sculptures" from nature with the various shapes, colors, and textures of fresh produce that were from Native American cultures that we use all the time, such as corn tomatoes, and potatoes.

Other teachers had been responsible for the colorful pictures already decorating the walls surrounding my project. Fortunately, Principal B. and parents liked the whole, cooperative endeavor and the entire fifth/sixth class created handmade and heartfelt thank you cards, which I still treasure today.

By December 1997 I received permission to separate the fifth/sixth and seventh/eighth music classes because of the large span of developmental differences. Learning went more slowly than it had in my classes at other schools. Also, soon after I had started working there earlier in February, I was told that about 15% of the students had some sort of learning difficulties, and there were a number of children on Ritalin, a medication commonly prescribed for attention deficit hyperactivity disorder (ADHD). I was told by one of the parents that it had to be dispensed at the school, but I never knew who was responsible for doing it. I don't know what the situation was after the upper grades were added.

On January 19, 1998 a letter from the school administration to the teachers read:

For the second semester of the school year we are interested in a different approach to how we are teaching subjects. We are looking for the classroom experience that incorporates music into the curriculum, such as history and geography. This unites the whole learning/teaching procedure and makes each classroom experience unique.

I had an appointment with T. for discussing it. I already had experience in teaching this way at St. James Academy. There had been good communication with the classroom teachers, and I had enjoyed doing it. I was fine with it for my new assignment and thought the meeting went well.

The theme that I had chosen for it was "Understanding the World Better through Music of Different Cultures" (Redundant though for music teachers because our resources come from many places and cultures.) All the children, except the pre-kindergarteners were learning to sing "America the Beautiful." The pre-kindergarteners were learning to count in Spanish and the rest of the students, sang songs in it since we lived on the shared border with Mexico. There was a celebration of the Contemporary period of San Diego through American songs of living in the city and going to the zoo, as well as movie songs from our neighboring Los Angeles area. There were the historical European Classical music periods. Contemporary American also included Leonard Bernstein of the twentieth century as well as American songs associated with Dr. Martin Luther King, the music of jazz, popular music such as "Butterfly", and the electronic studies sounds of the Moog synthesizer and electric guitars. The historical and geographical studies of the pre-Columbian Incan and Aztec cultures of Latin America were included in our studies of music and dance. The younger students had folders for music class materials and the fifth/sixth and seventh/eighth students were required by me to have loose leaf notebooks for their paper studies and to have them on display for the concerts.

February 27, 1998

Dear Seaview Community:

One of the unique opportunities that we have at our school is the ability to invite talented and creative individuals from throughout San Diego into our classrooms. Beginning this week, we will bring two exceptional child-centered educators into our Seaview family. Dr. D. and Ms. G. have joined me as part of an administrative team that will lead the school into the future. Dr. D. will become Executive Director, and Ms. G. will become Director. I will continue as principal through the remainder of the school year.

B.

We were told Dr. D. had spent a year teaching at Harvard, and had an accomplished background, including serving as executive director of an educational foundation. She was an expert at establishing technology for educational institutions, was a former teacher in schools lower than university level and had been a principal. Further, it stated that Ms. G. also had a strong background, having been an educational administrator in a large local area school system, an authority on curriculum instructional strategies, and arts education. I was looking forward to working with them, and incorporating some new tools, techniques, and resources for my classes.

Scrutiny began for what and how we teachers were conducting our classrooms and for part of our education for improvement we were taken on field trips by Dr. D. so we could learn what could be done to improve. We visited briefly an elementary charter school where she had been principal and the young children we observed had access to curriculum with computers and we were told older children were beneficiaries too because the benefits, including internet and multimedia applications, were from K-12. She had been the coordinator of technological training and support available for new and experienced teachers through a business/university partnership, which I thought could be helpful. Much of that had been accomplished through numerous public and private grants plus business partnerships. If computer technology had been considered for music classes at Seaview, the school administration would have had to find funding, which had not been mentioned while I was there or during this visit.

The only technology that I had at that time was the tape recordings I used for folk dancing and examples of the different styles of music. I didn't use recordings of children singing for our students to sing with them, as it was recommended to me by the Executive Director. The students in my classes had to use their ears and own voices to sing, without the distraction of recorded music, so they could hear their own voices better for singing in tune. Also during our visit, it was pleasant hearing a gathering of children sitting on the floor of a large room and singing with a teacher guitarist. It reminded me of a casual folk-style sing-along.

Next we were taken to a county wide administration center so we could view the large video conference room which Dr. D. had some responsibility in establishing. We learned later that she was considered an expert on innovative teaching and assessment, largely through technology. She had accomplished much, had received many accolades and was clearly the leader of the Triumvirate of herself, G., and T.

78. DISPENSABLES

UNFORTUNATELY, DUE TO MY emergency trip to care for Mother, the students didn't have music since the beginning of May. When I returned to Seaview from Las Vegas on May 19, I had to catch them up, so we were reviewing the pieces for their spring concerts. I had always cleared the dates early with the principals in the past, so had attempted to do the same in '98. It hadn't been easy finding Principal B early that spring before I had left for Mom's. He had by then been just part of the administrative team when I had asked him. When I had approached the other two, the Executive Director and Director, they were too busy to talk about the subject. It wasn't too much later that I had finally found the principal and then he was too harried and upset to talk about anything with me except, "I can't take it anymore—I'm leaving!" (By this he meant permanently from the school.) Then he walked away from me. What was going on? Seemingly, he had been *dispensable*, and I never knew what kind of treatment he had been getting from the Triumvirate—they hadn't told me, or even bothered to discuss that he had gone. From that time on, Ms. G., the Director, was taking the place of principal. Maybe the other teachers knew better what was going on—after all, I was only the music teacher!

March had been *The Month*, not only for the field trips for teachers, but also the beginnings of observations and vocal critiques of our classes from both Dr. D. and Ms. G. I don't know if either one of the women had any music education in their backgrounds, whether with private lessons, in their own schooling or teaching. I don't know if they knew what to look for. They could look at the guidelines from the State of California, the Core Curriculum, and Seaview's integrated music with classroom curriculum which I had been following and even exceeding. I wasn't asked *why, how or what* I did in teaching the students. They said I needed to improve, but they didn't provide enough details.

I had repeatedly asked the executives in the office for clearance of dates for the rest of the classes' concerts (K-6), and I was put off with no answers until finally, Dr. D. said I could not because she didn't want to "deal with the parents"! I went ahead and chose dates anyway.

While I was continuing to prepare the students, I learned that classroom teachers were extremely upset one day to find that their classrooms had been broken into by "vandals"! Their supplies, records and equipment were scattered and damaged! How much they were damaged further I wasn't told. On another day I came into my space for teaching, and it was cluttered to the point of my practically not being able to navigate through all the huge bean bag chairs and other furniture in my way! At first it appeared that I wouldn't be able to teach there, but I went about moving stuff enough to the sides so that I was able to do at least some!

The executives were not easy to find, and that included the times I tried to find them to ask if I was going to get a contract to teach the following year, which according to the contract, was supposed to be in writing by April 15, which had already passed. Any delays would make it difficult for any of us teachers to get jobs elsewhere. They kept telling me, into May, that they didn't know yet. It looked like they were trying to get me to quit, which would prevent me from getting unemployment insurance, so I refused to do what they wanted! Then in the other classrooms, there were "break-ins" again! I was so upset and busy with my own teaching I didn't know what the outcomes of the other teachers were at that time.

Shortly before I received the termination of my job, a new, acoustic piano was provided. Then I received a letter from Dr. D., Executive Director, with the date of May 27, 1998:

Dear Dolores: This is to confirm our conversation regarding a commitment for next year. At the present time, Seaview School is unable to offer you a contract for the 1998-99 school year. We appreciate your dedication to the children and your passion for music.

Orally I was told they wouldn't be offering music the following year, even though their July ad in the San Diego Family Magazine listed music specialist. I wondered what qualifications they would require of the new one, and what the pay would be.

None of the Triumvirate sought to know what my college education for teaching music was and that I had not only taught children, but had given workshops to teachers in two public school systems, one parochial school, and students at three universities. I had presented lecture demonstrations of my work to various groups, including the 1988 Ohio Alliance for Arts in Education Information Exchange in Columbus, an affiliate of the Kennedy Center for the Performing Arts in Washington, D.C. I had been a concert soloist in multiple concerts and had made a children's recording with other professional artists.

The person whom they brought in to demonstrate how music should be done was a young sixth grade teacher, member of the same Orff Music Association as I, had some of the same recordings as I, and had worked with Professor Phyllis Weikart. (I had worked with her both in Michigan and California.) I was pleased that he was teaching like I had been, using Orff and folk dance. If he were to be hired, the children could benefit from him. I hoped he would be treated better than the current teachers. The school could save money if it paid him for teaching sixth grade and not music if they considered music to be only part of his sixth grade teaching. I don't know what happened with him and all the other students who had been getting music.

We teachers at Seaview had no rights (and no benefits for me since I was part-time). I don't know if the classroom teachers had benefits such as medical insurance, or not. We were harassed and *dispensable.* (According to my contract, I could be terminated with no reason given, and I had freely signed it.) My contract also stated that teachers could be let go because of neglect of duty, which is reasonable, but I had no knowledge that I was guilty of that. Teachers could also be fired for the purposes of reorganization or the school's financial exigency, about which I had no knowledge. It was easier and possibly cheaper to just fire the principal and all the teachers. To do otherwise, would also consume more time, energy, patience and fairness than the Triumvirate was willing to give. I don't know if the board was involved. We had no access to communication with it. Our treatment was glaringly unprofessional, disrespectful, undignified, inhumane and bizarre! Seemingly, Dr. D. had excelled in technical aspects within a larger educational arena, but had failed miserably in the human aspects at Seaview. People were treated as chattel. Here was a glaring need for a teacher's union.

In a letter to parents, Dr. D. indicated that none of the classroom teachers or specialists would be returning, with *no* explanations as to why. We seemed to be invisible to the board and parents. The office secretary even resigned in protest. Plans for the coming year were going ahead with a June 17 *Seaview Parent Organization* board meeting with requests for new ideas and new energy; on July 1 there was a Director's Coffee, an open forum for all parents to ask questions and voice concerns (to the Triumvirate). The invitation stated that the goal of the parent organization was to increase communication between parents and the administration. *(There was none with the teachers.)* That evening's meeting goal was "to come to a better understanding about what is happening here at our school...growth and change never come easy." I never knew how the meeting turned out.

In June and July, the concerts of grades kindergarten through sixth went on with proud children interested in sharing with their parents what they had accomplished in their classes. The executives weren't interested in them, so didn't attend. T.'s fifth/sixth son performed in July when the Triumvirate, which included his mother, was away. I was proud of him because prior to the concert he had memorized his solo Mexican folk song in Spanish and had learned to sing it in tune. But when he started singing he lost confidence and reverted back to singing it out of tune. I was pleased, though, that he had continued with the piece anyway in Spanish until he finished it, so I complimented him when he was done.

There had been an invitation by the parent organization to a July 13 evening meeting for the parents to attend "to experience science and art, history and language arts, Spanish instruction, preschool, movement and music. Many of our new teachers for next year will be available for you to meet."

July 14 as per my usual custom, I sent a last letter to the parents at the end of the school year:

Dear Parents:

This is my last correspondence with you, since Seaview Administration informed me that it had decided not to have a music specialist for next year. I told the students today, and gave them their music notebooks to take home.

It has been a privilege and a joy working for you and your children. Peace and happiness to you all.

Sincerely,

Dolores Tate

Who are we teachers working for if it's not the children and their parents in both public and private schools? John and I have had many, many expressions of gratitude from both which have given us joy in teaching. On the last day of my teaching the children, I received a wonderful handmade card by a third/fourth grade girl on white paper with pencil drawings of floating, dancing notes and treble clefs (illustrated with great movement!) with the following words:

Thank you Miss Tate,

You were wonderful! Have a nice rest of the year. Don't stop singing.

Yours 'til the sky starts dancing,

T. V.

July 15 was the last day of classes and student J. J. brightened that day by singing in tune a song she had created herself. It was performed delightfully. Just as we all clapped and I thanked her, she said her mother learned what had happened to the teachers, so would not be sending her to school there next year.

The 16th was eighth grade graduation and that weekend we *Dispensables* gathered at one of the teachers' homes where she had graciously invited us to a party. We supported one another through food and other activities. It was fun when I was surprised with a Seaview Survivor Award "for exemplifying honor, integrity, and professionalism where there otherwise was none! Dolores Tate is hereby recognized for producing cutting edge, 'underground' concerts at Seaview." It was humorously signed by three of the teachers, one with the title of "Unemployment Counselor".

The high point of venting was throwing darts at a photo of Executive Director D. I was tired and not in the mood for doing it, so watched instead. I was sitting down with John who was not having the best time either — with his eyesight. By the end of the month we would learn that his life was in jeopardy again.

79. THE INVADER

ON AN EARLY SUNDAY morning in June, 1998:

"Dolores, will you come into the study?"

"Yes, what do you want?"

"I have a dull headache, and something screwy is going on with my eyes."

"What do you mean?"

"Well, I can't read the newspaper—the letters are scrambled, and I'm having trouble focusing. It's hard to describe. Parts of some of the words are missing, and the letters that are there are broken up on different lines."

"That's strange. You need to go to an ophthalmologist!"

He did and the results showed he didn't have eye disease. Next his doctor sent him to a physical therapist for his eyes who treated him for weeks. That didn't change anything, so he was sent to a neurologist on the 13th, who ordered an MRI which was administered on July 24. Shortly after, we were called into a surgeon's office to view the scan of his head. Dr. O.'s explanation of what we saw on the 28th wasn't good. There was bleeding in the brain area possibly related to a tumor! John and I were stunned into solemn passivity, not knowing what to say, with the desire that it was just a bad dream. But, we were both seeing the same bad, bright image in real life, which we couldn't escape.

Dr. O. kindly said, "John needs surgery immediately to remove it and to find out if it is malignant or not. I can schedule it for July 31st." We signed permission for it, hoping it was going to be just another episode in his health history that could be overcome. According to his other doctors, he was a healthy man. So, we weren't too worried then that the tumor would be malignant. It *had* to be benign!

I called the girls and Patti flew in the morning of Friday, the 31st to be with Carolyn and me for the 3:00 PM surgery. This one was, like the heart surgery, in Scripps Memorial Hospital in La Jolla. Time always drags when the emotional levels are tense in a surgical waiting room. However, I was absolutely sure and fairly serene that the tumor was going to be found benign.

But when the doctor came in and solemnly told us that it was a high grade, malignant glioblastoma multiforme tumor and that John had no more than about six months to live, an uncontrollable river of tears exploded and flooded my face. I was also disturbing the peace in the room with my wailing lament when a kind woman came to me with a box of Kleenex. Carolyn and Patti, also in shock, were stunned into silence until all our tears subsided and they finished helping me. The doctor said he wanted to tell John before we did, so we let him, thinking that was the common procedure.

Slowly, as the psychological numbness started to dissipate during that time, it was as though spirit-filled adrenalin was moving into its place. We all agreed that the prognosis was unacceptable to us because all his doctors, including this surgeon, verified that he was a healthy man in every other way! We five Tate girls had hope then that if we rallied forth with prayer and did everything within our power and that of the medical professionals to beat the Invader in the brain, we might extend John's life! This was the message we would give John when we would see him.

After the doctor left and we were admitted to see him, we greeted him with subdued smiles and quiet words of encouragement—trying to be optimistic—in order to give him hope for an improved future. John was quiet. We were with him only a few minutes and hoped we had buoyed his spirit, at least a little. With everyone in the room with moist eyes, we mentioned faith in God's help for the near future, kissed him and told him we would see him again soon. As we left his room, Patti said, *"This is the worst day of my life!"*

I felt rotten also. Our lives were in turmoil from the time of that depressing diagnosis in July, filled mostly with more disappointments. Even the room where they put him next was unpleasant—not like the accommodations for his heart surgery. He had to share an overly crowded, small room with two young men who were in comas, with no curtains to divide them.

However, we had a brief reprieve when Christina joined us on the weekend from Portland. Since John was able to leave the hospital on Sunday with directions for a post-op exam on the seventh, we five went Monday afternoon to Bazaar Del Mundo in Old Town for some relief with Mexican food because he felt good enough to do so. Patti left the next day for home and her job, and Christina left Wednesday for the same. As far as my own work was concerned, my job status had changed to caregiver so I had to cancel my appointment with the state unemployment office and never had another.

We had been told also by the first doctor that he was able to remove only 80 percent of the tumor, for to have done more would mean the risk of further damage to the brain. But then, Barbara found another neurological brain surgeon in the Los Angeles area who had such an excellent reputation, he was on the cover of Time Magazine. We contacted him, sent him John's records; and obtained an appointment with him. Amazingly, we had an acceptance for surgery, based on John's good condition for tolerating the surgery, in less than two weeks after the first surgery!

So it was that John had his second brain surgery by Dr. B. in Cedar Sinai Hospital in Beverly Hills on my birthday, August 12. Pieces of tissue were obtained at that time and sent to the neurosurgical lab for dendritic cell study culture. Carolyn drove the three of us there, and then she and Mickey generously paid for the luxurious Hotel Sofitel for our lodging, making it possible to walk John the short way to the hospital that morning. Again, Carolyn was by my side in the waiting room during the second surgery. My apprehension was worse that time around not knowing what we would be told afterwards. Thankfully, the doctor's words were comforting and encouraging because he was able to remove the rest of the tumor! The post MRI showed nothing where the tumor had been. But because of the nature of the high grade glioma, John would have to have radiation treatments on his brain to attack proliferation of migrating cells. At least there was hope of continued improvement for him.

Emotionally and physically exhausted, Carolyn and I sat down to order an early dinner on the patio of the hotel when Barbara called to get the news. We were pleased that we could tell her there had been success, and we thanked her for finding Dr. B.! Then, Barbara said I should order a martini to sooth my nerves and to celebrate my birthday. Even though I had never had one before, I ordered one and looked forward to anesthetizing my brain and relaxing, but then it was the worst, most bitter awful drink I ever had— I couldn't even finish it. The best parts of my sixty-third birthday instead were Carolyn's company, good news, good food and blessed bed.

The next day at Cedar Sinai was amazing! John was sitting up in his private room (all the rooms were private) while he was being interrogated by a speech therapist and neurologist because the Invader had been on the part of the brain which involve memory, speech, and thinking. We were advised that he would have to have the same in San Diego.

Barbara had learned about the Simonton Cancer Center with Dr. Carl Simonton in Malibu who was giving week-long retreats on the psychological aspects of cancer and healing. They were held in the serene setting of the Casa de Maria Retreat and Conference Center in nearby Montecito, California. We asked if it would be alright for John to go there before he started his radiation therapy in San Diego. We were given permission to do so before we left on the 15th and instructions for follow-up exams by Dr. B. and Dr. Y. at Cedar Sinai Medical Center on the 21st.

Besides having the staples removed satisfactorily from his shaved head that day, the exam also revealed that he was in pretty good shape. Only his brain wasn't. In July, his blood work and carotid artery check showed no disease. In L.A., eyes, cardiac condition, muscle strength in arms and legs were checked and found normal, with some neurological deficit in finding words to express verbally, and some lack of peripheral vision on one side. The Karnofsky test showed 80-100 %, which was a good score, indicating longer survival from cancer. On August 10, prior to the surgery, John had consented to the dendritic protocol, using his own tumor and blood dendritic cells for immunotherapy as a vaccine against the glioma cells to prevent a possible reoccurrence of the tumor. The therapy was scheduled to start two weeks after the completion of the radiation treatments at the end of October. Because of what was happening by that time, we had high hopes for the future.

Just as we were making the arrangements for Simonton, our beloved Aunt Vic died in Canton on August 26, and we were powerless amidst our grief to attend her funeral.

On the 30th, Eleanor was able to pick us up from the Santa Barbara Amtrak station and take us to the Casa (House) of Mary because she was familiar with Montecito. She and Glen lived there, and he still worked at Westmont, also in Montecito and the place of John's and my sentimental engagement. Our meeting for just the ride to the dorm was too short, but sweet.

The setting was everything conducive for a peaceful, spiritual and physical healing environment. There were narrow trails nestled under canopies of sun speckled California live oak and sycamore trees. Cats were leisurely crossing them and basking in the sun. Because it was located in the Santa Barbara foothills near the Santa Ynez Mountains there were large rocks and the San Ysidro Creek on its border cascading down its own stones to the ocean below.

There was a statue of Mary, mother of Jesus, beside one of the trails, organic gardens and orchards, as well as the Sadako Peace Garden, with rock carvings of cranes as symbols of peace. Prior to our visit there had been the annual memorial ceremony in August for a young Japanese girl, representing all victims of the Hiroshima and Nagasaki bombings in Japan, and co-sponsored by the Nuclear Age Peace Foundation, an organization founded in 1982.

The group of women who established Casa were dedicated and spiritually motivated, and still continue to be compassionate as they open their facilities to people of all faiths, in groups or as individuals through retreats. People in the arts, plus educational, personal growth and community service groups are also welcome.

Dr. Simonton, our (spouses were welcome) leader was a pioneer in how emotions affect physical health, positively and negatively. Negative ones, he said, break down the immune system, and positive ones can help in the healing process. He asked the half dozen cancer patients to list any nega-tive emotional stressors that they could recall in the last few years. John listed twenty! Just some were: the recent revelation about Aunt Vic, the ob-vious ones of being told he had very little time left to live; the two brain sur-geries where his skull had been cut and pinned together just weeks before this cancer retreat. Others were: the multiple promises of his principal for equipment for his student science labs and not delivering; the mistreat-ments of us teachers at Seaview; his kidney stone; my Mom's illness and surgery; the death in '97 of our twenty year old cat, Jasper— his only male buddy in a sea of women!

One of the biggest blows that went with the tumor was his inability to read books, magazines, and the computer screen, since reading had been one of his prior greatest joys in life. It was agonizing for me too as I watched my intelligent teacher husband's former abilities in these matters wane. Our girls pitched in and bought him a WebTV.

Simonton, trained as a radiation oncologist, acknowledged there were multiple causes for cancer, but through this work with patients he discov-ered, in addition to sensible diet and exercise, that the patients' commit-ments in helping to heal the emotional aspects, in some cases, had been beneficial for healing them. We already had the former in John's favor, and we were both working on the positive emotional factors, there, and at our house. While at Casa, we had meditation, massage, music, and visual imag-ery where we were imagining the desired outcome of wellness.

Son of a Southern Baptist minister, Simonton had helped improve the health of his father through meditation. The doctor said that eventually, when his father was near dying, he meditated into death, helping him to have a good death, meaning, a peaceful death. He said that was the ideal, and hoped that if any of his patients at Casa would not be able to survive the cancer, he wanted them to contact him at his office as one of their doctors, and he would help them toward a good death. We appreciated the offer—a good spiritual resource, made a note of it with his phone and address con-tacts, but hoped we wouldn't have to contact him for a long time. John was so opposed to leaving our family at that time.

One of the pleasantries on an evening in the middle of the week was visiting our niece Dawn and her family. They lived in Summerland, an ad-jacent community to Montecito, so after picking us up, we enjoyed snacks, dessert and conversation with her husband Gerald, their children Lukas, Lauren, and Kaila Rose, plus Dawn's mother and our sister-in-law Byrle.

By noon on the sixth day all the patients left, with our having felt that the Simonton experience had been a good one. We were thankful for it, and considered Casa a place worthy of our return. I looked forward to the five hour ride back to San Diego on Amtrak with John when we could have had a relaxing time enjoying the trip together—much of it along the ocean—but the poor guy was so exhausted, he slept all the way home, accidently causing me to not only worry, but also to feel so lonely until Carolyn picked us up.

80. LIFESAVERS

IN ADDITION TO THE surgeons that extended John's life a little, his primary care physician and his cardiologist contributed what they could. But there were even more people ready and willing to help us. Starting September 16 and finishing on October 29, radiation oncologists worked on his head approximately 5 days a week near Scripps Memorial Hospital in La Jolla. I welcomed our close friend Nancy's offer to take him one day, giving me a morning of relief. On a morning when the weather was particularly lovely I sang, "Oh, What a Beautiful Morning" from *Oklahoma* while driving down the highway to his treatment, hoping to give him a little cheer.

Carolyn helped by creating a loose leaf notebook for her and me to record John's daily activities, including what medicines he was taking, and how he was reacting to his food, his patterns of sleep or lack thereof. She took him to her house off and on to give me relief. I recorded his appointments and progress with the young speech therapist, three days a week, which I was pleased to observe, especially since he found it pleasant to be in her joyful company. We called her "Jolly Jan".

Also valued was the expertise of his acupuncturist, Loisanne. On September 17, while waiting for her to treat him, he started to get rather nervous, agitated, and confused. Then, it happened! He had his first seizure! Loisanne diagnosed it and helped us until it was over. I was so worried I started crying, and then called the neurologist, Dr. B., whom we had not seen or needed since the first MRI before the first surgery. I begged him to please take John as a patient again. After thinking about it for a few minutes, he consented, much to my relief, and told me to take him to the emergency room at Scripps Memorial. Since he was able to walk, I managed it, even though he continued to have muscular contractions involving his left side of his face, forehead, and eyelids, was mute and didn't recognize me or anything that was said to him. Dr. B. met us, examined him and ordered a CT scan. It showed a hemorrhage in the tumor bed. He was given an IV medication for the seizure, inflammation, and edema. His Dilantin was increased and Depakote was added.

He gradually improved. By the time he was discharged on September 20 he was ambulatory with a walker and was having no more seizures. John was conversant, able to answer questions but was having difficulties with even a little bit of writing. 'La Jolla' became 'La Hoya', and 'radiation' became 'radiacia'. We began a round of office appointments with Dr. B. which added to the hope that, with time, John would be able to recuperate enough for a more normal life. But by the end of September another MRI indicated that the tumor might be growing back. Since the dendritic cell immunotherapy therapy in L.A. was to help prevent regrowth, we were still confident that he could improve with that—we just had to wait until the radiation treatments were done.

Since John's tumor existed in May, even though none of us knew it at that time, we were fortunate that he hadn't had a seizure when driving us in Nevada and Arizona for Mom's medical care.

Carolyn had a birthday on August 18 and Cortland and Barbara were in town from New York. Barbara's gift for Carolyn was a t-shirt—not just any kind of t-shirt—this one was emblazoned with the customized decoration, LIFESAVER. She looked at it, emotionally hesitant, not knowing exactly how to respond. She didn't feel totally up to the title, but would keep on trying anyway.

At the end of September and lasting for a month until he was too tired to go the last time, John and I went to the Wellness Center, a group therapy place for cancer patients. He had multiple sessions of positive visualization with counselors, heard other patients' stories, and told his own.

I had to give up most of my singing in the Ascension Catholic Church chamber choir, but we still had emotional support and prayers from them. John could no longer be a Eucharistic minister at church so Joe, one of the others, brought him Communion at home.

Another Joe, a fellow social studies teacher when both he and John taught at Taft wrote:

Dear John,

I heard you were having a run of bad luck. I felt I had to write and let you know we back here in Canton haven't forgotten our friend. I can remember you didn't say too much, but you would get a humorous remark out quite often. I did enjoy your humor and friendship when we worked together.

I do hope my letter is uplifting, but an autographed picture from Pamela Anderson would be more uplifting! Nancy and I talked to Bill, and we were concerned about you. We were reflecting on the good old time at Taft when the Social Studies Department was at its best.

More recently they shipped Dave and me to the high school. I have taught almost every history they require there and love it!

Hang in there John, and remember your friends here are thinking of you and you are in our prayers. You can make it because you are blessed with a loving family and We Ohioans. When you get into town again make sure you call me or stop by the school. Dave and I are at the West Campus. Say hello to Dolores and the girls for me, especially my former student, Patti. Keep your chin up and write back.

Your old friends, Joe and Nancy

81. YO-YOS

DURING AUGUST JOHN WAS feeling decent most of the time. By the middle of September that situation and his personality began to change. So did our relationship. My usually mellow man was struggling with the effects of the seizure, radiation and medications. Off and on he exhibited irritableness, nervousness, dizziness, nausea, and tiredness. Since the radiation treatments and speech therapy sessions were in the mornings, he was able to take naps in the afternoons. When he tried to meditate he'd fall asleep.

One weekend Carolyn took him to Sweetwater Orchids Nursery for a walk in the greenhouses and the next day took him for a brief walk on Shelter Island, near her house. The sea air made him feel a little better. Encouraged by that, I took him to Shelter Island a couple weeks later, looking forward to a pleasant time that we could enjoy together. I was quickly disillusioned since shortly after we arrived, he was so irritated that he seemed angry at me, though he didn't say that directly, and asked to go home. With a lump clogging my throat and tears welling up in my eyes, I drove us home.

October 9 was better, though, for both of us. We attended the Ryan *Spirit of St. Louis* Rollout Ceremony at Gillespie Field in El Cajon, adjacent to San Diego. The replica plane was to be located at the San Diego International Airport—Lindbergh Field's Terminal 2. It was jointly sponsored by the Port of San Diego and the San Diego Aerospace Museum in Balboa Park. It had been built by almost 40 hard-working volunteer craftsmen at the museum, supervised by project manager Bob Greenaway. John, now a wearer of a hat, was able to walk with a cane. We heard interesting talks from museum representatives and Chairman of the Board of Port Commissioners who planned and implemented the construction of it and also from two grandsons of Charles Lindbergh. Everybody and everything was pleasant, including a tasty buffet, so it was a good break for us—we were glad we went, and doubly so for John who had loved planes since his youth.

John's 67th birthday was on the 28th of that month. Carolyn, Mickey and I celebrated with his usual favorite birthday foods—pumpkin pie and Mexican cuisine. Our girls who weren't there sent cards—Christina, John, and Cameron sent this card with their gift:

Dad—May all your wishes turn to dreams, and all your dreams come true. Happy Birthday—We love and miss you very much! You stay strong and we'll see you soon—Love.

There had been a heart-touching outpouring of so many get well cards that fall (too many to mention all.) They were from relatives in Ohio and other states, which had included myself, Mary Jean, Warren and his daughters, Mike and Aunt Vickie (in August just before she died). Friends responded, which included our Pittsburg reunion friends and their spouses: Nancy and Paul, Eleanor and Glen, Anna Marie and Oscar. Ascension choir members sent theirs, as well as other former teacher friends in Canton and here at St. Columba. Even Dr. M., who had removed his kidney stone, sent one!

There were many from St. Columba students, particularly those who had him previously for a teacher. They were hand made with thoughts of prayers, good health, and humor. Ginny, one of the teachers who had taught at St. Columba when John did, asked her third grade students to write and illustrate jokes to cheer him (..."wanted to make you smile"...), since she knew John appreciated humor. They were delightful. Her daughter, who was at that time a sophomore in college, sent him a card, also. She was his student during her seventh and eighth grade years.

Dear Mr. Tate,

During the difficult times in our lives, it helps to know that others care. I just want you to know that I do, and that I'm thinking of you. I hope that things will turn out for the best, but if for some reason they don't, I just want you to know that you have touched so many people's lives and I am one of those people. Remember, I'm your 'second best friend'—as part of our little joke—I know, your wife is your best friend, but it doesn't hurt to be second! I wish you the best, and you will definitely be in my prayers. Get well! I'm sending you a smile from me! Thank you for being such a wonderful person.

Love, Kelly

And then there was Mike:

Dear Mr. Tate,

I'm the red head you told to count all his freckles. That's when I first met you. I think you are very nice, and I don't want you to die.

Sincerely, Mike

I can just see the twinkle in John's eyes and his grin when he introduced the yo-yo into his classes. He loved science and found ways to encourage that interest in the students. One of those ways was the use of the yo-yo to illustrate concepts of physics. Not content to just stay with the science, he also applied a symbolic nature to it, representing the ups and downs of life.

Dear Mr. Tate

You need to get well. We need you to come and see us, so get better and bring yo-yos. You were the coolest science teacher ever.

Amber

Dear Mr. Tate,

I hope that you feel better soon. You're the coolest science teacher ever. Now there is a yo-yo club at school.

Love, Matt

Dear Mr. Tate,

Hi! Remember me, Melissa? I was in your last class @ S. Columba. Well, I want you to know I am praying for you and all of the 8ᵗʰ Grade still talks about how much we miss science with you. I want to let you know how great a teacher you were for me, Matt, and my older sister Marjorie.

Mellissa

Dear Mr. Tate,

I hope you feel better and get well soon. I will be praying for you and so will the rest of the students. Everybody loved you as a teacher and I wish you had never left.

Sincerely, Chris

82. CHEATING DEATH?

SOON AFTER THE RADIATION treatments were over I drove John to L.A. on November 11 for an early morning MRI scan and appointment with his doctors because the dendritic immunotherapy was scheduled to begin soon. It was a hopeful visit for us until Doctors B. and Y., visibly disappointed, told us that John was no longer a candidate for the experimental protocol because, unknown in the beginning by them, the requirement was for patients who had undergone only one surgery for the removal of the brain tumor. Compassionately, they apologized as they saw our disappointment and felt their own. Also, the MRI that morning showed that there was new tumor growth and excessive edema. It was assumed by Dr. B. that he had Decadron monitoring for proper dosage treatments for the edema during his radiation treatments, for it was standard procedure when done in L. A. He had some after that surgery there, which had been reduced. It was up to the San Diego physicians to remedy that. An appointment was scheduled to come back in January. John could understand enough what the situation was, so there wasn't much talk between us on the depressing ride home.

Climbing up the 13 stairs to our condo was getting more difficult for him, and for me to help him. Neighbors, Bill and Marcus, in two condos near us, kindly consented to be our "Good Samaritans" whenever each was home. A few days I even had Marcus's assistance in staying with John while I did some necessary errands. He was a *huge* help since I didn't feel comfortable in leaving John home alone anymore, and Marcus was in nurse's training. It was frustrating to me, also, that John didn't seem to be improving enough after all the therapy he had been getting. In fact, he was getting worse.

By November 20 he had to sit on each step on his way down to the bottom of the staircase on our way to La Jolla, for we had no other help that day. His usual morning appointment with his speech therapist had been cancelled and moved to 3 PM. Since we were both exhausted from that, ever so slowly getting back to the car and dealing with rush hour traffic, I decided to take him out to eat dinner at Trophy's across from University Towne Center.

Everything was fine until we had our meals delivered to our table. Then, to my dismay, John couldn't speak or feed himself well enough. He couldn't use his utensils at all and was eating everything with his hands—even spilling some on himself. He insisted on doing this as he didn't seem to understand his incapacities and my verbal and physical attempts to help him. As the struggle continued I was also getting embarrassed over the mess we were making and the whole situation. John couldn't help it, so then I felt guilty for the embarrassment. We left finally at 7:30 PM after the gracious help from the servers at the restaurant. Fortunately, we made it into our condo after I helped his six foot one inch frame crawl up the stairs.

This was a dismal situation, and I didn't know exactly what more we could do. There was a need for more help. Also, Thanksgiving was almost upon us and I didn't know what we were going to be able to do about it, if anything. Then, our angels for that occasion were S. and T. who invited us to their ranch for Thanksgiving dinner, along with Mickey and Carolyn, even though John was as sick as he was.

There were so many struggles amidst the abundant graciousness, kindness and hospitality of that whole family. John could hardly walk from the car to the house as he shuffled in small steps the best he could as he strained to move each leg. Once inside, he couldn't speak, and tried to smile occasionally. I don't know how much he was aware of all of us. I fed him the delicious food and helped with his other needs as I socialized in whatever limited fashion I could. Carolyn and others assisted too when they could (she had always been one of our angels ever since he had started getting sick). Nobody there seemed embarrassed by any problems John had. My gratitude for the compassion ran deep that day and into the evening when Mickey and Carolyn completed the blessings by helping John get up the stairs into our home.

John was too ill to go to speech therapy the next day. As Carolyn and I discussed John's situation, we decided we'd had enough on our own and needed more help. We called the ambulance to take him to Scripps Memorial and those great medics gave him a *ride* down the staircase.

When we arrived at the emergency room, besides meeting the emergency room physician we learned that John's neurologist Dr. B. was off for the holiday weekend and had a substitute, Dr. P., who came in and admitted John on the basis of his difficulty with using and understanding speech (aphasia) and inability to walk. Right after Carolyn and I met him we were stunned with his opening remark: "Why don't you just let this man die?"

Wow, did we get angry! Indignant, I fumed, "We were just trying to get him help with the hope of getting him better!" Anyway, he followed through with a CT scan that showed evidence of a recurrent tumor. There was also cerebral edema in the area where the original tumor had been and where he had been getting radiation treatments, so he placed John on a good amount of Decadron for the edema. He ordered an MRI for Saturday and it confirmed the same: edema and recurrent tumor on the left side. And, later that day, it seemed the Decadron was working already, because he was more alert and able to say words.

By Monday he was mildly disoriented, but his language and understanding had improved some more, and he was ambulatory in a halting way with a walker. The radiation oncologist had been contacted and given a report of his recent admission to the hospital and the diagnosis and treatment. She said she had not given him the Decadron during radiation treatments because she thought it was too strong, and that she didn't have any other plan of additional treatment for him.

By Tuesday, December 01, he had improved further, was alert and communicative, asking questions, and still ambulatory, so he was discharged by Dr. B. with further management as an outpatient. Carolyn and I thought *maybe* we had made the right decision after all.

The prescription added Scripps Home Health Care Services to his four medications. The Care Services included a physical therapist, occupational therapist, and a home health aide. Dr. B. also ordered a bench for the shower from a medical supplier. I rented a wheelchair and bought a removable shower head with a long chord. Things were looking up—the situation was now back to being more hopeful for John.

It wasn't easy, but we were managing better with the extra help. One of the emotional irritations I had, however, was getting notices in the mail from the managers of our condo that I was being fined for parking in the spots reserved for guests, which were closer to our condo than our carport. It helped me to park there and it wasn't high on my priority list to go to the monthly membership meetings to explain our situation, or even to think much about it, so I let it be.

By the second week of December John's walking was getting to be more of a struggle again, even with his physical therapy at home, but we were looking forward to a visit with Mary Jean, John, and their son Steve on the 13th. John was resting in bed until the doorbell rang, and then when I went to bring them in, John had risen by himself. I couldn't help him because he refused it—wanting so badly to walk by himself. It was so heart-wrenching as I watched him slowly shuffle and barely move those resistant legs and feet—but accomplish it he did! As soon as he was in the doorway to the living room, Mary Jean rushed to him, put her arms around him and sobbed, as he did with her as the two siblings sensed it would be the last time they would see each other. By that time all of us had wet eyes.

The invasive Glio was galloping ahead again. The recent MRI's confirmed a recurrent tumor which contributed to his problematic walking, but why, when the tumor was on his left side of his brain and it is the right side that controls motor movements? He didn't have the aphasia anymore, so why the continued trouble with his walking?

One night I lost it! I angrily slammed my fist on the bathroom wall adjoining our bedroom and pounded as I acted out my frustrations on the wall. It was as though subconsciously it represented blockage, because of John's lack of continued progress toward wellness. I screamed through my tears, "When and how did this damn Invader ever get started?"

I even forgot the fact that John was lying in our bed and saw me. Then I was sobbing and apologizing, feeling guilty for subjecting him to it as I went to his side. He wasn't angry at me as he asked haltingly, "You ever... get...upset... before this time?"

Stunned, I realized that the cheerful front we girls had put up to try to make him feel hopeful for healing *had* been a mistake. It had looked like we never had been upset. My tears then turned into a river of regret. I told him how the three of us had reacted after the first surgery to the doctor's upsetting news. I also shared that I thought it had been a mistake that the doctor was the first to reveal the diagnosis. We should have instead.

After that stormy outbreak at the wall and the calm that followed the revelations, our suffering spirits, too, were calmer when our entire lengths of our bodies felt the loving warmth of each other as we fell into peaceful, satisfying sleep.

Also in December, one of our girls had spoken with Dr. D's office in Newport Beach at Hoag Presbyterian Memorial Hospital where the neurosurgeon had a good reputation for doing Gamma "Knife" Radiosurgery for attacking cancerous tumors non-invasively, so it was not really a knife at all. The surgeon who had performed John's first brain surgery was capable of accomplishing that, but he had said the tumor at that time was too large. Supposedly, the earlier radiation treatments had shrunk the tumor that started resurfacing again, so maybe it was small enough yet to zap it with the highly focused low-level radiation on just that area. We met with Dr. D. on the 21st, and after viewing the MRI's said the tumor was small enough to be treated, and scheduled the treatment, which would be on an outpatient basis during the last week of the month. Was there hope again for John's improvement? Other brain tumor patients had been helped.

On Christmas weekend Mother, our two grandchildren, all our daughters and their husbands except Christina's John, joined us at our place. John the grandfather — with strained grins —seemed to enjoy the presence of us all— especially little Cortland and Cameron. Everyone was compassionately helpful with him, except Mother — who, with some dementia, didn't quite realize how ill John really was.

One of the get well cards from a St. Columba student was also a greeting for the New Year:

MR. TATE...HAPPY NEW YEAR

The day we heard that you were ill, there was a depression over the school. The rest of the day was odd and everyone sat in silence, mostly because we were thinking of you. We once again acknowledged your intelligence, how good of a teacher you were, and just what a wonderful person you are to be around. We really miss you. I wish you the best and hope you get better.

Your former student, Annette

Before we left for Newport Beach in Orange County, Patti and Eric took Mother to the airport for her trip home. Then the next day John's entourage drove in various cars to a hotel on Fashion Island near the Hoag Health Center where we all met and had dinner together before retiring for the night. John couldn't talk much or feed himself, but he had plenty of help.

Early the next morning John was given an MRI and prepped for the Gamma by being fitted with the stereotactic frame on his head. Carolyn felt she had a responsibility to be with me during the procedure. Eric and Patti went out to explore the surrounding area. Since their dad was to be done by afternoon, Barbara, Charles, and Christina took Cameron and Cortland to Disneyland, planning to return at that time.

Soon after Carolyn and I had settled down in the quiet, almost empty waiting room a despondent looking Dr. D. came to us. "Please follow me." He took us into an even quieter small room in dim light as he shared John's situation. "I'm so, so sorry because I can't help John after all. The difference between the earlier MRI's and the one we just took shows dramatic speed and invasiveness of the cancer. He has it now throughout his whole brain, so I cannot help you. The Gamma Knife will not help. Again, I'm so sorry." He definitely was truly sorry. "You need to call Hospice."

We had the answer to John's increased inability to walk.

At that point Carolyn and I were both stunned into crying as we thanked him for his services. I had another uncontrollable torrential downpour with audible sobbing as the doctor quietly left. That was the moment *hope died.* We had to accept it. Any attempts for further life extension would have been *cruel.*

Carolyn and I could only hug each other through our tears. When we were able to stop we called the family and told them. Barbara said when they received the news they were near Sleeping Beauty Castle just as she was remembering her Grandpa Arnie's role in that place. Suddenly everything felt so surreal. They left Disneyland immediately.

Before we left for San Diego, Carolyn and I took John for a ride in his wheelchair by the waterfront at Newport so we, and especially he, could breathe some sea air. I could hardly talk, so Carolyn took over the major part of that to give John some sense of normalcy.

Once together at our place again, the family was unanimous: "Mom, you cannot take care of Dad anymore. He's getting totally incapacitated and he's too heavy for you to lift. You must get more help." San Diego Hospice was called the next day and shortly we had two staff members with us who analyzed John's situation. "We have only one room available at our only in-patient center in San Diego, and with your permission, we will reserve it for John. You need to know also that we do not treat the illness, but provide only palliative (comfort) care for the patient. Once in a while a patient improves enough on their own to come home again. Most do not. Most patients there have terminal cancer, but they receive round the clock excellent care with doctors, nurses and other caregivers. There are chaplains of your choice and guests are welcome. Each room is private and there is a couch that opens into a bed for a family member." Everyone decided that the inpatient center was the best place for John. Until he was there several days later, the good care he had been receiving at home from Scripps continued.

He was given a pleasant room the first week of January directly across the hall from a nurses' station and a shared wall with a lounge/coffee area for guests. The three daughters from out of town said their tearful last good-byes to him individually. They were deeply genuine words and feelings of love, since they had been experiencing the give and take of that all their lives. He was leaving us too soon since he was only 67, but we thought we were all fortunate in that he had survived two close/near death situations before and that we were given time to say good-by. As he left us this time for his next level of life we hoped we would see him again. By the time they left for home we were all at a loss and puzzled as to how this could have happened to our otherwise healthy man.

As we prepared further for John's death, Carolyn visited almost every day, bringing sunshine into his and my lives with her smiles, sweet conversations and fresh bouquets of flowers as he quickly lost all ability to communicate. I couldn't smile nor talk much. As long as we could, we wheeled him outside on a bed that could help him experience the lovely yard and view from that vantage point on the hill, of Mission Valley below and beyond to Mission Bay.

He was put on a regime of morphine, which Carolyn and I hesitated to accept on his behalf at first. We hadn't known prior to his admittance to Hospice that it was standard therapy for terminally ill patients. It didn't take us long to consent to it, believing then that the alternative was worse.

I was sleeping 10 hours a night on the bed in his room, going home every few days to get the mail and pick up clean clothes. On one of those days, our neighbor Mary invited me into her place to relax and sleep a bit. I did, as she refused—even my daughters—from interrupting that by any phone calls.

One of the most touching events was the visit one evening into his room of the entire Ascension Chamber Choir. While one of his favorite CD's—a gentle, soothing Chinese piece—played, each member in the line stopped to give him quiet, soothing words. John seemed to sense their presence and why they were there. He had subtle tears of appreciation, and even more so when Angela touched his arm. Other times there were the friends from Ascension who visited to sit compassionately, prayerfully and patiently by his side for a while such as Rodger, Carlo, Phil (from choir) and Ceil—a married couple—who sat together.

All the staff at Hospice was outstanding and compassionate with his care. He had strong men who would take him to warm water therapies, food servers and a chaplain who brought him food and Communion until he could swallow no longer. There was harp music. The doctors and nurses were ever vigilant, but there was one problem they couldn't solve—raw skin. He had to have suppositories which were irritating his skin, and nothing they used to sooth and heal worked. Finally, I talked to the doctor about it and asked him to please give John a high potency topical d-alpha vitamin E a try, because I knew it could heal even ulcers on skin. He then ordered a pharmaceutical potency and after it was applied for a while, it healed.

Since he was expected to pass away that month of January, I started making funeral plans. I called Tony, the principal who had hired John to teach at St. Columba, to give the eulogy. He came into the inpatient center from St. Augustine High School where he was assistant principal, visited John and accepted very graciously after learning from me all that had happened. Marianne, my choir director, also came into the lounge area where we planned the music for the Memorial Mass.

During one of my tearful vigils by his bed I spoke of our family members who had passed and that he might be seeing them soon, identifying them individually, such as his dad. It happens commonly that dying people have visions of deceased loved ones greeting them. I don't know if this happened to him or not, or if he was capable and aware of that. Because of his condition and the morphine he never reacted to my being with him near the end, except that one night he threw my hand away—off of him—as though he hated it! I didn't always have my hand on his while sitting with him, so when he did that, I was crushed emotionally. I needed to remember his condition and should have not let it bother me so much. I didn't mention it to anyone at the time and later I thought that maybe it was part of the shedding phenomenon that the medical staff had told me could happen. It is common, as the spirit is leaving the body that the patient tears off his or her clothes, blankets and sheets. It did happen to John and the rest of us were on watch that no visitors were coming in at those moments.

If we dared to have any tiny shred of hope while he was there, it was to hope that he wouldn't die on Barbara's birthday. That was January 13, and thankfully, he didn't. Hospice staff told us that patients usually leave this life when their friends or relatives leave for a short while.

I awoke suddenly on the morning of January 17 when the blood pressure machine squeaked across the floor as the nurse rolled it to John's bed. She attached it to John and then ran out of the room to the nurse's station across from his room to get the doctor. Startled, I looked at him from my bed across the room and he looked like he was breathing because his chest was moving up and down, so I assumed he was alive. The nurse said to the doctor, "John Tate has no blood pressure!" He came immediately, examined him, and pronounced him dead at 8 AM.

I broke down again because he was gone and I had not been at his side. Then they also became tears of relief as well as I recalled my prayer the night before that John would not suffer anymore. My Love, who had been easy for me to love was at peace now, 12 days after entering Hospice. Thankfully, The Source of Everlasting Love was now embracing him, in that place where speech is unnecessary. Within John's limited sphere of influence he had treated creatures and our planet with compassion, causing it to have been a better place for a while.

I called Carolyn and she came with Mickey as soon as possible, toting a breakfast that we ate together. We waited until John was taken away for cremation and then met with the staff briefly. We walked without words to the small gazebo on the Hospice property overlooking Mission Valley and ate quietly with wet eyes and few comments.

Just as we were walking to the car in the parking lot to go home, we accidently met Angela, Marsha, Lyn and Stephanie from choir just getting out of the car with the aim of visiting John. It made me feel better just seeing them during that brief encounter while we told them John was gone. They came to my place later in the day to help me. They did a marvelous take-charge job of feeding me and doing the dishes. They wanted to stay with me through the night and I appreciated their offer greatly, but surprisingly even to myself, I wanted instead, to be alone within the double quietness of prayer and sleep. (They left with the parting understanding that we would stay in touch.) Then the lonely lamentation of my heart and mind cried out to Mary, Mother of Sorrows (Dolores) to pray for me, for she would understand.

This was taken before we left home to celebrate our 42ⁿᵈ wedding anniversary by dining and dancing to a big band.

Del Mar, California.
We had a picnic at Seagrove Park on the coast, complete with
Tiramisu for dessert. It was our 43rd wedding anniversary.

Mom & Dad,

Happy Anniversary!

44

Eegads! How did you do it? ☺

Thanks for being such good role models!

Love

Carolyn & Nick

1998

San Diego, California 1998.

83. KINDNESSES AND APPRECIATIONS

AFTER JOHN'S PASSING, ALL the plans fell into place easily. We had created a trust two years before. Rosecrans Cemetery was where we had the interment ceremony on January 29 with Father Jim from Ascension, but without the military gun salute so graciously offered by the staff. I didn't want it because I thought it was more appropriate for a career military person, and John had not been. But it was good to receive the American flag in such a well performed, ceremonious way. The people there that day before the funeral consisted only of our immediate family; John's sister Mary Jean and her son Steve; Pat; Nancy and Paul; Nancy's father Doc Vriend, who at 98 years old wanted so much to be there and was still able to walk across the cemetery. I sobbed so loud when I placed John's ashes into the crypt, those wailings could have disturbed the waters and boaters in the bay below. Steve softly quipped "I think I'm going to become a nasty rogue so everyone will hate me and not to have to go through this when I die!"

The location was perfect for John's remains (and eventually mine) for it was in the area of that "favorite place" of his, overlooking the vast Pacific Ocean in the city he loved—San Diego. Tree lover that he was, there is a huge, sturdy pine nearby with others in the distance.

Just as John was so special, I wanted his memorial service to be the same. It had to reflect best what he was like in such a short time. I couldn't do that in the typical few days in which most funerals are planned. I had already started choosing the music with Marianne; the rest I felt would be finished later in the month. It was held then on Saturday, January 30.

I went to a florist shop in the Hillcrest area part of San Diego because I had often admired it as such a beautiful place. The exuberant and kind young man helped me order exactly what I wanted for the large, cascading bouquet of yellows, golds, tans and greens to be placed near the altar. The only hitch was that the shop was going out of business the day of the funeral. Fortunately for us the owner still wished to do it and had the beautiful creation delivered in time for the Memorial Mass of the Resurrection.

As each guest entered the sanctuary they were handed a program of the service. One of John's photographs of Yosemite in winter graced the front with a quote at the bottom by Indian poet Rabinadrath Tagore, "Death is not extinguishing the light—it is putting out the lamp because the dawn has come." Inside we had a happy photo of middle-aged John. There was a duplicate of it in a frame on the altar. There was no casket.

The celebration of John's life began with European prelude music, played on the baby grand piano by extraordinary Maria, who had just returned from living again in Finland, her native country. She started with Beethoven's *Moonlight Sonata* and ended with contemporary Andrew Lloyd Webber's *Pie Jesu* (Blessed Jesus) sung so beautifully by Marianne and Angela.

The liturgical prayers to the loving, merciful God were for John, the Church, peace in the world and all who work for justice and peace, and all who suffer in mind and body. David, who came to be with us as cantor added much with his rich voice, as did also soprano Angela J. who joined the choir. The readings from the Old and New Testaments were of mercy, the Beatitudes, and hope of eternal life. Nancy and Paul, who are Baptists, brought the bread and wine to the altar for Communion.

Stephanie from choir offered some of my thoughts because I could not get up and talk during the service. "From the seas to the stars, John loved the beauty in nature and gained strength, comfort, and joy from it. He and Dolores had fun riding the seas together on the Calypso ship with explorer-conservationist Jacques-Yves Cousteau while watching him on TV. John wondered, along with astrophysicist Carl Sagan, at the vastness and mysteries of outer space and universes."

Father Jim, as Celebrant for the Memorial Mass, gave comforting words in his brief homily; Tony, in celebrating John's life in his eulogy touched all the family deeply as he spoke of his life as teacher, husband and father. He shared how he found him to be when he had worked with him during his first year at St. Columba. He described John as possessing a quiet grace and a spiritual peace that disregarded impulses of anger and hate so he could be free to love others, wanting the best for them and seeing the best in them with an 'agape' love. In defining a gentleman as a polite, considerate man, having regard for the needs and feelings of others, he described John as a teacher who not only knew how to communicate data and information well, but also knew how to live a lifestyle of a Christian Gentleman.

Along with Patti, Carolyn and Barbara, I was stunned when shortly before the memorial Christina announced that she wanted to talk about her dad at the service. None of the rest of us felt that we could do it, and we had never seen her talk with a mic in front of a group.

We all asked by phone, "Are you sure you can do it?"

"Yes!—I've already written it!"

We didn't know what to expect when she left her seat and arrived at the pulpit. Evidently her son Cameron, who had just turned four, had the same reaction, because just as she started talking he started wailing, as he had never seen such a scene either. "It's okay, Cameron, you can come here with me!" Since he was in the front row, he was there in an instant. She held him on her hip as she read:

When I think about my dad, his smile is the first thing that always comes to mind. It was kind of like this closed-mouth grin with lots of expression in his big, brown, warm eyes. I have never met anyone else ever, who just always seemed to glow. His moods were contagious. I don't know anyone who didn't like him—he was loved by many people and also pets! Aside from being the best dad in all of history, he was an exceptional human being! He was handsome, brilliant, and spiritual— kind, compassionate, patient, loving— and did I mention patient? That quality just wasn't passed on to me through his genes!

He was hard to beat at Trivial Pursuit, gentle, strong, open-minded, cultured and funny—a big fan of The Three Stooges!? A nature lover, he was also a lover of Mexican food and my wonderful stuffed cabbages! A loving grandpa, and an awesome teacher with a wonderful sense of humor with his students—and did I mention patience?

A lover of life, nature and Mom was part of that as she said he was a great husband, and she does not lie! I loved my dad very much and I'm going to miss him terribly as I think of him daily. He will always be in my heart. Most importantly, I'm going to tell my son Cameron about his grandpa and how much he loved him.

When she was done, I could smile.

The Twenty-Third Psalm, traditional in many Christian requiems, was sung beautifully by my choir as *My Shepherd Will Supply My Need*. Since John had taught American History, Government, and Justice in Urban America in his strong social studies curriculum, I also wanted music that reflected America. One of his favorite songs, like for many Americans, was *Amazing Grace*, which was used for the processional, and sung the best way in African-American Gospel style, as was *Soon and Very Soon*. The southern folk song hymn *Jesus Walked This Lonely Valley* was added and we concluded the service with everyone there singing the recessional hymn, *America the Beautiful*. By that time Barbara could not hold back her choked up emotions any longer and sobbed.

As people were streaming out they took funeral cards that, in addition to John's life span, displayed five different choices of outdoor scenes with the well-known prayer of naturalist-saint, Francis of Assisi. There were more attendees than we had anticipated, because we had lived in San Diego a little less than 10 years. As I met some of them I learned that there were even former students of his who were in college and had come for the funeral. There were 95 people accounted for, and two of those were Doc Vriend, a senior chiropractor, and Miles, our younger chiropractor at that time. Laurie flew in from Ohio and our nieces and Marcus came with Byrle. All six members of Mickey's family were there. It was quite moving and deeply appreciated by our family.

We had a catered Mexican buffet lunch on Ascension's patio to help people recover and played one of John's favorite recordings as people came. It was Louie Armstrong singing "It's a Wonderful World". Paul, a retired public school principal and former teacher who had known John since the 1950's created the following poster which we exhibited:

Washington, D.C.: ...a place of high expectations and at times, of low achievement.

John was a realist. He knew that the democratic process was sometimes slow and imperfect, but he was also an idealist. As an American History teacher, he believed passionately in the ideals of our democracy and took an active part in shaping our contemporary history. He established the 9ᵗʰ grade 'Justice in Urban America' curriculum for his Canton, Ohio school system; took 8ᵗʰ grade students to Washington annually for a decade; he worked for interracial justice and Christian ecumenism.

World geography, including international cultures, was another of his specialties. He could always be counted on to inform anyone who asked, what the latest new country was and where it was located.

While John valued his own roots, which began in Romania, he also celebrated that which was positive in many other cultures of the world. He recognized the power of the arts to bring people together. He was pleased and proud to be invited to perform with a Romanian-American folk ensemble as a dancer, right next to a professional Romanian folk ensemble at the Smithsonian Institution's Festival of American Folklife. It was for the 1976 American Bicentennial Celebration. In celebration of that history, America invited people from all over the world to celebrate their arts on the National Mall. John got an emotional "high" from all that and also where he, the Romanians and Africans were performing—in front of the Lincoln Memorial. This was Washington at its best!

We girls felt closure by the time we donated the flowers to Hospice, where individual vases of flowers were made up for the patients. The caterer delivered the large arrangement in the van, and confirmed John's and my belief that there are so many kind people in the world who often respond compassionately when asked, and even when they are not asked. After learning about John's death, the board members of our condo association forgave my penalty parking fee. Our cardiologist Dr. G., who had liked John so much and had helped save his life with the emergency heart care, called to offer his condolences over the family's loss and to let us know how sad he was that the medical teams had not been able to save John's life the second time. We received almost as many sympathy cards as people who came to the Memorial. One of them was from our dentist Dr. L. and his staff. He also forgave John's unpaid balance of his bill.

84. SORROWS TRANSFORMED

Gentle, Dancing Rain—

Sparkling droplets, feign
Dragonflies' stained glass wings
Raindrops' tears, plus Sunrays' hope,
Mirror
Life's spiritual rainbow, as Nature
Sings

In Harmony—

SPRING COMES AGAIN

1999 CONTINUED AS AN extraordinary year. After the rest of the family left at the beginning of February, Carolyn and I attended Founders' Chapel at the University of San Diego for a Mass in John's name, given by her friend Lisa. It was an appreciated gift that could still be given for John and comfort us girls still in recovery. Hospice was helpful for me by providing several one-on-one grievance counseling sessions with one of their counselors and a support group session that was helpful. Then Lent began.

As we had done other Lenten times, our Ascension Chamber Choir sang special music, and one that we had appreciated doing was the beautiful *Vere Languores Nostros* by Antonio Lotti. Translated into English, it appears as *Surely He Has Borne Our Griefs*. Usually when Marianne would pass out the music either for choir practice or performance, she would say, "Let's do Shirley and Dolores!" Not really disrespectful, it was our pleasant inside understanding of what we were about to sing. "Shirley" was really Surely, which in Latin is Vere, and "Dolores", which means sorrows in Latin, is sung three times. We would sing it with sad feeling in Latin: "Vere languores nostros et dolores nostros" and also in English: "Surely He has borne our griefs and our heavy sorrows". If there was any time in my life that I could feel this so personally, this was it. Jesus, who had suffered so horrendously, could understand John's suffering and my sorrows.

That first Sunday in Lent I woke up suddenly at 5 AM. Then I heard my name—spoken with the tender elevation of the second syllable more beautifully than any other time of my life—just, "Dolores" by John in his deeply mellow baritone-bass voice! He couldn't be seen, and no other words came.

301

Hearing him speak, when he couldn't before he died, meant everything to me, causing me to have a joyful assurance that he was healed and at peace.

Shortly before we were to sing the song that morning in church I said, "Marianne, I don't know if I can sing this morning, especially my name in 'Surely'".

I told her of my experience with John, wondering if she might have thought I was losing my mind. Unruffled, she answered, "That's okay, Dolores. Besides, you won't be able to sing anyway if you're crying. You can stay if you like and see how you feel and if you need to leave, that's okay, too." I sang the other music with the altos and just when we were going to sing "Surely", I braced myself, took a prayerful deep breath and started. I not only started, but sang through it to the end, so thankful and feeling stronger than I had at any other time of singing it. *My healing had begun.*

The music therapy continued. I would be given various songs to sing that first six months that had been used for my dad's and John's funerals. Sometimes it was as part of the choir at Ascension, other times it was at other occasions and places, culminating lastly at the July 1999 FinnFest in Seattle. Earlier when I would discover a piece, my first reaction was "Here it is again—why does this keep happening to me—should I sing it?" Then I would clear my throat, eliminate the beginning tears, sing and then feel strong. I didn't know what the music would be when I first joined the FinnFest choir because I decided to attend at the last minute, and it was too late to send me the music. After I arrived and looked over the music, the three pieces were not surprising for a Finnish *and* Finnish-American gathering. They included a song from Finland which I didn't know, in Finnish. Fortunately for me, the other two were in English and I had sung both. One was *America the Beautiful* (John's funeral); the other was *Finlandia* (my father's funeral). It was my first time of singing in Finnish and it helped that I stood between two Finnish speaking women. When done, I had achieved peacefulness as well as strength.

The symphony performance of Sibelius's *Finlandia* with Seattle area musicians and a conductor from Finland, was the best I'd heard, whether performed live or on recordings—and the percussive parts were never more powerful. It had been as though Dad, John, and that Spirit which we Christians call Holy, were there to help me celebrate this part of my journey into healing and help me understand what it was taking to get me there.

Because of my mother's first cousin's son Ed Bissell, I met another distant cousin and her husband Frank at their home in Seattle. They treated me to a scrumptious Northwest style salmon dinner, complete with an elegant, rich Swedish cream cake, and I met their grown children. Ellsbeth, a native of Sweden and a retired nurse at the Swedish Hospital in Seattle became a possible resource for me whenever I do more family genealogy.

There were more sun rays of hope and healing as I struggled in and out with the lack of joy that missing him brought. I mentioned it to choir member Su one day and she said, "It'll come back." Pat, another choir member, took me to lunch at an Italian restaurant and Stephanie took me to a live theater performance of *Les Miserables*. Getting a good report on my health status from Dr. G. after echo-stress tests helped my mood in June, as did a Hospice memorial service with sacred dance at the Unitarian Church which honored John and all who had died in 1999.

My girls took me under their "wings" after I had wondered to myself how they would respond to me and be able to bounce back too from the death of their father. Girls seem to have a special attachment to their fathers if they have been treated well by them. As it turned out, there was no reason for me to be concerned. They were so attentive to me, even though there were issues with their own healing.

On a 1996 trip to Ohio, M. J. at the CAI made the comment to John and me that John looked like the tenor, Placido Domingo. After John's death, Carolyn and I watched a concert by him on TV while I was at home, and she was at hers. It was like crazy-real! It was as though it was John himself—except for the higher voice. Even the mannerisms were similar. Carolyn and I sobbed together while our saline waters washed away some of our collective grief and splashed onto our phone receivers as we haltingly commented into them.

All three daughters outside of California asked me to visit them that year and the trips started in the spring when I went to see Christina, John, and Cameron in Oregon. It was adventurous while exploring great public transportation, sights and scenery in the Hillsboro/Portland areas.

Cousin Ed and his wife Jean, who lived in Portland, took me to the Oregon coast to experience the beautiful scenery and sea air. We went to Cannon Beach, Ecola State Park and the town of Seaside where we were greeted with pink blooming cherry trees. Another day Ed took me to the Portland Japanese Garden and it was solace for my soul— an experience as real as a serene, picturesque visit in Japan. Downtown we visited the cherry tree decorated Japanese-American Bill of Rights Memorial at Waterfront Park, which had been dedicated to the Japanese Americans who were incarcerated into camps on U.S. soil from 1942-1946. It had been beautifully created with sculptures, engraved histories and haiku. I was a child at that time in California and didn't know about it until I was an adult, even though the Japanese were taken away from their homes, businesses and farms from California, Oregon and Washington.

In the summer I was visiting parks in 100 degree heat with Barbara, Charles, and Cortland in New York along with Patti and Eric who had flown in from Colorado. Surprisingly, we survived the heat better than I thought we would.

Marian Clover, my writer friend in Ohio called during the summer and shared that she wanted to celebrate the Millennium by visiting the Sequoia Redwoods in the Sierras, something she had never seen. I had seen them, but I jumped at the chance to see them again, because they are so precious a treasure. So for several days in September we took train, bus, and van rides to accomplish our goal with an Elderhostel group. Being in the quiet presence of those huge trees is a spiritual experience, respecting that meditative communication between plants and people as our spirits ascend together in that beautiful sacred space. Bonuses were the folk dancing she and I taught, and the sing-along which I led. Unforgettable also was the John Muir impersonator and viewing the large, flat rock in King's Canyon where the real Muir used to stand and talk to people about nature.

Also in September, I brought Mother to San Diego to live after selling her Arizona desert home. It turned out to be very different than I thought because her dementia was worse than I knew. All her activities of daily living were suddenly up to me. It also included medical and spiritual care. That all contributed to another story of caregiving which lasted eight years. I was fortunate that I had experienced some healing by then, because it was the only way I could deal with all her problems and still appreciate her good qualities. My own healing slowed down as it wasn't the priority.

By October I was invited by Joyce Hatfield to sing in a women's vocal ensemble, the "San Diego Choral Club." I enjoyed it thoroughly and felt fortunate that it was led by expert musician Catherine Fisher, pianist and director.

After getting temporary care for Mom I flew on a red eye one night in late December to see Patti and Eric in Boulder. It was important to us to close out the year together. In January when John had died, so had our marriage. While thinking of that and more that had passed since then, I also had hoped to sleep—even though I had never been able to sleep on planes before. Maybe it helped that it was night and I was exhausted that I did fall asleep. When I awoke I recalled vividly a puzzling dream. It was a hand that looked similar to John's—strong and angular with slender fingers—clutching a single, beautiful daisy. When we arrived at the house, Patti informed me that cousin Ed had died suddenly of a heart attack the day before.

It was a stunning disappointment and loss to us. He had seemed fine in April. He was the one who did the most genealogy research for our Swedish family. Christina had called to tell Patti. Because Christina lived nearby and the rest of us could not attend the funeral, she volunteered, representing us all with flowers and her presence. I don't know for sure if the daisy dream had been about Ed, but I like to think it had been.

Patti took me to one of my favorite places—Estes Park. We walked in the snow around a lovely lake nearby. We went to the historical Stanley Hotel where we could see one of the best views of the mountains and valleys and explored the gift shop. She bought me a shimmering millennium scarf with 2000 decorated on it to celebrate the new, as we ended the old.

85. OTHER INTERLUDES THAT HELPED

I HAD RECUPERATED A lot by June 2000. That month Mom and I attended Doc Vriend's hundredth birthday party in San Diego since we had known him since the 1950's. My first chiropractor was amazing! He was still slender and had beautiful posture .He looked younger and was still handsome with white hair and moustache. Not only did he walk unaided, he all of a sudden grabbed me as I was speaking to him and led me in a ballroom dance! That caused a flurry of flashbulbs from cameras and moving video shots that rolled with the dancing. Some of the scenes arrived in the Netherlands, his birthplace.

August had me watching my four and five year old grandchildren Cortland and Cameron romp on Barbara's expansive Long Island lawn at dusk. Their mothers and I watched as they collected fireflies in glass jars and then released them quickly to freedom. Since it was my sixty-fifth birthday week, Barbara and Christina treated me to dinner in Manhattan.

Then when I flew from there to Washington, D. C. for a visit with my brother Warren, I teased him that it was so great of him to have such a distinguished museum celebration on my birthday evening, August 12 (when it didn't have anything to do with me)! *The Washington Post* staff writer Adrian Higgins headlined the August 10 article about the viewing stones as *Rock Stars*, and accompanying it were three beautiful examples in photographs. Warren by then was curator of the North American, Japanese and Chinese Penjing Bonsai Museums at the National Arboretum. It was he who planned and directed the stones on exhibit as art forms.

The appreciation of viewing stones (gongshi) comes from centuries long traditions in China and Japan and just recently have societies been established in North America. Sculpted outdoors by nature, connoisseurs such as Chinese Scholars choose those that are aesthetically pleasing and mount them on specially designed stands. Impressive were the abilities of the stones to balance on them without being attached.

The museum had its own collection. However, there were none from China, so this event was special in that Kemin Hu of Newtown, Massachusetts, donated three large gongshi from her Chinese Scholar father, the late Hu Zhaokang Kemin. After one of Hu's interesting tours I was pleased that I had been privileged to meet the gracious and generous lady.

The next day I had a private tour with Warren showing me the huge collection of beautiful bonsai in all three museums. The Japanese pavilion was built in 1976 to accommodate fifty-three bonsai from the Japanese people as friendship gifts for our country's bicentennial. Three were from the

Emperor of Japan's private collection and one white pine in particular was exceptionally special. It was donated by the Yamaki family of Hiroshima, who had lovingly cared for the oldest member of their family for almost 400 years! It survived the 1940's war between the United States and Japan and has become an international symbol of strength and peace. Miyajima—the Peace Tree—is named for the island where it was born.

A terrific story for young children is the newly (2015) published book *The Peace Tree from Hiroshima, The Little Bonsai with a Big Story*. It is written by Sandra Moore, illustrated by Kazumi Wilds and published by Tuttle Publishing.

The Chinese pavilion was added in 1986 following the gifts of penjing (miniature plant sculptures) from China. Soon after that time and before Warren arrived the largest of the three, the North American pavilion was established and named after Japanese-American John Naka.

Shortly before Warren retired in 2000 he went to Japan in October, representing the Arboretum and our country's friendship. The purpose of his trip was to visit with a number of Japanese bonsai masters, tour their nurseries and learn about current bonsai practices in Japan. His first visit was with his mentor and friend the now deceased Mr. Saburo Kato, who then at 85 years old was the most respected bonsai master in the world and President of the World Bonsai Friendship Federation. He had also helped in the development of the Washington bonsai museums.

When asking another Japanese man on his trip why he didn't seem to hate Americans for our use of the bomb, he said he was grateful that our country didn't punish them for their part in WWII, and helped them recover instead.

I was so fortunate that many people had helped me get through my loss, so by spring of 2001, I felt good—in fact, healed enough to plan and perform in a jazz concert for a scholarship in John's name and Marian's, another teacher. A couple had provided it in appreciation for all that John and Marian had done for their son, a student at St. Columba. The gift would go to a student planning to attend St. Augustine, the college prep boys' high school in San Diego. The scholarship was for excellence in science and math.

When I approached Peter Rubacalva, an outstanding singer-guitarist, and asked if he would be interested in performing with me in a jazz concert for the scholarship, he enthusiastically said yes! He also volunteered to get the jazz musicians. He led the music at St. Columba Church and school and had worked with John and his classes. John had liked him very much, so Peter was the perfect choice! I invited Stephanie, another alto, to join us. Father Scott, who liked Peter and his singing, gave us permission to have it at

Ascension. It was held May 27, 2001 with the three of us, plus Hans, pianist; Andy, bassist; Christopher, flautist/saxophonist; and Wayne, the drummer. It was a joyful affair for us. Marian joined us since she was the honoree. I considered it the final closure for me.

But by the end of summer I was beginning to feel the black hole of John's absence again. Loneliness was creeping back. Every time I would see an older couple walking together and holding hands, I'd get a lump in my throat as I was reminded how I used to assume John and I would be like that someday, enjoying our old age gracefully together and lovingly taking care of each other. When I would sing in the rehearsals for the *Pacem Choir* at St. Paul's Episcopal Church I would check out the older men, admiring some of them without their knowing it. Then reality would set in and I assumed most of them were married and maybe there were some available who would need a caregiver soon, which immediately squelched my interest!

Soon after the horrible losses on 9/11, I was introduced to Simon Mayeski in October by a mutual neighbor of ours. While we were chatting casually about some of our recent activities and I mentioned the scholarship concert, he mentioned that he, too, was a graduate of St. Augustine. I learned that we both attended Ascension Parish. He spoke well, seemed bright, and had a great speaking voice. He was single and had been married. I thought it might be interesting to know more about him. He felt the same way about me. Jazz came into our future together on our first date at his suggestion. Then we wanted to know each other so much more—and that's another story!

86. SLAM DUNK

AS FAR AS I know, John never knew what caused the disease in his brain. At most, he may have only sensed or guessed what might have been responsible. Besides, as sick as he was, knowing might have caused him to be even sicker, sooner. Before the tumor however, whenever he would go to a new doctor for his medical exam, he would mention casually, "By the way, when I was 20 years old, I was exposed to radioactive fallout from atomic bomb tests in Nevada." The doctors would always respond with, "If you develop illness, it will be leukemia." That never showed up, so we never worried about it. Also, in the fifties, he and the other exposed military participants had been given a booklet at the test site entitled *Armed Forces Talk*, which was for all five branches: Army, Navy, Air Force, Marines, and Coast Guard. Fifteen pages long, it was full of text, photos, and drawings of Camp Desert Rock at the test site to give information about what to expect from being near an atomic bomb explosion. In mentioning lingering nuclear radiation from deposited bomb material, it stated it was so small that it was not a hazard and to disregard it. So we did.

In the San Diego Union-Tribune newspaper on September 20, 2004, there was an article entitled "Atomic veterans fight for benefits" with a large color photograph of a widow of an atomic veteran, Merrilyn Holl. At issue was the struggle veterans and spouses were having with the federal government over benefit claims. The article stated that in 1988 a law was passed by Congress granting compensation for nuclear radiation exposure because cancer loomed large in this group. Included were many thousands of service members who participated in atomic bomb tests in Nevada, the Pacific Ocean and those who were prisoners of war near the Hiroshima and Nagasaki detonations. Immediately after reading it I realized that John was one of those atomic veterans.

Then my mind raced back to another news clip that I saw the year John passed away, also from the Union-Tribune. I saved it because it stated that there were higher than usual cancer rates among atomic test participants. The kinds of cancers listed were leukemia, prostate, and nasal. I was especially interested in the nasal because that area was close to the brain.

The 2004 article stated that at that time there were 21 different cancers related to atomic radiation and acknowledged by the government. Four were specifically mentioned: pancreatic, many forms of leukemia and multiple myeloma (cancer of the bone marrow), as well as brain.

When I spoke to a woman on the telephone working for the Veterans Administration about benefits, she asked, "What kind of cancer did your husband have?" When I told her 'brain', she answered, "That's a slam dunk!" I was pleased to learn that benefits were available to spouses of deceased vets, as well as living ones. All I had to do was prove that John had participated in the tests, and she said that wasn't going to be easy!

I noticed also in the paper that there was an organization called the National Association of Atomic Veterans (NAAV) and it was having a convention at the end of that week in San Diego. I was especially interested in that Robert "Doc" Campbell, the vice commander of the group and planner of the conference was a resident of Santee, a community just over the hills from where we lived in Tierrasanta, our neighborhood in San Diego. I waited until the conference was over and called him, hoping he would speak to me about John. He did, and was so kind and helpful.

"We have the highest cancer rate than any other group except Agent Orange Vets. It seems your husband's experience qualified him for benefits, and I'm sorry he didn't live long enough to get them. You should apply for yourself, but you'll have to work hard to get them. The government puts you through hoops and some denials, but if you stick with it you might be compensated. Do you want to try?"

"Yes, I do!"

"The first thing you have to do is contact his Air Force records in St. Louis. Also, the NAAV has a website where you can get the information you need. If you have any more questions, don't hesitate to call."

"Okay, thank you so much!"

* * * *

Patti went to the website and printed information for me from her computer in 2005, and then said she couldn't go any further because I was the one who had her dad's military and medical records which had to be sent to the government. When I requested his military records from St. Louis by phone, I was told they had been destroyed in a fire in the 1970's. In fact, the lady there apologized and asked me to send what I had of John's. All that I had were his discharge papers, and sent them. When I contacted the Department of Energy in Las Vegas, I was informed that it had no record of John's participation in the bomb tests.

In February, 2006, I accidently found in a box of papers in the garage the previously mentioned two letters that John had written to me from the test site in Mercury, Nevada in 1952. They were inside the envelopes that had his full test site address on the envelopes. I was so elated to find them, first of all, for his sentiments and nuclear information, and then also for the addresses—all proof that he had been there! Some things that happen seem to be guided by God. I'm a bit agnostic about being absolutely sure, but I was spontaneously saying prayers of gratitude!

Until doing the research on participants in the tests, I didn't know that the military and government had sworn them to secrecy after they were involved in the fallout. John never told me anything about them after sending those letters and showing me the booklet. Up to that time the activities at the site were so public that casinos in Las Vegas were even advertising the mushroom cloud bomb explosions as entertainment for prospective customers and there were radio broadcasts of them!

On February 2 2006, I wrote to the Defense Threat Reduction Agency (DTRA) in Fort Belvoir, Virginia and told that he was sent there from Camp Stoneman in Pittsburg, California, and that it no longer existed. I also gave DTRA a listing of the other bases where he had been stationed briefly before he was at Stoneman. I included that he had been a guide at a viewing site for top military and government officials for the atomic bomb tests and sent his Mercury based letters. Upon request, I also sent his surgical medical records from Scripps Memorial and Cedar Sinai Hospitals and his death certificate.

By February 24, 2006, I had a letter back from the DTRA, which confirmed that John had participated in Operation TUMBLER-SNAPPER, conducted at the NTS in 1952. That involved 8 detonations from April 1 through June 5, and John was there for them all! The government sent me the paper, supposedly, with John's dosimeter (radiation exposures) readings, but that paper is blank. Either the readings were too damning with high levels, or they have been thrown away. Another page had his orders to travel to Mercury and back to Stoneman, and then there was the one that was mostly blank with the statement that information had been redacted (removed). The DTRA is the executive agent for the Department of Defense Nuclear Test Personnel Review, and I was recommended to contact the Department of Defense for compensation. Congressman Bob Filner contacted the Department of Justice and Department of Veterans Affairs on my behalf.

Shortly before Christmas, 2006, I received the news from the U.S. Department of Justice that my claim for compensation had been approved. The $75,000.00 was deposited into my credit union account February 13, 2007. I divided $40,000.00 of it with my daughters, for they had suffered so much, too. Even in death, John had helped his family.

We thanked everybody concerned, and thought it was a bit of justice for us from the government. When I called "Doc" Campbell to thank him, I learned he had already passed away in his 70's from his cancer, so I was only able to give sympathetic condolences to the family and tell his widow how much I had appreciated his help.

87. FINALE

WHILE PREPARING THIS BOOK I read photo journalist Carole Gallagher's documentary *American Ground Zero: The Secret Nuclear War* (1993) as background reading on the atomic veterans who became ill and died from ionizing radiation exposures caused by nuclear bomb tests detonated by the United States. In addition to writing about veterans and rural down-winders, she also included Nevada Test Site (NTS) workers who suffered the same tragic results from their exposures. All the stories contained heart-wrenching testimonies and photographs from people who told of their or their spouses' horrendous experiences. The information on the test site workers and their wives suggested that there might be possible nuclear connections to my parents' illnesses as well, adding more agony to that which I had with John.

Complicating any evidence of radiation poisoning here is the fact that both my parents had been smokers. Dad was until he died, and Mom until her larynx cancer was diagnosed in 1988. How much disease was attributed to their smoking, and how much to the bomb tests, I will never know. However, I think the following information merits a mention.

My dad worked on and off at the NTS for about 6 years, from 1968 until 1974. He was willing to work because the pay was good and he wasn't old enough to retire yet. According to Gallagher's information, the radiation risks were never issues, according to the authorities. That's what all the workers were told. The dosimeter badges registering the exposure levels weren't of much help, since the handling of them was often ineffective or irresponsible. Sometimes they worked, and sometimes they didn't. Many were thrown away when they didn't, and if they were working, very high levels registering from the workers were sometimes thrown away also, and instead of the workers being removed for a while, they just gave them new ones! I assume Dad probably wore one, and if his registered high levels, he may have been removed from the area for a while. But then, even low levels have been found to be killers. According to other workers, if they talked about what they did at the site to others not there, they could lose their jobs. That's probably why we never knew about Dad.

The atmospheric bomb tests were banned by the government in 1962, but then they literally went underground, involving tunnels as well. According to his employment records Mom had saved, Dad was working at the test site in December, 1970 when a huge underground bomb explosion went wrong, sending massive levels of radiation debris as a plume through a vent into the atmosphere for 24 hours, polluting greater than 40 other vented ones! The identifying name was "Baneberry", according to Gallagher's book.

I don't know for sure whether Dad had been affected, but the highly radioactive cloud created by it polluted areas of Nevada, Wyoming, a part of California, and snowfall over ski slopes in Utah.

Walter, a bus driver, and the only Baneberry worker interviewed, had been exposed heavily. So were the other workers—they were not in the tunnels at the time, but outside. According to Dad's work records, he had been assigned to a nearby site. Radiation monitors were run over the other workers' bodies and the radiation levels were higher than the dosimeters could show! They gave each and all of the men *nine* showers to get the pink dust off, until the levels went down. Even so, two years later Walter eventually suffered cancer of the larynx and lung, intense, interior burning pain and skin cancers all over his body. He had surgery that removed one of his lungs. Soon after the explosion, before symptoms, the doctors at Mercury said he was in good health.

Curiously, Dad was told by the doctors there in 1974 that he was in good health too, and gave him permission to work. Then in 1975 he was diagnosed with his extremely diminished lung capacity, as I mentioned before, putting him on oxygen therapy. His pneumonia in 1977 could have been related to the test site, as it also had been a result of working there by others. Then there was his heart disease.

Gilbert, an Atomic Energy Commission (AEC) monitor worker, traveled constantly in Utah and Nevada distributing radiation dosimeters to people in those areas after he chased fallout clouds in his car. Besides bladder cancer and other health ailments, he suffered two heart attacks. Heart attack and cancer deaths were common also among downwinders (rural people of several states who received radioactive fallout from the bomb tests. Their animals and crops were also destroyed.) In addition, more illnesses surfaced because the radiated fallout also compromised immune systems. Dad's health problems actually started to deteriorate in the fall of 1970 with the flu and bronchial asthma. After that he kept having one health problem after another, failing to recuperate fully. He never recovered from his 1978 open heart surgery, unlike his friends who did. But those friends had not worked at NTS.

What about Mother? After Dad died in 1979, she became, unofficially, one of a group of women who had the dubious distinction of being Test Site Worker Widows. Their husbands had all died of multiple kinds of cancers. Not only that, but they were getting various cancers themselves. They would wash their husbands' contaminated work clothes and Mother had been used to washing Dad's paint overalls, so might not have thought anything of handling and washing those dusty ones from the test site, not realizing the dust was radioactive. Since he would come home on weekends, it's possible she had more than one pair to do at a time because of his five day work weeks. Plus, there was contamination on his hard hat and shoes, which he brought into the laundry room, and onto his pickup truck.

Cancer of the larynx was one that she and others suffered, including test site workers and down winders. She fared better than Jack, the test site worker whose cancer was too advanced to have surgery and just had the larynx scraped of it. His tongue swelled so much that it burst out of his mouth and covered his nose shortly before he died.

In 2005 she was diagnosed with inoperable lung cancer and passed away from it in 2007. The breakdown of her lung(s) with the lung infection in 1998 that almost killed her may have been test site related. The infection could have weakened them enough that cancer cells found it easy to proliferate there. Her doctors in San Diego, including the oncologist at the Moores Cancer Center, were puzzled by it. They could only suggest that it may have been related to her cancer of the larynx, which had been declared gone in 1989 after her treatments.

Cancer didn't run in Mother's family of siblings and parents—she was the exception. None of us family members knew how toxic the test site legacies were that we received from the Fifties through the Seventies.

I've shed torrents of tears for these three loves in my life. But the tears only help my own physical and emotional release, leading me toward healing and compassion. I must continue, as I have in the past, to be in solidarity with people of good will everywhere in the world who *relieve* rather than *cause* suffering.

After World War II, there was a realization among leaders worldwide that the power for massive destruction of civilian populations with nuclear weapons was greater than with any previous armaments. Nevertheless, other countries decided to create them as well, starting with the Soviet Union in the late 1940's with their first detonation in 1949. Consequently, a lack of trust between us and the Soviets resulted in a "cold war" mentality. A race began for superiority in national security, manifested by building more nuclear weapons for use if a "hot war" broke out. Testing put living people and animals in nuclear testing harm's way in order to learn what the results would be in war. The lack of remorse over the civilian casualties of our 1945 Hiroshima and Nagasaki atomic bombings (which took only one relatively "small" bomb to produce extreme fireballs that cremated them alive) is beyond my comprehension. Instead both Soviet and American governments, along with their respective military personnel, scientists, and nuclear weapons industries, created an agenda for proliferation. American tests began by proclamation in 1951 by President Harry Truman. Succeeding presidents continued them because the scientific facts regarding the risks for were ignored. This was the situation by the time John became involved in 1952 on Nevada land belonging to the Native American Shoshones but taken over by our federal government.

The other three of the Big Five nations (United Kingdom, China, and France) rapidly gained nuclear capabilities. Over time, four others followed suit: Israel, Pakistan, India, and lately North Korea. The weapons today are much more powerful than the WWII ones. Fortunately, since the 1980's some stockpiles have been reduced and some countries have given up the notion of having them, but currently the U.S. and Russian ones are the largest and can launch them in less than ten minutes. The Big Five are currently modernizing their supplies and making them "more efficient". In the 21st Century, only North Korea has been detonating nuclear weapons and that has been underground.

So far just our own testing has produced dramatic human casualties over more than one generation in Nevada, Utah and the Pacific Marshall Islands. It is likely testing in other countries has done the same. I support all our national and international efforts to prevent future testing, manufacturing and stockpiling nuclear weapons globally and countries to abide by the involved treaties. To do otherwise is extremely unsafe to life on a planet already in jeopardy with climate change and terrorists who value death more than life. How can we be sure they never have access to use them? Nuclear governments need new paradigms for thinking about national securities. Obviously we are safer without nuclear weapons than with them.

We also need new paradigms for job opportunities. We don't need workers who mine uranium and those who process it in factories to inevitably get poisoned from exposures. We also don't need servicemen and civilians in places like the Middle East to continue getting cancers and other ailments from depleted uranium in current weapons. Rather, training in green jobs technology is critical for human and environmental survival.

Where is the nuclear toxic waste from past and present going, whether it is derived from weapons, power plants or medical procedures? American servicemen are having health problems from "cleaning it up" and there are still radiation risks from the 2011 Fukushima plant in Japan and in the Pacific Ocean. Medical professionals have to conscientiously monitor for safety the amounts of ionizing radiation their patients receive.

Because it was the United States, my country which I love and where I have thrived, who first released the nuclear genie upon the world, it is the one who needs strong leadership in eliminating it. Not doing it is inexcusable.

* * * *

For years I hadn't been able to recognize any good coming out of John's death. I am hoping now that this book might be an answer to that if anyone might be enlightened or helped by anything I have shared.

There is a sign in Berlin on Rosenthaler Strasse (Street): *Das Leben ist kein Ponyhof—life isn't easy.* But with love, laughter, compassion, faith and the arts life becomes easier as we continue the struggles for a better world. While John's beautiful brain was healthy, he would have agreed.

If he had lived longer, he would have continued to improve that future for the family he adored. He would be enjoying the company of our grandson Christopher, the latest addition to the family in 2008. As it is, we now only have memories of his spirit, his love and compassion. They inspire me to better the futures of our children, our grandchildren and people everywhere as John's rich legacy continues.

Santa Barbara, California
Christopher, son of Carolyn and Mickey, 5 months old

Made in the USA
Las Vegas, NV
03 September 2023

77012314R00184